Ideologies of Forgetting

SUNY series in Feminist Criticism and Theory

Michelle A. Massé, editor

Ideologies of Forgetting

Rape in the Vietnam War

GINA MARIE WEAVER

SUNY
PRESS

Published by State University of New York Press, Albany

Printed in the United States of America

For information, contact State University of New York Press, Albany, NY
www.sunypress.edu

Production by Eileen Meehan
Marketing by Michael Campochiaro

Library of Congress Cataloging-in-Publication Data

Weaver, Gina Marie, 1980–
Ideologies of forgetting : rape in the Vietnam War / Gina Marie Weaver.
p. cm. — (SUNY series in feminist criticism and theory)
Includes bibliographical references and index.
ISBN 978-1-4384-2999-1 (hbk. : alk. paper)
ISBN 978-1-4384-2998-4 (pbk. : alk. paper)
1. Rape as a weapon of war—Vietnam—History—20th century. 2. Vietnam War, 1961–1975—Atrocities. 3. Rape victims—Vietnam. I. Title.

HV6569.V5W43 2010
959.704'38—dc22 2009017939

10 9 8 7 6 5 4 3 2 1

For Bil, Rachel, and Will

Contents

Acknowledgments

I would like to thank my family—my husband and my parents—for their support as I worked on this manuscript in graduate school and after. I am indebted to Krista Comer at Rice University for her invaluable readings and feedback on various forms of the manuscript as well as her encouragement regarding the project's importance. Many thanks also to Gwen Hackler at Southern Nazarene University for her mentorship and encouragement throughout my academic journey and to my colleagues at SNU for shouldering so much of my workload during the last crazy semester of wrapping up this book and preparing for Will's arrival.

Preface

A Postwar Look at Vietnam

> Nearly one-third of female veterans who sought V.A. healthcare in 2003 reported experiencing rape or attempted rape . . . in the military.
>
> —Corbett, "The Women's War"

> Of the 3,038 investigations of military sexual assault charges completed in 2004–2005, only 329—about one-tenth—of them resulted in a court-martial of the perpetrator.
>
> —Corbett, "The Women's War"

While searching for a dissertation topic in 2004 and having recently become fascinated by Vietnam War literature, I taught the Literature and Film of the Vietnam War: Nationalism and Identity at Rice University. The course coincided nicely with the presidential elections, and I planned for our critical focus to be on nationalism and the construction of patriotism and masculinity as we read or viewed the primary texts I had selected. However, as the semester unfolded, an unintended theme in the literature and films I had chosen materialized: neither I nor my students could help but notice the repetitive occurrence of sexual abuse perpetrated by U.S. soldiers against Vietnamese women. I was a bit surprised at this emergent theme, as I had not yet noticed a discussion of sexual violence in the secondary texts through which I was just beginning to sort. After a half-year's worth of research turned up very little in the way of critical discussion of war rape in Vietnam, I began to suspect that I had stumbled into every PhD candidate's dream: a critical blind spot waiting to be investigated.

Though rape by American soldiers has never been a subject that the American public—or academia, as I discovered—wished to acknowledge, the fiction and memoirs that arose out of the Vietnam War repeatedly show it to have been a persistent problem. Larry Heinemann's National Book Award–winning novel, *Paco's Story* (1986), presents a prime example of the kinds of perpetration-induced trauma that Vietnam veterans frequently relate in literary and oral accounts of their war experience. In the novel, Vietnam veteran Paco returns to make a life for himself in the United States but remains haunted by memories of the war. The unnamed narrator—revealed later in the novel to be the collective ghost of the company with which Paco served in the war and that was wiped out in a single accident of friendly fire[1]—seems to embody the haunting memory that is keeping Paco from successfully reintegrating into society. The narrative leads readers to assume that because Paco is the lone survivor of the accident at Fire Base Harriet, he suffers from survivor guilt. However, in the penultimate chapter, the narrator reveals the memory at the root of Paco's emotional problems: the gang rape of a female Viet Cong prisoner. The narrator observes as "[Paco] suddenly remembers the rape of the VC girl, and the dreams he has had of the rape. He winces and squirms; his whole body jerks, but he cannot choose but remember."[2] After Gallagher, the soldier instigating the rape, ties up the girl,

> There was considerable jostling and arm punching, jawing and grab-ass back and forth, and everyone formed a rough line, so just for that moment Paco got to stand there and take a long look. A peasant girl, not more than fourteen, say, or sixteen . . . And when Gallagher finished, Jonesy fucked her, and when Jonesy was done, half the fucking company was standing in line and commenced to fuck her ragged . . . [A]nd Jesus-fucking-Christ, she had her nostrils flared and teeth clenched and eyes squinted, tearing at the sheer humiliating, grinding pain of it . . . Dudes still ambled over to the doorway to watch, to call out coaching, taking their turns, hanging around the side of the building after—some getting back in line. (pp. 179–81)

The narrator spends a total of eleven pages (a considerable number in a terse novel) narrating Paco's memory of the rape, culminating when the girl is shot execution style, and the soldiers "looked at her and at ourselves, drawing breath again and again, and knew that this was a moment of evil, that we would never live the same" (p. 184). Thus, the reader becomes aware that Paco's problems result not from garden-variety survivor guilt, but from the terrible guilt of the crime committed by his company in the rape and murder of the Vietnamese woman. With this information, the accident at Fire Base Harriet is reformulated as a moment of justice for the woman, and Paco is unlucky in having escaped it; instead, readers may now see him as condemned to remembrance of a collective crime.

As is generally the case with texts interested in sexual trauma perpetrated by American soldiers in Vietnam, this shockingly brutal scene of gang rape is not widely addressed in works of criticism and reviews despite the fact that the disconcerting heart of the novel turns on the revelation of the rape.[3] This absence is even more often the case among popular critics. In fact, one of Amazon.com's "Top 50 Reviewers," Orrin C. Judd, openly criticizes the rape scene's inclusion, apparently entirely misunderstanding the novel: "The story itself is kind of an amalgam of clichés from the popular culture's rather deranged view of the war. In particular, there's one scene in which he participates in a gang rape that is purely obligatory, rather than growing organically out of the story. The author is a Vietnam veteran, so I'm hesitant to simply dismiss it as pandering, but one senses that it is there because Heinemann thinks the reader expects it to be."[4] Judd's assumption that the gang rape scene is an "obligatory" part of "popular culture's . . . deranged view of the war" and is probably just "pandering," rather than a depiction of a brutal, widespread activity that was tacitly condoned during the war, demonstrates how little he and reactionary mainstream American culture understand about the war and the desire of the American public to turn away from such nasty actions of fellow Americans. The review also reveals the extent to which popular views of the war have changed since the war years. Perhaps Judd considers the rape a "cliché" because it appears in so much of the best Vietnam War literature.

The fallaciousness of Judd's understanding of war rape as mere cliché becomes apparent when one has a fuller knowledge of the cultural artifacts of the war. Volumes of testimony verify that rape was far from a literary device. As early as the International War Crimes Tribunal, a 1967 panel sponsored by Jean Paul Sartre and Bertrand Russell in Stockholm, American, and North Vietnamese soldiers, as well as Vietnamese women political prisoners, reported the sexual abuse of women by Americans and their allies. These participants' reasons for testifying were expressed by Russell's opening words, "We are not judges. We are witnesses. Our task is to make mankind bear witness to these terrible crimes and to unite humanity on the side of justice in Vietnam."[5] The Winter Soldier Investigation (31 January–2 February 1971), a forum to speak on the atrocities of the war that was initiated by and presented witnesses from the Vietnam Veterans against the War (VVAW), gave horrific and detailed accounts of sexual violence[6] toward women by U.S. soldiers. This testimony included extraordinary instances of brutality. Sergeant Scott Camil of the First Marine Division describes how, after an American sniper had shot and wounded a Viet Cong woman, his lieutenant "said to kill her. So he ripped off her clothes, they stabbed her in both breasts, they spread her eagle and shoved an E tool up her vagina, an entrenching tool, and she was still asking for water. And they took that out and they used a tree limb and then she was shot."[7] Many veterans also gave witness to the everyday atrocities committed against women such as "routine" searches, in which "the women would have all their clothes taken off and the men would use their penises to probe them to make sure they didn't have anything hidden anywhere; and this was raping but it was done as searching" (p. 13). Such testimony suggests that any understanding of war-related rape by Americans as a mere cliché is facile and a dangerous refusal to acknowledge the terrible crimes committed by Americans—yet based on primary and secondary texts concerning the war, responses like Judd's seem to be the norm of American belief.

By the time I finished my dissertation prospectus, I had come to believe the topic of sexual abuse in the Vietnam War would not only provide the opportunity for original scholarship but that bringing to light this overlooked issue was of vital importance to a more accurate history of the war, to a complete understanding and acceptance of the Vietnam veteran, and to the lives and memory of Vietnamese women victims. Furthermore, as I began working on the manuscript version of this project in 2007, the consequences of America's refusal to acknowledge our actions in Vietnam became quite apparent as recently released statistics revealed that staggering numbers of female American veterans experienced rape during their time of service, often at the hands of their fellow soldiers. These figures speak to the relevance of this project's excavation of soldiers' sexual aggression even now, more than thirty years after America's war in Vietnam. For it is, I argue, Americans' refusal to acknowledge our military's capacity for sexual abuse that enables the current situation in which U.S. female soldiers find themselves victims of their fellow soldiers' sexualized violence.

Just as I will demonstrate in later chapters that the public remained willfully ignorant of sexual abuse committed in the Vietnam War, as the war in Iraq drags on and politicians vie to out-do one another with promises to bring troops home or stay the course, the statistic that nearly one-third of female veterans who sought V.A. healthcare in 2003 reported experiencing rape or attempted rape while they were in the military quietly goes unnoticed.[8] Of that group, 37 percent reported being raped multiple times, and 14 percent experienced gang rape. While the Department of Defense is well aware of the problem and began training victim advocates on major military bases in 2005, its awareness has done little to stem the tide of rapes or to punish the perpetrators of such crimes. As the epigraph above notes, only about one-tenth of the 3,038 investigations of military sexual assault charges in 2004–05 resulted in the court-martial—the equivalent of prosecution in civilian court—of the perpetrator. Over half of the charges were dismissed for lack of evidence or because an offender could not be identified, and about 20 percent were punished administratively by such measures as demotions and letters of reprimand (Corbett, p. 4). The leniency of the military toward sexual assault crimes is not representative of current American civilian culture, where approximately 80 percent of people arrested for rape are prosecuted.[9]

The military's laissez-faire attitude toward the sexual harassment and abuse of its female soldiers is well known among insiders. In response to the ninety acts of assault (many sexual in nature) that occurred at the infamous 1991 Tailhook Convention, no participants were convicted as a result of the navy's investigations. The navy's so-called zero-tolerance policy toward sexual harassment[10] is belied by the reports of such women as navy veteran Amorita Randall; Randall explained to *New York Times* reporter Sara Corbett that she did not report her rape by a petty officer because, "You just don't expect anything to be done about it anyway, so why even try?" Such attitudes suggest that the majority of military rapes may go unreported. However, unlike rapes committed in civilian society, the female soldier must continue to live among and work closely with her rapist, which frequently leads to an increased sense of powerlessness, leaving the victim at a greater risk for additional victimization. And, as the Department of Veterans Affairs points out itself, "sexual victimization that occurs in this setting often means that victims are relying on their perpetrators . . . to provide for basic needs including medical and psychological care."[11]

For soldiers living in a war zone—and about one in seven of U.S. soldiers in Iraq is female—the stakes are even higher.[12] As more than twenty female veterans of the Iraq war told Salon.com reporter Helen Benedict, "the danger of rape by other soldiers is so widely recognized in Iraq that . . . officers routinely told [women] not to go to the latrines or showers without another woman for protection."[13] Not only are sexual assault victims forced to have continued contact with their perpetrators, but these perpetrators are the teammates on whom the victims' very lives depend. Because the military is a closed, hierarchical society, no woman who reports a rape will remain anonymous. If she seeks psychological counseling, it will be noted in her permanent record. Most probably she will be resented by her fellow soldiers, some of whom believe "the military sends women over to [Iraq to] give the guys eye candy to keep them sane . . . [I]n Vietnam they had prostitutes to keep them from going crazy, but they don't have those in Iraq. So they have women soldiers instead."[14] If her victimizer is a superior, the female soldier may feel unable to say no or report any abuse, for fear of punishment.[15]

Thus, "[b]eing sexually assaulted by a fellow soldier may prove extra-traumatic, as it represents a breach in the hallowed code of military cohesion" (Corbett, p. 5). Susan Avila-Smith, director of the female veterans' advocacy group Women Organizing Women, asserts, "It's very disconcerting to have somebody who is supposed to save your life, who has your back, turn on you and do something like that . . . You don't want to believe it's real. You don't want to have to deal with it. The family doesn't want to deal with it. Society doesn't want to deal with it" (qtd. in Corbett, p. 5). In this statement, Avila-Smith points to the reason U.S. society has thus far ignored the sexual abuse of women in the military: it suggests that something at the core of the military—its base of camaraderie and "brotherhood"—is diseased.

The *Denver Post*'s three-part series "Betrayal in the Ranks," published in November 2003 after a nine-month investigation, pointed to this diseased core, citing "studies and surveys [that] showed a military culture that demeans women," as they clearly revealed the sexual assault and domestic violence that run rampant through all branches of the U.S. military. Perhaps even more damning, however, is the "Profiles" section of the series, which chronicles the narratives of some of the more than sixty women *The Post* interviewed. These women detail rapes committed against them by their military comrades even as far back as the fifties, suggesting a decades-old military culture that relies on the rhetorical abuse and devaluation of women. Their individual stories are supported by various studies conducted by the VA. A 2004 study of all women veterans from the Vietnam War forward found that 71 percent of those seeking treatment for PTSD suffered rape or sexual assault while in the military, and a 1992–93 study of Gulf War and earlier female veterans found 90 percent reporting sexual harassment while in the military. Thus, over the same period the military has continually promoted itself as a career field with endless opportunities for women, through its subornation of the sexual harassment and abuse of its female soldiers, it has damaged the lives of women veterans across several generations.

However disconcerting the fact of the widespread sexual abuse of American military women may be, it is a trend that should have been noted and predicted based on research, testimony, and literature that came out of the Vietnam War. The continuance of sexual abuse in the military even in today's more gender-issue savvy society and despite the occasional reports such as *The Denver Post* and *The New York Times'* exposés and calls for hearings by Congress, reveals the imperativeness of digging to the root of the problem: a violent masculinity as the basis of the American military character. This book will foreground evidence from the Vietnam War that will allow more wide-ranging and meaningful changes to be made to the military to make this sort of abuse unthinkable for our soldiers. This foundation of military identity based on gender differentiation and misogyny must be eradicated if we are to make the military a safe environment and population in which American women may fully participate and for the international female populations with whom our military comes in contact. In order to begin this process, scholars and lawmakers must, for the first time, truly listen to the voices of Vietnam veterans and Vietnamese women as they speak to the sexual violence that American military society perpetuates, whether intentionally or unintentionally.

Thus, while this book is about the Vietnam War, the rapes that took place there, and the sociocultural systems in place during the war years, it is very much a postwar book in terms of its goals. As feminist scholar Cynthia Enloe has pointed out, "The post-war era in any country is a time fraught with gendered decisions. Memories are being fashioned in museums out of selected images. Lessons are being set in reports and school books out of presumptions about masculinity and femininity. Militaries and labour forces are being reconstituted according to officials' gendered anxieties and popular gender-inattentive impatience."[16] If the United States is ever to achieve its goal of gender equality, it must pay attention to the facts of the Vietnam War, begin to reconceptualize its history there, and, moving forward, reconstitute its understanding of the military character. This understanding would provide a fuller acceptance of the Vietnam veteran and, importantly, a national sharing in responsibility for the aggression perpetrated in Vietnam, a recognition of the suffering inflicted upon Vietnamese women, and the ability to make the U.S. military safe for both the women who belong to it and those with whom it comes into contact.

1

Silencing

Erasure of Rape in the Vietnam War

> [A]lthough rape is one of the most widely used types of violation against women and girls, it remains the least condemned war crime.
>
> —Coomaraswamy, *Common Grounds*

Before we can understand the role rape played in the Vietnam War or the reasons and means by which it has been erased from narratives of that war, it is helpful to contextualize war rape more generally. Especially important is a recognition of the fact that, after many years of work by feminists, war rape has finally come to be recognized as an international war crime. Within the global and historical contexts of warfare, however, women's sexual abuse by soldiers is not a new phenomenon. Throughout history, women's bodies have constituted an important part of the spoils of war. For example in ancient sources such as Homer's *Iliad* the women Chyseis and Briseis are captured and enslaved as concubines, and Plutarch's *Lives* details the rape of the Sabine women as part of the founding of Rome. However, the effect of war on women has changed dramatically as warfare in the twentieth and twenty-first centuries has become total war. While during World War I "the ratio of military personnel killed to civilians killed was 8:1," this ratio changed dramatically during World War II to 1:1. In the many wars worldwide since 1945, the ratio has been 1:8.[1] Within the context of total war, women suffer not merely as "collateral damage," but their bodies have also taken on strategic importance. They have served as "toilets" for the Japanese military,[2] unwilling child bearers for the Bosnian Serbs and Rwandan Hutus, and symbols of the conquering military's honor (and the dishonor of the defeated), as well as targets in and of themselves. Military sexual slavery has continued throughout the twentieth century, and "systematic" or "strategic" rape as a military policy played an important role in both the Bosnia-Herzegovina and Rwandan civil wars (pp. 8–9).

In spite of the increased importance of women to the strategies of modern warfare, however, women's sexual trauma as a result of war has been little studied or even mentioned until recent work by feminist scholars has begun to gather primary accounts of women's abuse in war as well as to publicize and theorize its oversight. Anne Lewellyn Barstow's collection, *War's Dirty Secret: Rape, Prostitution, and Other Crimes against Women* (2001) seeks to do just that, joining the ranks of such works as *Common Grounds: Violence against Women in War and Armed Conflict Situations*, edited by Indai Lourdes Sajor (1998), and *Mass Rape: The War against Women in Bosnia-Herzegovina*, edited by Alexandra Stiglamayer (1994). These works mark the increasing attention being turned specifically toward sexual violence against women in war, particularly after the recent horrific and very well-documented sexual assaults on women in Rwanda and Bosnia-Herzegovina, as well as the "coming out" of the Korean comfort women in 1991. This latter group of women includes those impressed (either through trickery or kidnapping) into servitude in Japan's military brothels in World War II.

This recent work finds its foundation in previous feminist research that sought to reveal the importance—both literally and rhetorically—of women to the military. In 1983, Cynthia Enloe recognized the importance of women and their bodies to the military as soldiers, mothers, and victims in *Does Khaki Become You? The Militarisation of Women's Lives.* Her subsequent work has continued to investigate the strategic rhetorical and physical use of women, particularly in emergent nations, such as the Philippines, Bangladesh, Sri Lanka, and Kashmir.[3] Even more foundational is Susan Brownmiller's landmark text, *Against Our Will: Men, Women, and Rape* (1975), which contains an important chapter on the role of rape in war, making this book one of the first to link the law, the military, and the nation's tacit approval of woman abuse, especially in a military situation. Her "War" chapter opens with statement made by General George S. Patton during World War II that he knew, "in spite of my most diligent efforts, there would unquestionably be some raping, and . . . I [asked] . . . to have the details as early as possible so that the offenders could be properly hanged."[4] Brownmiller thus points out the obvious attitude about rape in war, one that all contemporary feminist critics of war have since worked to prove problematic: the common belief that there shall "[*u*]*nquestionably* . . . be some raping. Unconscionable, but nevertheless inevitable" (p. 31).

Brownmiller suggests that, unlike other wartime atrocities such as a bomb's hitting a civilian target, rape is qualitatively different in that "rape in war is a familiar act with a familiar excuse. War provides men with the perfect psychologic [sic] backdrop to give vent to their contempt for women. The very maleness of the military . . . confirms for men what they long suspect, that women are peripheral, irrelevant to the world that counts, passive spectators to the action in the center ring" (p. 32). Though an early critique and a book that lacks nuance in other areas,[5] current statistical data confirm Brownmiller's analysis of the reasons behind war rape. Madeline Morris notes a clear and significant "rape differential" when comparing military personnel's rates of rape to other crimes. In a study comparing U.S. civilian to U.S. military records from 1944 through 1945 and again from 1987 through 1992, Morris found that enlisted personnel's rates of rape and other aggressive crimes (murder and aggravated assault) were lower than civilian rates of these crimes during peacetime; Morris notes, though, that rape rates did not drop as sharply as did other crimes committed by military personnel. However, "[m]ilitary rape rates in the combat theater . . . climbed to several times civilian rates, while military rates of other violent crime were roughly equivalent to civilian rates. Thus, in both the wartime and the peacetime contexts studied, a rape differential exists: The ratio of military rape rates to civilian rape rates is substantially larger than the ratio of military rates to civilian rates of other violent crime."[6] This research bears out Brownmiller's claim that war provides men an excuse to carry out a peacetime crime, and clearly, as both Brownmiller and Morris suggest, the military's organization or training enables and/or induces men to perform this particular, woman-directed crime much more than other aggressive crimes.

If rape has played an increasingly important role in modern warfare, it has not, until fairly recently, received much attention. Clearly, the budding recognition of war rape in the 1980s and especially the later 1990s correlates with the strides made by the women's movement in the United States, Europe, and around the world since the 1970s in alerting the public to rape as an important issue generally, which, in the U.S. context, can be seen in the establishment of victim's rights legislation and rape hotlines. Another reason war rape in particular has finally begun to garner attention from the media and scholars is the crucial work feminists have done to change international understandings of war crimes; until 2001, rape, while a crime within individual countries, was not considered to be a war crime and therefore not internationally litigable. Thus, the prior lack of interest in women's trauma in war until recent years was enforced by international definitions of war crimes. For instance, though testimony and other evidence indicated that not a little raping occurred in both the European and Pacific theaters during World War II, the International Military Tribunal in Nuremberg did not mention "rape" once in its 179-page judgment, subsuming this particular, women-directed crime into the more general category "ill treatment of the civilian population."[7] Thanks to pressure from feminists around the world, however, the international community's understanding of war rape and sexual exploitation is slowly beginning to change. During the trials of Rwandan leaders, the International Criminal Tribunal for Rwanda "articulated a broad, progressive definition of rape, defining it as a 'physical invasion of a sexual nature, committed on a person under circumstances which are coercive'" and declared that rape does constitute torture and is therefore a war crime.[8] Following this new designation of rape as torture, the first successful international conviction of soldiers (three Bosnian Serbs) for the crime of rape finally occurred in 2001.

In spite of these progressive changes in international law's definition of war rape, unfortunately the sexual abuse of women in war continues to be dealt with inequitably and to be used for varying purposes by states looking to bolster feelings of nationalism or desire for retribution. Looking not only at how an abusing military uses women, but also at how nations rhetorically exploit their own female citizens' status as victims, Enloe claims that "[r]ape and prostitution have been central to many men's construction of the nationalist cause. They have permitted men to hear the feminized nation beckoning them to act as 'her' protectors . . . Too often missing in this gendered nationalist scenario are the voices of the actual women who have suffered rape or have been compelled to seek an income from prostitution."[9] Though such women are "rarely asked to help build the identity of the new nation, . . . news of their rapes . . . mobiliz[es] the anger of [the] men" to fight for the nation.[10] Thus, often when war rape has been trumpeted by the states of victimized women, neither the crime itself (and the institutions that enabled it to occur) nor even the victims, is the focus, but rather the victims are symbolic of the nation itself, and the crime symbolic of the undeserved aggression against the nation as a whole.

Even when feminists have fought to have rape recognized as a serious war crime, brought to light, and punished, they have often silenced unintentionally the women who have experienced war rape, the very women they hoped to help. As Karen Engle reminds us, feminists who argued that the rapes of Bosnian women in the Bosnia-Herzegovina war were acts of genocide tended to view all Bosnian women as victims, not only "incapable of fighting in the war, but also of speaking truthfully about whether they had been raped." Similarly, activists who emphasized rape as a gendered crime (rather than as a part of genocidal strategy), focused on women of all sides of the Bosnian-Herzegovinian war as victims, again shutting down possibilities for any of these women to have been active agents in the war.[11]

America's Dirty Secret: Rape in the Vietnam War

Complicating recognition and prosecution of war rape is the obvious fact that not all militaries that commit this crime will find themselves subject to an international war crimes tribunal; additionally, when the "losers" of a war have been the victims of such crimes, these rape victims do not garner the same recognition as more sympathetic victims. A case in point is German women who were raped after World War II, primarily by occupying Soviet forces. Though numerous rapes (some historians describing them as being of "massive incidence")[12] of German women occurred, they have not received much attention from international audiences. Hesitation to recognize crimes against German women is surely due to the legitimate suspicion of historians of the German past toward "any narrative that might support postwar Germans' self-perception as victims insofar as it might participate in a dangerous revival of German nationalism, whitewash the Nazi past, and normalize a genocidal war."[13] Thus, this case provides an excellent working example of historians' fearing the very purpose of a nation's open discussion of rape that Enloe pointed out—a revitalization of nationalism. However, in this case fear of the symbolic utilization of the crimes doubtless stymies research into the real, sociohistorical conditions that precipitated these rapes and their effect on their victims.

Not unrelated are the war rapes committed by militaries that never find themselves forced to submit to the jurisdiction of international tribunals. This is the circumstance that describes the widespread rapes by American GIs against Vietnamese civilians and POWs that occurred during the Vietnam War. However, not only did international juridical discourse overlook these crimes against Vietnamese women by U.S. forces directly after the time of the war, but recent feminists and other activists working against war rape as well as historians have continued to ignore this well-documented crime. In the aforementioned *War's Dirty Secret*, in which sex crimes against women in World War II, Bosnia-Herzegovina, and Rwanda are discussed in some depth and in which there are independent chapters devoted to non-American military brutality toward women in Guatemala, Nicaragua, and Haiti, the crimes against Vietnamese women are given only cursory notice in the introduction (Barstow, p. 5). After criticizing Seymour Hersh's convenient forgetting of the rapes that occurred at My Lai as an example of the ubiquitous omission of rape from histories of war, the editors then themselves neglect to include further information on the frequent rapes committed in Vietnam. In spite of the fact that there is certainly enough information on this subject to fill an entire section of chapters and that it is a much more recent occurrence than the sexual abuses of WWII, not even one chapter is devoted to discussing the sexual exploitation of women in the Vietnam War. Even more astonishingly, this oversight occurs in a book whose purpose is to change the trend in research and reportage to overlook, forget, or deny violence against women!

To my knowledge, Brownmiller's chapter on war in *Against Our Will* contains the most in-depth exploration (at thirty pages) of the U.S. military's sexual exploitation of women in Vietnam, a rather revealing fact since much more evidence of this exploitation and abuse has become known since 1975. Thus, Brownmiller's work demands recognition for its willingness to bring accusations against the U.S military (and implicitly the government) for its participation in this world-wide phenomenon. Her work is the exception, however, to a persistent inclination not to make sexual violence in the Vietnam War a topic of research or discussion, even though a wealth of irrefutable evidence of such violence exists in the primary sources, including testimony given in public hearings during the war, court proceedings and military investigations, oral accounts collected for publication both during and many years after the war, and literary works—including poetry, novels, and memoirs. These sources will be discussed in detail in the following chapters in an effort to reverse the trend toward academic erasure of these acts. Although precedent for erasing women's sexual assault during war has continued to exist despite recent feminist intervention, I will claim that none has remained as unrevealed as that of the Vietnamese women by U.S. armed forces. This refusal to recognize abuse by American GIs is important because the longer Americans do not acknowledge this history, the greater the potential grows for such abuses to recur and the longer veterans will remain unhealed from unexplored sources of traumatization.[14] Importantly, as pointed out in the preface, the refusal to address the fact of American war rape and its causes has surely had devastating consequences for a large percentage of our female GIs, who will only find themselves further victimized as their numbers increase in the U.S. military.

One is left to wonder what has precipitated, even in an era of burgeoning interest in women's war-related sexual trauma, this odd silence about and erasure of Vietnamese women's sexual abuse at the hands of American GIs and their allies. It is especially troubling that even well-meaning academics, such as Barstow and colleagues, uphold the same patterns of disremembering. One might claim that there is a lack of evidence from the Vietnamese women themselves. While it is true that extensive interviews with abused women, such as the kind conducted by aid workers in Bosnia-Herzegovina and Rwanda, do not exist for the Vietnam War, it is not true that there is a complete lack of evidence. On the contrary, there are at least two very important sources—Le Ly Hayslip's *Between Heaven and Earth* and Martha Hess's *Then the Americans Came*—giving voice to women who were sexually abused during the war. While the amount of evidence written by the women themselves is not nearly as great as it is for the atrocities that occurred during the 1990s, there is clearly enough to warrant further inquiry into the matter and more extensive information gathering from the women involved.

This work therefore contests the claim that inadequate information exists, demonstrating that literary and testimonial accounts from Vietnamese women as well as American veterans make sexual violence a topic often enough to warrant extended investigation. In fact, it is this very abundance of material that reveals the ideological underpinnings at the heart of forgetting women's trauma. The underlying reason for the lack of coverage of Vietnam War sexual violence is (usually) an unspoken decision by producers of cultural narrative—be they historians, filmmakers, literary critics, journalists, or politicians—to keep silent about and even deny such atrocities. To restore the comfortable myths of American exceptionalism, it has been necessary for such producers to "forget" particular instances of racial and gender hatred and violence that are evident in the history of the Vietnam War. For to admit these violences would demand that the militarized American exceptionalism from which such behavior sprang was problematic at its very core.

Even in academic circles, where attention to such events should be represented because they are part of the historical record, acknowledgment of Vietnamese women's sexual abuse is conspicuously lacking. Thus, even those whose special job it is to remember such events participate in this erasure. Seymour Hersh, who won the 1970 Pulitzer Prize for his reporting on My Lai, provides an example of this tendency toward disremembering. As Barstow notes, although the Peers Commission investigation and the court martial records of Lt. William Calley revealed that at least twenty women were raped during the massacre and confirmed that rape was a widespread practice, when Hersh wrote a thirtieth anniversary piece, he did not recall the rapes. Writing about the mass murder of civilians, especially of children, and dwelling on the mutilation of corpses, Hersh neglected to mention the rapes at all (p. 5). Thus, even the most celebrated reporter of the Vietnam War seems to have fallen prey to an ameliorated narrative of the war.

It is one of the large claims of this work, then, that, though a central fact of the war, rape and sexual violence against Vietnamese women have been effectively written out of historical scholarly critical memory and, even more consequential for popular memory, filmed out of the national narrative of the Vietnam War. I will show that these acts of forgetting have been necessary steps in the rehabilitation of the Vietnam War veteran. As cultural critic Keith Beattie argues, representations of the veteran in the early seventies "crudely depicted [him] as an inarticulate psychopath."[15] In the late 1970s and especially during the eighties and Reagan era, however, the Vietnam veteran was reconstructed. He became "an authentic [and sympathetic] spokesperson" on the war, though "he was permitted only a limited range of topics, predominantly . . . concerned with the common-sense notion of cultural unity. In this way the veteran emerged as a hero, valorized, in effect, not for his war experience but for his ability to contribute to the maintenance of cultural homogeneity and holism" (p. 61). Beattie argues that this rehabilitation and use of the veteran as a ventriloquist for messages of unity was one of three strategies of unity, terminology he uses to evoke the work and material effects of the ideology of unity within national culture since the later sixties. The strategy of veteran as ventriloquist was used to successfully "heal the wound" wrought by the Vietnam War, the wound being cultural division, which although it had long been a characteristic of U.S. culture, became widely attributed to the war and its effects (p. 7).

With Beattie's assessment in mind, it will be my goal in this book to posit an additional role for the veteran, one beyond that of cultural unifier; I am speaking of the role of valiant and true victim. Not only is he the only authentic spokesman on the war. More important, the Vietnam veteran is a traumatized guerilla warrior, victimized both by the "old, white men" who drafted him and sent him to a war with "one hand tied behind his back" and by the "spitting" countercultural protestors who did not support him.[16] As Arthur Egendorf put it in 1985, Vietnam vets by the early eighties were "tragic victims of a war that went bad, in a time of cultural change and conflict . . . Anyone could root for the good guys who did their duty and didn't get a fair shake. These feelings were stirred by the media . . . [And] [s]ympathy for the Vietnam veteran . . . joined motherhood and apple pie as a hallmark of true Americanism."[17] The conception of the veteran-as-victim is not without cultural or political significance; rather, it has enabled the conservative revisioning of the Vietnam War, a revisioning built on rehabilitated American exceptionalism.[18]

I argue that through its conferral of extreme victimhood and metonymic representation of the national "wound" upon the Vietnam veteran, American national culture enabled itself to appropriate the veteran's victimhood. Through the traumatized body of the veteran, national rhetoric and popular memory transformed America's role in Vietnam from a bloody attempt at neoimperialistic domination to the nation's victimization by its own weak and corrupt leaders. Further, this revisionist memory of the war suggests that American citizens' own "self-loathing" as they came to doubt the promises of American exceptionalism during the war was both a contributing factor to losing the war and a self-inflicted trauma from which the nation must heal.[19]

Necessary to the rehabilitation of American exceptionalism was a concurrent redevelopment of nationalist masculinity. The traumatized veteran of the early eighties provided the nation with a convenient response to the women's movement, which had flourished throughout the seventies. In answer to the movement's claims that America was a sexist society in which women comprised an oppressed majority, the Vietnam veteran represented a male who was a victim. Veterans' amputated limbs, scars, and shattering symptoms of PTSD proved much more visible signs of victimization than the types of oppression the women's movement pointed out, which were frequently subtle or hidden from public view, such as discrimination in the workplace and domestic abuse. Moreover, according to sociologist Jerry Lembcke, in the mythical stories that proliferated in the eighties of returning Vietnam veterans being spat upon in airports, the antiwar spitter was almost always "a girl or male 'longhair,'" a telling image that clearly represents the veteran as a victim particularly of activist *women*.[20] The refiguring of the veteran as sympathetic victim (both of combat trauma and aggressive women at home), however, covered the excesses of masculinity apparent in American soldiers' actions in Vietnam.

When I initially conceived this project, trauma theory seemed an obvious analytic angle from which to approach the fact that the rhetoric of veteran victimization had overwritten Vietnamese women's sexual trauma. However, rather than providing a means to better understand the trauma veterans wrote and spoke of in relation to their aggressive actions, I came to see and will here argue that the very development of current trauma theory with its emphasis on the medicalization of PTSD, together with its theoretical blind spots, has been crucial to American culture's reconceptualization of the veteran solely as a victim, which in effect erased the trauma of the veterans' Vietnamese victims. That is, the currency of trauma studies within mainstream American discourse actually was catalyzed by the 1980s reconceptualization of the victimized veteran.[21]

A genealogy of trauma studies shows that much ground-laying work in trauma had been done in the late nineteenth and early twentieth centuries by theorists such as Josef Breuer, Pierre Janet, Sigmund Freud, and later clinicians. They struggled to cure World War II soldiers who experienced "combat fatigue," while psychoanalysts working with Holocaust survivors identified chronic complexes of problems they variously named "concentration camp syndrome" and "survivor syndrome." But none of these attempts to clarify or treat the effects of profound trauma aroused the widespread American interest in trauma that came with the rehabilitation of the Vietnam veteran. It was not until psychiatrists, social workers, activists, and veterans themselves engaged in a struggle for the political recognition of the postwar suffering of Vietnam vets that *psychological trauma* and *PTSD* became household words in the United States. The medicalization of his condition would prove the turning point for representations of the Vietnam veteran. While in the seventies, returning veterans' sometimes-erratic behavior earned them the reputation of being dangerous and even psychopathic, in the eighties, the much publicized, debilitating symptoms and toxic behaviors of some returned veterans were now seen as part of the complex posttraumatic stress syndrome. In 1980, PTSD was first recognized as a serious disorder by the American Psychological Association and included in the association's third edition of the *Diagnostic and Statistical Manual of Mental Disorders* (*DSM-III*). This medicalization of the effects of veterans' psychological trauma gave the stamp of "objective" scientific approval to the national reconception of the Vietnam veteran as symbol of the American wound and legitimized veteran sufferers' mental health problems to the VA.

The newfound interest in the veteran as a victim suffering from PTSD only proved to be another means of ignoring the war's events and the veteran's role in it, however. In fact, James William Gibson suggests that the discussions swirling around PTSD and dioxin poisoning of veterans in the early eighties actually allowed

> [t]he war . . . to [disappear] as a topic for study and political consideration and instead bec[o]me dispersed and institutionalized in the complex of medical, psychiatric, and legal

> discourses. It was as if a new series of medical and judicial problems with no traceable origin had appeared in American society. Or rather, although it was acknowledged that Vietnam was the origin, once the word "Vietnam" was mentioned, the war itself was dismissed and discussion moved on to how an institution could solve the problem . . . In this way the war became progressively displaced and repressed at the same time it was written about.[22]

Just as discussions of institutional problems allowed the politics of the war to be erased, the veteran's victimized masculinity[23]—which relied on these medicalized narratives as well as popular representations of the "vicious feminists" of the antiwar movement—allowed the behaviors associated with American militarized masculinity to be buried. Because the veteran's plight was a lightning rod for anxieties and animosities provoked by the women's liberation movement, it neatly symbolized the wound of disunity "caused" by Vietnam. His trauma—and the need to heal it—came to be used to reinforce nationalism, as the American people were told they must heal the wound of Vietnam in the name of unity. During the buildup to and in the wake of the victory of the first Gulf War, George Bush Sr. jubilantly spoke of "kicking the Vietnam Syndrome," and Americans were encouraged to support with yellow ribbons and ceremonial parades the Gulf War vets as a means of doing their part to heal the Vietnam-era wounds of disunity.[24]

The national adoption of the veteran-as-victim mindset, however, was not without consequence. The most obvious effect of displacing national conversation about the war onto the medical and psychological issues of the Vietnam veteran was, as I have been pointing out, the suppression of the traumas of the truest victims of the Vietnam war—Vietnamese civilians, namely, women. This suppression was absolutely necessary though; for acknowledging the aggressive and atrocious actions of American soldiers in Vietnam would certainly mitigate—possibly destroy—Americans' ability to view the veteran as simply a victim. This national appropriation of the veteran-as-traumatized-victim reveals the pernicious power struggles that characterize national culture. As trauma theorist Ann Cvetkovich warns in *An Archive of Feelings*: "'the nation is a space of struggle,' . . . and forms of violence . . . are forgotten or covered over by the amnesiac powers of national culture, which is adept at using one trauma story to suppress another."[25]

The veteran-as-victim paradigm not only smothered American recognition of Vietnamese trauma, however. It was also, at a deeper level, a refusal to truly understand the trauma of the veterans themselves.

As Kalí Tal notes, "As a society, we have effectively inhibited Vietnam veterans from speaking in terms other than those we have defined as acceptable, silencing those whose stories fall outside the boundaries of convention."[26] Drawing on the work of Michel Foucault, Tal points out the political significance of the nation's refusal to hear veterans witness to their Vietnam War experiences: "Once codified, the traumatic experience becomes a weapon in another battle, the struggle for political power . . . The speech of survivors, then, is highly politicized. If 'telling it like it was' threatens the status quo, powerful political, economic, and social forces will pressure survivors either to keep their silence or to revise their stories. If the survivor community is a marginal one, their voices will be drowned out by those with the influence and resources to silence them, and to trumpet a revised version of their trauma" (p. 7).Tal's perceptive analysis of the means by which survivors' speech is molded, revised, and used by dominant culture can clearly be seen in the way national culture—in both popular and academic realms—has responded to the testimony of Vietnam veterans. Even when veterans themselves were willing to admit it, the public at large has refused to hear what many of these veterans have to say: that they were as much aggressors as victims. It is only when veterans were reconceptualized entirely as victims that they received the "warm embrace, [the] welcome home, . . . [and] a long-overdue recognition of gratitude" from their fellow Americans.

It will be one goal of this project, then, to show that many veterans themselves sought to bear witness to the true events of the Vietnam War—even their participation in atrocities—some to the point of publicly asking to be tried as war criminals in the Winter Soldier Investigation. Veterans' endeavors at such witness bearing, however, have been perpetually thwarted. Attempts during the war were squelched and resulted in the Nixon administration's harassment of veteran witnesses. Subsequent postwar efforts have been ignored or misinterpreted, subsumed into the veteran-as-victim representation or muted by it. I further posit, therefore, that in its refusal to truly listen to, share in, and bear responsibility for the nation's complicity in Vietnam veterans' actions in the war, American culture retraumatizes its veterans. America's much vaunted, open-armed acceptance of the wounded Vietnam veteran, which welcomes him home even as it turns a blind eye to the history of the war and our soldiers' actions in it, is only yet another wounding of the veteran. He will be denied healing until his witness is finally heard by his country.

Neither psychologists' medicalization of the veteran's trauma as PTSD nor what Cvetkovich calls "[t]he amnesiac powers of national culture" is solely to blame for America's uncomplicated understanding of the victimized veteran. His rehabilitation and the subsequent appropriation of his trauma have been facilitated by the theoretical shortcomings of contemporary trauma studies itself, for it does not adequately theorize the trauma of a person who is both a victim and a victimizer.[27] Rather, trauma studies has tended to approach the traumatized subject as merely—and simplistically—a victimized subject. This tendency toward either/or conceptualizations of the subject is problematic even when applied to the other favored subjects of trauma theory, rape and incest victims and Holocaust survivors, for the boundaries between complete victimization and complicity/agency are rarely as clear cut as such classification implies. The grotesque implications of this binary become only too obvious when applied to many combat-experienced veterans. Take those who participated at My Lai as an example. While they certainly may have been traumatized by the endangerment of their lives and the deaths of close comrades, and in this sense are "victims" of violence, they also committed horrible acts of aggression against other human beings, including mass murder and possibly sexual abuse. Surely no one could classify the My Lai aggressors as simple "victims." And a review of the testimony and writings of veterans reveals that much of the "trauma" Vietnam veterans as a group experienced was indeed a product, not of proximity to combat, but of the deleterious psychological effects of having committed atrocities. Given the exclusive focus of most trauma theorists on the victimization of veteran sufferers, however, such critics have failed to theorize the complicated situation of the victim-victimizer, who is not only traumatized by combat, but who also has experienced the devastating effects of committing violence against others.

One theorist in particular comes in for criticism in this project: literary scholar Cathy Caruth. Caruth, a psychoanalytic critic with post-structuralist allegiances, is an extremely influential critic whose theory informs most literary avenues of trauma studies. She has grounded her claims about trauma and the nature of traumatic memory in the neurobiological approach employed by neuropsychologist Bessel A. van der Kolk. Based on his scientific studies of flashbacks, Van der Kolk explains PTSD and the human response to trauma in terms of an "implicit or non-narrative traumatic memory"—an "imprint memory" of which the trauma victim cannot be consciously aware or verbally narrate its events. Rather than a narratable past event, van der Kolk sees the implicit traumatic memory as more akin to "bodily . . . reflex actions . . . that lie outside verbal-semantic-linguistic representation" (Leys, p. 7). Drawing on van der Kolk's work, Caruth claims that victims cannot truly understand and testify to the trauma they experienced, either to themselves or to others. All they can do is repeat the trauma as if it were happening continually, namely, in the form of flashbacks and nightmares. Paradoxically, it is the victim's failure to narrate his or her trauma to him/herself that enables its transmission to others who can then imaginatively comprehend the trauma as well as literally share in the suffering of the victim.

When applied to the Vietnam veteran, Caruth's theory suggests that the meaning of the Vietnam War and the American experience there can only be performatively communicated to the nation through "the suffering of those who 'listen' but were not there" (Leys, p. 254). And once sharing the suffering of the trauma victim, those who were not there become, through this shared suffering, participants and co-owners of the traumatic event.[28] On the surface, co-owning a victim's trauma seems a viable means for trauma victims to heal through the supportive understanding of their community. However, because of the fundamental flaw in Caruth's theory—the uncomplicated, binary understanding of trauma victims solely as victims, which necessitates a suppression of veterans' trauma of aggression—the practical result has been the co-ownership of victimization rather than responsibility. What is more, in its transference from victim to those who would co-own it, the trauma itself achieves an iconic status, as evidenced in Caruth's quoting of Van der Kolk when he suggests "sacrilege" might be committed against a memory of trauma. From this perspective, "trauma in its literality, muteness, and unavailability for representation becomes a sacred object or 'icon' that it would be 'sacrilege' to misappropriate or tamper with in any way" (Leys, pp. 252–53). The influence in American culture of this theory of trauma, which confers a sacredness and inviolability to a victim's trauma, may be seen in the trend Egendorf noted in which sympathy for the Vietnam veteran has become a necessity for "true Americanism."

A further problem with Caruth's assessment of trauma is that, as an answer to critiques of poststructuralism, it itself eliminates "moral meaning"[29]: it shuts down ethical and political assessment regarding soldiers' actions during the war. Authorized by scientific, neurobiological discourse that claims traumatic events cause physiological changes in the brain, veterans' actions in Vietnam cannot be critiqued on the basis of morality or ethics; rather, they are only important as traumatic events that cause such changes. Further, as Cvetkovich points out, "By consistently stressing questions of epistemology and trauma as structurally unknowable, [Caruth] flattens out the specificities of trauma in a given historical and political context" (p. 19). It is this flattening of specificities that enables Vietnam veterans and Holocaust survivors to operate on a concurrent plane of victimhood in most discussions of trauma. In the case of Vietnam veterans, this model implies that all who have experienced trauma, whether those who suffer from PTSD caused by combat or those who suffer similar symptoms as a result of overwhelming feelings of guilt from their participation in atrocities, are both victims of an external trauma that "causes objective changes in the brain in ways that tend to eliminate the issue of moral meaning and ethical assessment" (Leys, p. 7). Thus, for veterans, the very immorality of the acts they committed creates the inability to assess the morality of these acts after the fact.

A further detrimental consequence of Caruth's driving interest in trauma as representative of "a rethinking of reference" is her exclusive focus on trauma as a catastrophic event, a focus that severely hampers her theory's application to the complex subject position of the Vietnam veteran.[30] She and similar critics ignore victims who suffer from more everyday kinds of trauma, such as racism or sexism. These "systemic traumas," as Cvetkovich calls them, do not necessarily have the intense focal moment or period that car accidents and rapes do, but they can be equally damaging as they occur over lifetimes and generations. In opposition to Caruth's model, Cvetkovich argues for a "sense of trauma as connected to the textures of everyday experience. Moreover, . . . [C vetkovich] resist[s] the authority given to medical discourses and especially the diagnosis of traumatic experience as . . . PTSD" (p. 4). In *An Archive of Feelings,* she proposes a different paradigm for trauma studies, one that "forges a path between a debilitating descent into pain and the denial of it" (p. 6); her "investigation of 'trauma cultures'—public cultures that form in and around trauma—means that ultimately [her work] is not only focused on texts as representations of narratives of trauma but also concerned with how cultural production that emerges around trauma enables new practices and publics" (pp. 9–10).

Building on Cvetkovich's theorization, I form an analysis of the trauma witnessed by various survivors of the Vietnam War that attends not just to the moments of catastrophic trauma veterans and Vietnamese women experienced in the war, but also the systemic traumas of which they were victims long before the war. My analysis enables, therefore, a nuanced understanding of the particularities of the traumas experienced by those who suffered in Vietnam, both Vietnamese women and American veterans. It allows for a complex conception of the veteran, not just as victim, but also as a perpetrator of trauma. Moreover, understanding the systemic traumas of which veterans were themselves already victims, such as racism, violently enforced ideals of masculinity and heterosexism, and classism, can then inform a critique of the underlying causes for GI participation in violent abuses against the Vietnamese. This analysis is based upon the veterans' own writing and testimony and finally allows their own quite sophisticated critiques of American culture to be heard rather than "silencing those whose stories fall outside the boundaries of convention" (Tal, p. 14).

In constructing this analysis of the veteran's complicated role in perpetrating violence in Vietnam and the ways in which his testimony to this role has been ignored and erased, it is my hope that, by recognizing the damaging systems that prepared American GIs to commit terrible abuses, by facing these atrocities head-on rather than denying them, and by understanding the ways national culture attempts to cover over such events, readers will realize that the potential for similar abuses exists and that steps must be taken to prevent them. Perhaps most important, this process opens a means for true healing of veterans. Unlike Caruth, I would suggest that veterans are fully capable of testifying to and understanding their trauma; they only require an audience that will allow them to narrate their trauma, not just of victimization but also of aggression. Especially, society must hear their analysis of the deep societal roots of the atrocities committed. The key to this process is the creation of new publics, which are willing to truly listen to veterans. These new publics—as opposed to those that failed to listen to the veterans in the decades during and after the war—must be sensitive to the veterans' narratives of gender and racial violence. Rather than suppressing such narratives as disunifying, these publics must accept them as an essential part of the American story. In this way, such publics will be integral to veteran healing; they will be the vehicle permitting veteran narratives of the war to be recognized in American culture and the veterans themselves finally to be accepted.

In chapter 2, through an analysis of histories, oral accounts, and novels, I will highlight the voices of Vietnamese women who speak about their sexual abuse during the war, contesting the implicit claim that inadequate evidence exists to conduct valid research in this area. Through these voices and an analysis of the women's histories, readers will hear the women suggest causes for the abuse they suffered. Relying extensively on the memoirs of Vietnamese American immigrant Le Ly Hayslip, this chapter will also reveal why Vietnamese women were particularly vulnerable to sexual abuse from an invading army. I will also analyze traditional and contemporary gender relations in Vietnam to explain how and why the subject of Vietnamese women's sexual abuse at the hands of Americans has not been more vocally discussed in Vietnam itself or by the Vietnamese in the global context.

Chapter 3 will continue this speculation concerning why American men felt entitled and sometimes compelled to commit acts of brutality against Vietnamese women, but in this chapter, I will analyze the voices of non-Vietnamese, particularly those of American veterans, as they spoke in public forums against the war. Not only do these witnesses give important testimony proving that sexual atrocities took place on a daily basis, but in these transcripts, one sees young American men and women struggling to understand the complex motivations behind GI actions in Vietnam; they begin to propose reasons for this behavior, forming critiques of American culture as racist, sexist, and classist. Veterans particularly point to their brutal experiences in basic training as life-altering, although they suggest the modes of thinking, such as violent forms of masculinity, which were exploited and exacerbated by their drill instructors, had been instilled in early childhood. This chapter will also note the ways in which the nascent women's movement interacted with the veterans' antiwar movement, encouraging veterans to think critically about their conception of women, and I will suggest that much of the veterans' critique of the Vietnam War and their behavior in it was drawn from and informed by the concerns and problems beginning to be voiced by the women's movement.

Chapter 4 analyzes literary writings of veterans as they began to reflect on their war experiences from the perspective of the postwar years. The thinking in these writings is much more nuanced than that found in the war-years' testimony, the intervening years having given the veteran authors time to fully analyze the causes and consequences of their behavior during the war. The authors whose works I analyze were chosen for their importance in the Vietnam War literary canon and for their works' interest in gender relations during and after the war. In these works, the authors point to the various problematic systems at work in post–World War II American culture mentioned earlier, but they explore much more deeply how these systems were at once deeply traumatizing to them as children and young men and then how the transplantation and exaggeration of these systems into the war environment of Vietnam enabled the military to condone and even encourage monstrous behavior by its soldiers, especially toward women. The chapter ends with an analysis of W. D. Ehrhart's memoirs, which suggest the consequences of soldiers' behavior toward Vietnamese women far outlasted the war and reached beyond Vietnam.

In chapter 5, I turn to the important question of how these narratives that make clear and public the atrocious sexual acts of American GIs in Vietnam have come to be erased in popular American conceptions of the war. By studying filmic representations of the war, particularly those that are based on works discussed in chapter 3 (and thus ones in which representations of woman abuse in Vietnam are ubiquitous), including *Platoon, Full Metal Jacket, Casualties of War,* and *Heaven and*

Earth, I argue that Hollywood productions of the war are leading sites of erasure. Though the works from which these films were adapted provide important examples of rape and sexual abuse in Vietnam, such events are erased in the film. Rather than the victims of rape and abuse, Vietnamese women are depicted instead as greedy prostitutes and wholly unsympathetic characters. The importance of these films to popular understandings of the war cannot be overstated, for it is from Hollywood that U.S. citizens have—for those coming of age after the war—come to understand the history of the war in Vietnam and—for those who lived through the war years—to reremember it. This is especially true because, as films based on "true events," such as *Casualties of War* and *Heaven and Earth,* or taken from the memories of Vietnam veterans—as in *Platoon*—these films have attained a particular ability to speak about the war with an air of authority because of their billing as based in the reality of some veteran. Using Anthony Swofford's definition of "warnography," I will suggest that the Vietnam films have produced a pernicious formula for representing gender relations vis-à-vis war, one that will continue to affect new generations of American boys and their concepts of masculinity.

2

Vietnamese Voices

Accounts of War-Time Sexual Trauma

Although this book focuses primarily on the accounts and evidence from American soldiers and records regarding the rape of Vietnamese women, I wish to frame this evidence within the context of the experiences of the women directly affected by these soldiers' actions. Thus, my project begins by forwarding what Vietnamese women themselves have said about their treatment during the American War, as they refer to it. The lack of major research on American veteran accounts of the sexual abuse of Vietnamese women during the war has led to even less analysis of what these women have said about their sexual abuse. Silence in the academy does not necessarily indicate systemic discrimination or blindness to women's issues. As discussed in the previous chapter, feminist scholars recently have produced much important work regarding women's under-recognized roles in war. Rather, I suggest the inability to see women's trauma in the Vietnam War has occurred because—unlike the wars in Bosnia-Herzegovina, Rwanda, and Latin America, about which women's writing has proliferated—the Vietnam War involved the United States. As I have been arguing, American discourse about the Vietnam War has, from the beginning, largely focused on the cost to America and its citizens. This focus has effectively discouraged the acknowledgment of non-American views of the war. Moreover, in the insidious method noted by Kalí Tal, national rhetoric has used the trauma of American Vietnam veterans to silence the trauma of Vietnamese women. For to acknowledge Vietnamese women's trauma would threaten U.S. national interests by pointing out the violent excesses of militarized masculinity, a concept the veteran's trauma has been used to rebuild.

As Renny Christopher notes in her excellent work, *The Viet Nam War/The American War: Images and Representations in Euro-American and*

Vietnamese Exile Narratives (1995), America's ethnocentric and nationalist rhetoric surrounding the war has "caus[ed] America to turn hermetically around and around about itself so that the same notes—a few notes from the Left, a few notes from the Right—are sounded repeatedly and no new understandings can be reached. These polarized positions share an ethnocentrism that conceives of the war as an American 'experience.'"[1] Soldiers mythologized Vietnam in a John Wayne cinematic conceptualization from the very beginning, and the mythologizing of the "Vietnam experience" has continued to the present through political rhetoric and, I will argue, especially through Hollywood representations of the war. Additionally, long-standing American cultural mythology that emphasizes the individual and the primacy of personal experience encouraged national narratives of the war to focus on the individual soldier's war experience.[2] Because the Vietnamese experience lies far outside the American soldier's experience, their views are seen as unimportant and extraneous to the war as an American cultural "experience." Thus, Vietnamese representations of the war have been largely ignored, including those published in the United States by Vietnamese refugees.[3] Christopher suggests not only are representations of the war that focus on individual experience at fault in the reinforcement of this ethnocentrism, but so also is literary criticism, which has celebrated and valorized such representations.

As a corrective to the tradition of analyzing various aspects of the war only from the American perspective, this chapter will consult Vietnamese sources for firsthand accounts and evidence of the sexual abuse American soldiers claim was meted out on a regular basis. Drawing on these sources and scholarly accounts of gender relations in wartime and contemporary Vietnam, I will also suggest several reasons rape and sexual abuse receive so little comment, even within Vietnamese accounts. As trauma theorist Ann Cvetkovich notes, "[b]ecause trauma can be unspeakable and unrepresentable and because it is marked by forgetting and dissociation, it often seems to leave behind no records at all."[4] While this is true of any trauma, sexual abuse victims frequently find speaking about (and thus leaving records of) their abuse extremely difficult because of its deeply private nature. Even more, women victims of sexual trauma are made to feel responsible for their victimization, for they have been "taught to believe that they provoke men to assault them . . . They are taught that there is a thin line between seduction and rape, and that it is their responsibility to keep men from crossing that line."[5] Even in the United States, the justice system favors those *accused* of rape or sexual abuse, forcing victims to prove that the sexual contact was not consensual, thus increasing victims' fear of the "social, psychological, and personal consequences" of prosecuting their abusers.[6]

If this is the case in the United States, rape and sexual trauma are even more unspeakable in cultures more openly repressive of women, such as Vietnamese culture of the war years and even today, which Vietnam studies scholars continue to classify as "charged with feudal relations of power . . . structured around the veneration of elders and filial piety," despite reforms to equalize gender relations."[7] The innately private nature of sexual trauma coupled with Vietnamese attitudes toward women makes it very difficult for female victims to speak out about their trauma in that culture. To explore these women's complex situation, I will begin with a brief discussion of women's historical positioning in Vietnamese society and show that the historically accepted oppression and sexual abuse of women continues to haunt contemporary Vietnam. I will highlight women's role in Vietnam's American war, noting how roles differed for women of the North and the South, and then I will turn to the reasons both Vietnamese women and Vietnam as a nation might be reluctant to place women's sexual abuse during the war on the stage of international debate. After this sociohistorical contextualization of sexual violence toward Vietnamese women, I will analyze literary sources that offer evidence of rape and sexual abuse by Americans, including two celebrated Vietnamese novels as well as the collection of Martha Hess's interviews with South Vietnamese peasants; these sources testify to the veracity of the memoirs of Le Ly Hayslip, the most well-known and celebrated of Vietnamese American writers. The chapter ends with an analysis of Hayslip's works.

Gender Relations and Sexual Abuse in Vietnam: Historical and Contemporary

Women have filled varying roles during Vietnam's long history, and the social constraints placed on them have shifted dramatically over time. In earlier centuries, women held crucial leadership positions; for instance, during the Lê dynasty (1428–1788), Princess Đoan Trang was named *nu tong binh* (female commander) and led her army to several military victories.[8] Similarly, Vietnamese folk history celebrates the Trung sisters, who, leading the Vietnamese military forces, drove out Chinese invaders in the first century. Women's earlier active involvement in governance and the military came to an end in the nineteenth century, however. The reigning Nguyen dynasty emphasized Confucianism, which, with its patriarchal strictures, placed much more repressive social constraints on women than had previously existed. As scholar Lê Tuan Hùng explains, "Confucian ideology propagates a system of gender roles in society:

a social role for men and a domestic role for women." Through the "concepts of *tam tòng* [three submissions] and *tu uc* [four virtues]," Confucianism oriented women, particularly those from established urban families, toward domestic affairs only. The "three submissions" mandated a woman's obedience first to her father, then to her husband after marriage, and finally to her oldest son after her husband's death, thus defining women and girls only in relation to their male relatives. Never could a woman be truly independent. The "four virtues" were designed to complement the three submissions; they encouraged women to perfect their "domestic skills, beauty, calm speech, and virtuous character."[9] Women's adherence to these virtues determined their value within the family unit and in society. Particularly important for her standing—and relevant for this book—is the final virtue of good character, which decreed that a woman's sexual intimacy be reserved for her husband.

Further complicating these unequal gender relations were the stresses of colonialism. During the period of French occupation of Vietnam (1883–1954), women not only occupied a subordinate position within their families due to religious and cultural tradition but also found themselves made particularly vulnerable to exploitation because of their need to seek employment outside the home in order to avoid poverty. "In Vietnamese texts on this period, there are allusions to the sexualization of women; women became prostitutes or were victimized by rape and what we know as sexual harassment in the workplace with no recourse" because of their need to retain employment.[10] Lynne Goodstein notes that "the legacy of rape, prostitution, and sexual harassment" begun under French rule continued through the wartime period with the United States (p. 278). Even with the advent of socialism, these repressive values have continued to be subtly encouraged by the state. "*The Women's Newspaper*, the official voice of Vietnamese women, still stresses that protecting women's interests means educating them to dress appropriately, remain chaste, maintain a decent way of life and exemplify the gentleness of Vietnamese women."[11] As feminist and Vietnam studies scholar Kathleen Barry notes, the "[u]nchanged marital feudalism in private relations [that persists in Vietnam today] leaves women with either male dominated marriage and the family or prostitution."[12]

These attitudes toward women have allowed terrible abuse of various kinds to be culturally accepted. Physical abuse of wives was common in Vietnamese households during the war years,[13] and, as scholar Le Thi Quy reports, even "forty years after the liberation from the colonial and feudal yoke, vestiges of the Confucian attitude of honouring men and despising women still linger and have even regained vitality in some places. This attitude creates a kind of terrible violence against women."[14] Family violence has been and remains by far the leading cause of divorce over the last two decades.[15] Based on Hayslip's memoirs, rape during the war years by Vietnamese men does not appear to have been uncommon; as we will see in her narrative, Vietnamese women and girls during wartime met with conflicting demands—at once they were expected to be willing and pliant, submissive to all men, and yet they were also expected to protect their sexual purity for the husbands and future husbands.[16]

Although Goodstein notes that little is known about rape in Vietnam—earlier in its history or currently—due to an "[a]bsence of research and silence on the subject," there is good reason to believe that the demands Hayslip narrates persist in Vietnam today (p. 276). While the "generally accepted position [among Vietnamese scholars is] that 'rape is not a major problem in Vietnam'" that belief reflects such scholars' characterization of rape as only occurring between strangers and the fact that there is a relatively low rate of stranger rape reported in Vietnam (p. 284). However, coupled with the anecdotal evidence from women's narratives (such as Hayslip's), the high domestic violence rates, and women's subordinate position in the family, Goodstein's proposal that "the state of contemporary Vietnamese thinking about rape is similar to the state of Western thinking before the issue became a rallying point for feminist activism and scholarship in the 1970s"—when rape was believed to occur only among strangers and the concept of acquaintance rape or husband rape seemed preposterous—is quite reasonable (p. 285). Indeed, she notes that when asked about the frequency with which husbands force "their wives to submit to sexual advances against their will, one Vietnamese scholar gave a terse but clear response, 'Everywhere'" (p. 285). Additionally, "Vietnam continues to maintain conventional standards of conduct with respect to sexuality," standards that have lost much force in the West since the sexual revolution. Just as Hayslip notes in her memoirs, it continues to be the case that "sexual victimization . . . bring[s] shame to women victims and could have serious ramifications with respect to their chances of marriageability" (pp. 283–84). Understandably, this perhaps unintentional, but nevertheless existing, societal punishment of the victim results in women's tendency to endure sexual abuse without complaint to authorities.

Similarly, Khuat Thu Hong's more recent 2004 report, "Sexual Harassment in Vietnam: A New Term for an Old Phenomenon," stresses the historical continuity of such attitudes. Using the folkloric verse, "Flowers are made for people to pick,/Girls are born for people to tease," Hong suggests the long existence and naturalization of Vietnamese male harassment of women (p. 117). Though the scope of her report is narrowly focused on sexual harassment, its assessment of cultural gender roles and expectations is useful in my discussion of sexual violence. Hong notes that while Vietnam's *Đổi mới* (renovation)[17] of the eighties "has brought a greater sense of openness [about sexual matters], many Vietnamese are still not prepared to discuss sexual harassment. Victims rarely talk about it because society fails to protect them. If women complain about sexual harassment, they risk losing their reputation, their employment, or they face other serious consequences because of social mores about women and taboos around sex" (p. 120). Hong notes that sexual harassment has been linked to sex rather than gender power relations; this linkage makes women's reporting of harassment damaging to their reputation, which "is closely attached to her sexual purity and virtue." As one Vietnamese woman put it, "We women do not dare to talk about [sexual harassment], but that doesn't mean it does not exist . . . We fear that once these stories are told, women may lose their reputation or value" (p. 120). If admitting to being sexually harassed opens a woman to serious aspersions against her chastity, how much more so would being the victim of sexual violence in which a woman has been physically violated.

As noted earlier, the societal attitude that permits men to take what they want from women in terms of sexual favors was extant before the war with the Americans; this is why stories of rape during the war frequently involve not only American men, but Vietnamese men as well.[18] However, a history of sexual abuse in Vietnam does not excuse or explain American men's participation in this abuse. Understanding the role sexual abuse plays in Vietnamese culture, however, aids in understanding why the rape of Vietnamese girls and women apparently raised so little outcry from the victims. The historical and continuing abuse of women in Vietnamese culture also suggests that the Vietnamese government itself has a stake in maintaining women's silence on their abuse, for a critical assessment of women's abuse at the hands of Americans must inevitably lead to an analysis of Vietnam's own endorsement by willful ignorance of male sexual violence against women.

Women's Role in the American Conflict

Thus, while historical women heroines such as the Trung sisters continue to be celebrated in Vietnamese culture, from the nineteenth century onward, women have been deemed inferior to men; defined by their relationship to men and relegated to the domestic sphere, they are valued according to how well they fulfill the feminine virtues. As historian

Karen Gottschang Turner explains, a woman coming of age during the Vietnam War era was taught that

> as a woman she was an inferior member within the family and society, a person of lesser value than a son no matter what she managed to accomplish by virtue of her talents and character. This doesn't mean that daughters were unloved or neglected in all Vietnamese families, but sons were preferred for economic and religious reasons . . . In traditional society only men could serve in public office; they alone could use their power to protect their family interests. A woman's only security rested in her ability to manipulate the affections of her father, her husband, and her son if she had one. If she did not bear a son, she faced a sad old age.[19]

Even progressive men were fearful of women's independence. One male writer wrote in a 1917 essay advocating women's education, that "[w]hen men lack virtue, it is harmful to society; but not as harmful as when women become unsound, because unsound women damage the very roots of society" (qtd. in Turner, p. 43). Thus, rather than arguing for new potentials for women's contributions to society through education, this writer claims that women's education is important because it will ultimately support prescribed ideals of feminine virtue.

Despite the attitudes that so narrowly circumscribed women's position in society and family, however, the country called upon women to carry out not only their established domestic duties but also men's duties during Vietnam's long half-century of war.[20] And perform they did. In the urbanized North, women filled many support service roles and even served in active, frontline military duty. Military historian Nguyen Quoc Dung estimates that the number of women in the regular North Vietnamese Army (NVA) together with those participating in the militia, local forces, and the professional teams was almost 1.5 million. Women composed between 70 and 80 percent of the youth making up the volunteer youth corps, an untrained "shock group" who served in the most dangerous spots along the Ho Chi Minh Trail (Turner, pp. 20–21). They were charged with keeping open the strategic roads and guarding key points while they were under attack; from 1965 through 1975, the youth corps built six airstrips, defused tens of thousands of bombs, shot down fifteen airplanes, and transported tens of thousands of pounds of cargo, weapons, and foods down the trail (p. 35). In the South, in which the population was largely rural and agricultural, peasant women took on the duties of their husbands and fathers as the men volunteered or were conscripted by one side or the other. As Hayslip notes in her first memoir, "No man was believed capable of earning a living and raising children at the same time, although, as my sister [whose husband joined the NVA] was finding out, this was regularly expected of women in the same position" (*Heaven,* p. 20). Not only did women care alone for their homes and children, but they cultivated and harvested several rice crops a year;[21] as their farmland (and means of livelihood) was destroyed or their families were removed from their land to "strategic hamlets," many women also turned to black market sales, menial labor on American bases, and prostitution to support their families.

However, women's advance into the male sphere, even temporarily and under dire circumstances, was not always accepted with approbation. In a 1966 article in *Nhan Dan*, the Communist Party newspaper of North Vietnam, one author argued that the numbers of women party members must be increased and that women must be given more responsibility. His call for egalitarianism within the party, however, reveals men's reluctance to accept women as their equals. As the author explained, "[T]here are Party branches which have not for years admitted any women members . . . Many Party members do not want to admit women because although they think that they are courageous and diligent, they also believe 'women cannot lead but must be led'" (qtd. in Turner, p. 125). As hinted at in this passage, in which men "think that [women] are courageous and diligent" but should not lead, women in Vietnam were often held up as exemplary members of society, even as their lives and activities were harshly circumscribed. Similarly, in Vietnamese depictions of the war, nationalistic rhetoric idealizes women as sacrificing mothers, emblematic of the Vietnam's sacrifice for unification. Positioning women as stoic sufferers, such rhetoric denies women's agency and their active roles during war. As is the case with war widows everywhere, since the war, the women of Vietnam have provided a national symbol of "women's capacity to offer up personal happiness for the welfare of the state and its people" (p. 156). Of course, women's usefulness as a rhetorical symbol does not translate into financial support or recompense for their service and sacrifice during the war, as male combatants are generally rewarded.[22]

Symbolic Use of War Rape in Vietnam

Women's stoic suffering in war is not the only emblematic use made of their war experience. Feminist political scientist Cynthia Enloe importantly points out that "[r]ape and prostitution have been central to many men's construction of the nationalist cause. They have permitted men to hear the feminized nation beckoning them to act as 'her' protectors. The external enemy is imagined to be other men, men who would defile or denigrate the nation."[23] This strategy was used frequently throughout Vietnam's history, as many of the tales of heroic women involved their rape or prostitution in service of the state, perhaps most famously in the long narrative poem, *The Tale of Kieu*.[24] Ho Chi Minh himself, when attempting to foment nationalist feelings to overthrow the French, linked the oppression of Vietnamese women to the nation's colonial oppression by the French. In a 1922 appeal, he wrote, "Colonialization is in itself an act of violence of the stronger against the weaker. This violence becomes still more odious when it is exercised upon women and children." Connecting this metaphor to lived experiences, he then told the horrible story of French soldiers' rape and torture of two women and an eight-year-old girl (qtd. in Turner, pp. 28–29).

The nation's symbolic use of women's sexual abuse begs the question of how a society such as Vietnam that is extremely repressive of women, demanding strict sexual purity, can incorporate victims of rape back into society. The words of a Yugoslavian victim of the Serbian mass rapes are instructive in answering this question: "Although our people are very conservative, these [raped] women are accepted and understood. [The scale of] rape in this war has been so massive that it ceased to be a taboo. And, besides rape, other very serious crimes happened . . . massacres, torture. The most important thing for women is to be well accepted in their families."[25] Similarly, it appears that in the South, rape was so common that, in many ways, the sexual defilement of women by soldiers seems to have lost its taboo. For this reason, rape victims appear to have retained their position in the fabric of everyday life; however, because of the lingering taboos against discussion of sex as well as the idea that women are responsible for their sexual impurity, even when sex is forced upon them, women are, for the most part, silent about the sexual abuse they experienced. And unlike Korea, which recently used the speaking out of their comfort women to make reparation demands of Japan, Vietnam is not interested in publicizing the rapes in an international context. Rather, in the interest of repairing their political and economic ties to the West, a course of action Vietnam has pursued since the end of the war, Vietnam and the Vietnamese people generally take the attitude that war memories should be forgotten or at least put away.[26]

Another reason women's sexual abuse remains unpublicized by the women who experienced it is the fact that political power in Vietnam continues to reside in and emanate from the North.[27] Because of their rural location and poverty, southern peasant women have never gained access to the means of publicly witnessing to their plight during the war. And southern women are those who experienced the brunt of American and ARVN sexual aggression. Though those living in the North suffered terrible privations throughout the war years, and though northern women participated in the military and support groups in much greater numbers than did southern women, southerners lived on the land on which the ground war was fought. And without a knowable enemy at which to point their aggression, soldiers, both American and ARVN, often turned their frustration and anger toward the civilians at hand, most of whom were women. Therefore, in order to hear the voices of the women who can speak to the behavior of American soldiers, one must seek out the women who came in close and frequent contact with them—the southern peasant women.

In her excellent work *Even the Women Must Fight: Memories of War from North Vietnam* (1998), Turner exclusively interviews and focuses on northern women's activities during the war. Her reason for this is that the "situation in the South is better known in the United States through refugee accounts, oral histories from Vietnam, and two recent women's books" (p. 10). I disagree with this statement, at least in terms of the typical woman's experience. The refugee accounts Turner cites are perhaps representative of *urban* South Vietnamese. Most of the people able to refugee from Vietnam were urban and/or wealthy southerners who had connections with the Republic of South Vietnam's administration or the ARVN. Refugees were not often the rice-growing, village peasant who had no political ties or may have supported the New Liberation Front. An exception to this is Le Ly Hayslip, whose memoirs are widely read and who does fall into this latter category. However, it was only because she eventually ended up in Saigon, where she made American contacts, that she escaped to the United States. Also, the oral histories from Vietnam that Turner claims illuminate the southern story are most generally not women's histories, and many of them are, in fact, North Vietnamese.[28] Thus, I would suggest that for the most part, Americans are not familiar with the southern woman's trauma during the war. In the remainder of this chapter, I will analyze Vietnamese narratives of rape and sexual abuse, including those by northern authors, though I will focus on the experience of southern women in particular so that their sexual trauma may be recognized.

Vietnamese Literature

As is clear from the above discussion, rape and sexual abuse are topics not easily broached in Vietnamese literature. However, in relation to the war, two of Vietnam's most famous writers have managed to speak openly on the subject. Duong Thu Huong, one of Vietnam's most celebrated (and censored) authors, opens her *Novel without a Name* (1995)—set during the American war years—with the gory remains of a gang rape. Quan, the novel's NVA-regular protagonist, investigates a terrible odor his platoon smells in the forest. Instead of the expected corpse of a dead soldier, he finds "six naked corpses. Women. Their breasts and genitals had been cut off and strewn on the grass around them . . . The soldiers had raped them before killing them. The corpses were bruised violet. So this was how graceful, girlish bodies rotted, decomposing into swollen old corpses, puffy as dead toads. Maggots swarmed in their wounds, their eyes and mouths. Fat white larvae. They crawled over the corpses in waves, plunging in and out of them in a drunken orgy."[29] Readers never discover the affiliation of the soldiers who committed this crime. The narrator does not assign blame to anyone; rather, Duong uses this incident to set the tone for the rest of the novel, a bitter description of the terrible waste of war.

Her refusal to assign blame seems appropriate in a novel that is not concerned with decrying American actions but rather with the ideology of war that drove the Vietnamese to make terrible, destructive sacrifices. With this horrific image, Duong explodes the sentimental Vietnamese idealizations of women sacrificing their bodies for the greater good, to save their country. Here, instead of being portrayed as beautifully, poignantly noble, the "sacrificed" women are bloated, decomposing—revoltingly likened to dead toads. They have been senselessly tortured, mutilated, and murdered. This is no meaningful sacrifice, but utter waste and mindless destruction. Furthermore, the author links death and decomposition with sex, as the maggots "plung[e] in and out of [the corpses] in a drunken orgy." This linkage bitterly condemns the Vietnamese national pride and mythology that exalts death in service to country, making death the ultimate act of "intimacy" with one's land.[30] Reversing the "nobility" of this final intimacy, Duong reveals the grotesqueness of such ideology through the devouring "orgy" of maggots, who, like the nation, thrive on the women's death.

While Duong describes rape's aftereffects with ghastly detail, she mentions the rape itself almost casually with a complete lack of interest in who committed the crime or why it occurred. While her nonchalance attests to the frequency of this type of crime, Duong does not focus on the specificities or causes of the rape/murder because she uses the women's suffering much as nationalistic rhetoric does: not important so much as a crime against women, but as a metaphor. Herein lies the problem with such literary representations of rape. This northern woman writer, who was herself part of the Volunteer Youth Brigade and present on the front lines of the war, portrays the sexual abuse of women, not to bring attention to its occurrence, but as a metaphor for the entire war and its effect on the generations of Vietnamese touched by it. There is no sense of a call to action for future prevention of sexual war crimes or recognition of and recompense for those who suffered that fate during the war.

Similarly, Bao Ninh, author of *The Sorrow of War* (1991; English translation, 1993)—internationally the best-known Vietnamese work of fiction on the war—structures his entire novel around a wartime rape. The novel slips and slides through time, fluidly mixing the protagonist's experiences in the prewar, interwar, and postwar periods. It is clear that the protagonist, Kien, suffered trauma that left him deeply bitter and unable to relate to others. Readers assume the trauma resulted from his war experience: after ten years of fighting, he was the sole survivor of his once large military unit. This seems to explain his inability to reunite happily with his former fiancé, Phuong, when he returns home. However, in the final pages of the novel, readers learn the true nature of Kien's trauma. Phuong, while accompanying Kien to meet his unit when he first joins the military, was raped by a North Vietnamese man in the chaos following a train accident. Overwhelmed and distraught by these events, Kien blamed his fiancé, calling her a "whore" and eventually abandoning her to make the return journey on her own.[31] With this final revelation, readers understand that the trauma from which Kien suffers is actually the guilt of his terrible, inexcusable reaction to Phuong's rape.

This understanding casts new light on an incident narrated earlier in the book (though chronologically occurring long after Phuong's rape) in which an American patrol brutally gang raped Hoa, a female guide of Kien's military unit. Choosing to sacrifice herself to protect Kien and a group of wounded NVA soldiers, Hoa shot the tracking dog who could have revealed the other soldiers to the patrol, allowing herself to be seen and caught by the American enemy. Kien watched powerlessly as

> [w]ithout losing their control or lifting their voices, [the American soldiers] set about stripping Hoa and, the dog handler first, roughly fucking her. Some of them stayed back, but the way they had all come to a standstill, and with others waiting their turn, it appeared they would end their patrol with the rape . . . As the almost silent but barbarous multiple rape of young Hoa continued in the small jungle clearing in the dying minutes of that harrowing day, Kien crept away from them, towards his wounded men . . . Not one of them

> asked about Hoa. At first he found it disagreeably strange. Then, with its acceptance, he too began to forget about her. Was it that such sacrifices were now an everyday occurrence? Or that they were expected, even of such young people? Or worse, that they were too concerned worrying about their own safety to bother with others?[32]

I quote this passage at length because it asks very similar questions to those this chapter attempts to answer. The physical and psychological trauma to which women were subjected because of the war—figured here and in national rhetoric as sacrifice—have been forgotten and ignored, just as Kien began to forget Hoa's sacrifice almost immediately. He gives three possible reasons for this forgetfulness, all of which seem equally valid. First he suggests, as did *Novel without a Name* and as will American accounts, that rape was an "everyday occurrence," not requiring explanation or much notice. This is certainly a possible reason women victims and others would not mention rape—it was so ubiquitous it did not require comment. Another possibility Kien suggests is that women, as others, were expected to quietly accept the trauma visited on them, as their contribution to the war effort. Still again, he wonders whether the stresses of war (and we might add the economic and physical hardships of the postwar period) enabled people to focus only on their own survival to the extent that they ignored or forgot the hardships of others.

In light of the eventual revelation of Kien's harsh rejection and abandonment of Phuong after her brutal rape, this last answer seems most probable. Not only did the war put Phuong in the dangerous situation in which the rape occurs, but it also seemingly justified Kien's inexcusable behavior toward his fiancé—he had to catch up with his unit to avoid punishment and join the fighting rather than helping traumatized Phuong travel home to safety. Thus, Bao's narration of the guide's gang rape has a double function. First, the combination of Kien's acceptance and near instantaneous "forgetting" of Hoa's trauma as a necessary action of war with his terrible reaction to his fiancé's rape emphasizes the horrible callousness war demands. Yet—unlike the horrific scene of murdered and raped but anonymous women in Duong's work—his detailed and sympathetic description of Hoa's and Phuong's rapes forwards their suffering as individuals and women. Even as Bao uses these episodes to reveal the dulling touch of war on human feeling, he ignites deep sympathy for the suffering of these women. He forces readers to ask if war can ever be worth the sacrifices it demands and the alterations in emotional capacity it causes.

Duong and Bao, both war veterans, are two of the few contemporary writers of Vietnam who deal with the American war in their writings, and they are part of an even smaller group who broach the topic in a nonpropagandistic way. Because of her bitter writings on the war and postwar Vietnamese politics and society, Duong, though a war hero and celebrated author, is considered a dissident and was ejected from the Communist Party. Her works have been banned (*Novel without a Name* has never been published in Vietnam), and all copies of one of her documentary films have been destroyed. She cannot leave Vietnam. Thus, even North Vietnamese authors with important political connections cannot openly write of the terrible events connected with the "War of Unification," suggesting that fear of state reprisals may also contribute to the silence regarding women's abuse. For as I have been suggesting, an open discussion of women's abuse at the hands of Americans during the war must certainly point out the abuse women have suffered from Vietnamese men as well.

Oral Histories

Because South Vietnamese writers have not produced a body of literature on the war and the Vietnamese government appears uninterested in taking the history of the southern experience of the war, Martha Hess's collection of oral accounts, *Then the Americans Came: Voices from Vietnam*, is an invaluable resource in researching women's war experiences. Her book is composed of interviews with Vietnamese she met while traveling across Vietnam in 1990 and 1991. Rather than interviewing war veterans selected by government officials, she drove about with a guide from the national tourist office. She explains her approach to locating interviewees: "Often we would just stop on the road and approach people who appeared to be of an age to remember the war. One person led to another and onlookers joined the conversation."[33] Instead of guiding interviewees by asking specific questions about the war, Hess only asked what they remembered from the war, leaving the direction of the answer up to the interviewee. The result of this is what we might call "a peasant's view of the war," a view not replicated in other sources with the exception of Hayslip's memoirs. For readers knowledgeable regarding American combatant accounts, however, these southern narratives only reaffirm the terrible daily realities of those living in the war zone.

Hess includes accounts from both northerners and southerners, dividing the accounts into sections entitled, "North of the Seventeenth

Parallel" and "South of the Seventeenth Parallel," with a final section including accounts from permanent residents of war hospitals. A comparison of the accounts in the "North" and "South" sections confirms my earlier assertion that war experiences were very different for northerners and southerners. While northerners report a great deal of deprivation, terror, physical destruction, and death because of the constant bombings, they do not report the intimate, personal crimes that southerners do. Southern peasants describe a life of terror in which they never knew how the Americans would react to them, handing out candy to children on one village sweep and then committing a massacre on the next visit. Rape, a crime obviously requiring close contact, is reported only once in the thirty-three northern accounts, and this northern woman, who experienced rape and sexual torture while a political prisoner, was assaulted while living in the southern capital, Saigon (p. 85). In the southern accounts, however, rape is mentioned in 32 percent of the histories.

The apparent frequency of reported rapes by South Vietnamese villagers agrees with the testimony veterans gave at the Winter Soldier Investigation, which will be discussed in the following chapter, and with the remembrances of American veterans in oral account collections such as Mark Baker's *Nam: The Vietnam War in the Words of the Men and Women Who Fought There* (1981). The types of sexual violence against women reported in Hess's collection can be divided into three approximate categories: sexual torture of prisoners, rape, and murder rape (often associated with mass killings).

While sexual torture was used upon male prisoners as well—namely, the use of electricity on the genitalia—sexual torture of women appears to have been equally common and often progressed much further than did the sexual torture of men, resulting in rape and mutilation of the sexual and reproductive organs. As Le Thi Dieu, a villager arrested by the Americans in 1965 and 1967 and imprisoned for a total of four years, reported, "They put electricity in my vagina, on my nipples, in my ears, in my nose, on my fingers. Blood came out of my vagina" (p. 151). The sexual nature of the torture became more overt as it progressed.

> They took me to a little house . . . and one American tried to rape me. I started screaming, and he took my hair, which was very long, and he dragged me and beat me. A Vietnamese interpreter came and said, "Why do you struggle against the Americans? It won't do any good." And I said, "They arrested me, they tortured me and beat me, and now they want to rape me. How can I not cry and struggle?" The next night the American came back, when I was alone. I

> cried again, but he forced me to the floor and put a cloth in my mouth. He took off my pants. I couldn't scream. I went faint, and he raped me, and I couldn't do anything more. Later, the interpreter returned, and removed the cloth from my mouth. I was raped again, and I didn't feel anything more. (pp. 151–52)

Truong My Hoa, the northern woman mentioned earlier who was imprisoned while attending school in Saigon, confirms this kind of prison abuse, asserting simply, "They had all kinds of sexual torture for the women" (p. 85). Huynh Phuoc Tinh reports that when one woman in his village was interrogated and refused to give information, the Americans "beat her, tortured her, and cut off her breasts" (p. 142).

This kind of sexual torture was well documented even during the war years themselves. In the 1967 International War Crimes Tribunal, an American attorney named Hugh Manes testified about depositions he had taken in Vietnam during 1967. One woman, Tran Thi Van, whose testimony he relayed, gave extended descriptions of the torture she suffered as a political prisoner, tortures she was told by her guards were not "the ordinary French tortures, but rather the tortures learned from Americans." Much of the torture was sexual in nature. Van recalled being tormented by a man who "stripped her, tied her arms, and thrust his hand into her vagina until blood came and she cried out in pain." She also informed Manes that her sister too, bore "scars all over her body, including her genitals, from many tortures." Further, Van testified that "her niece died after a broken bottle was inserted into her vagina."[34]

A second category of reported sexual abuse was the widespread rape of village girls. These rapes were not used as torture for the supposed purpose of eliciting information, nor were they necessarily committed during mass atrocities. Instead it seems many field soldiers raped village women simply because they wanted sexual gratification and felt, as one veteran expressed it, "like I was a god. I could take a life, I could screw a woman." He specifically asserted, "You had the power to rape a woman and nobody could say nothing to you. That godlike feeling you had was in the field."[35] Another soldier callously explained to Baker why rape became so ubiquitous in the Vietnam War, "Let's face it. Nature is nature. There are women available. Those women are of another culture, another color, another society. You don't want a prostitute. You've got an M-16. What do you need to pay for a lady for? You go down to the village and you take what you want" (p. 206). The Vietnamese voices in Martha Hess's collection confirm these veterans' statements. Phan Xuan My, of Binh Trieu Village, reported that when the Americans launched "mopping-up operations in our villages . . . They raped the women in secret, one at a time, because they didn't want to get caught by their officers. They even raped pregnant women . . . The young girls had to hide in the daytime" (p. 159). Such rapes not only provided a release of sexual aggression on the part of American soldiers, but they were also used to humiliate the Vietnamese. Huynh Thi Pham recalled that people of her village "were brought out in the sun, pushed to our knees and made to draw up our arms, as they cut off our hair. With older people, they pulled out their beards. They were laughing as they did this . . . Women were raped. In Bin Duong village across the river, twenty-one women were raped in an afternoon by Americans, not just once but one after the other. Some died on the spot, and others died later" (p. 169).

Soldiers committed other rapes, such as those occurring in conjunction with the My Lai massacre, with the intention of ultimately killing their victims. A villager from My Lai, Ha Thi Qui, explained how, after the massacre, she went to locate her relatives and found her sister-in-law dead and her niece—"a fifteen-year-old girl, [with] all her clothing torn off and her legs were spread open—raped by Americans" and then shot (p. 130). Similarly, Huynh Phuong Anh, from Nha Trang, remembered passing "though villages where [the Americans] had been . . . find[ing] only bodies—in the trees, on the ground, and women with cloth stuffed in their mouths" (p. 119). The rape and murder of Vietnamese women was so common that American soldiers had a special term for the soldiers who committed the acts in conjunction: *a double veteran* (Baker, p. 321).

While American soldiers remember with either amazement or apparent callousness the ubiquity of rape and the attitudes that enabled it, the emotion that most stands out in Vietnamese accounts of rape is their rage-tinged perplexity as to why such torture and cruelty were meted out to noncombatants. In one typical passage, Ha, the woman who discovered her raped and murdered niece, ended her account by saying, "The Americans had lived alongside the Vietnamese people, and we did nothing to them. We worked, spent all our lives in the fields. How could they come and kill us that way?" (Hess, p. 131). Surely the worldwide erasure of women's abuse in the Vietnam War and the Vietnamese government's willingness to let it be forgotten contribute to the villagers' rage. In their accounts, readers see these victims struggle between their knowledge of and need to witness to these terrible violences and the world's refusal to hear. As a coda to his narrative, southerner Tran Van Nhan noted succinctly, "Many women were raped, but they never talk about it" (p. 108). This silence indicates not a forgetting by the victims, however, but a silent seething. Villager Ngo Thi Dao reveals the inability to forget sexual atrocities, even as she desires to heal relations with Americans, saying, "The war has been over for a long time now and I don't like to talk about it, for the American people to know, but when a young girl in one family is raped by Americans or South Koreans—how can we not be angry, even now? They should help to rebuild our country, but what can we do? So we try to forget it. It was terrible for us . . . How can we forget? But for life, for peace, for the future, we try to forget" (p. 181). In her reflection, Ngo faced the quandary in which Vietnam finds itself—should recognition and recompense for women's suffering be demanded from those countries responsible, or should it be forgotten, silenced, in deference to goals that could have wider implications? Clearly, the state of Vietnam—bolstered by its unwillingness to address its own culture's tacit approval of woman abuse—has determined that in order to placate the United States and gain a place in the international economy, it must not require an admission of guilt from the United States or pursue war crimes charges. However, as Ngo expressed it, it is not easy for the Americans' victims to forget these crimes; she clearly felt deep anger many years later, and because she recognized this anger as just, she was loathe to release it.

Thus, the invaluable accounts in *Then the Americans Came* give voice to a people whose traumas have been willfully forgotten, even by their own country; and their testimony reveals that the South Vietnamese peasants suffered the brunt of the Allied forces' abuse. These voices provide evidence that corroborates the testimony of American soldiers regarding rape and sexual abuse in the Vietnam War, which will appear in subsequent chapters. Unfortunately, to my knowledge, no statistical research has been conducted on the topic of women's abuse, with the result that the only information on women's abuse in the war is anecdotal, both from the Vietnamese and the American perspectives. However, the fact that witnesses from opposing sides give corroborative evidence suggests the validity of the testimony and also begs for further formal research to be conducted.

Le Ly Hayslip's *When Heaven and Earth Changed Places*

Le Ly Hayslip's memoirs—particularly the first—fully develop in the specificities of one woman's life the incidents and stories reported in Hess's collection and the current scholarly research on the dangers Vietnamese women face within the family and the workplace. These memoirs are important, not just because they flesh out and give detail to one "typical" southern woman's experience, but also because they intentionally reveal the influence of social values and restrictions on women in Vietnamese culture. Hayslip's internal dialogue regarding the sexual abuse of which she was a victim allows readers to see the ways in which women internalize negative and oppressive cultural attitudes about themselves, an internationalization that often causes them to act against their own best interests. Her memoirs enable readers to understand why, even if they were encouraged by the government, Vietnamese women would find it difficult or impossible to publicly discuss their rape and sexual abuse in the war. Additionally, Hayslip's writings are important because Oliver Stone adapted them into the final film of his Vietnam War "trilogy," *Heaven and Earth,* which will be discussed in chapter 5. Thus, an analysis of Hayslip's narrative voice is important to fully appreciate the subtle but vital changes Stone makes in his cinematic adaptation. For his shifting of her story downplays the extent of Hayslip's sexual trauma—particularly that occurring at the hands of Americans—erases her political message and call to action and reverses her critique of American culture into doe-eyed awe and wonder.

Though Hayslip's memoirs recount with agonizing emotion the sexual abuse she repeatedly experienced as a young woman—the trauma actually structuring and moving Hayslip through her story—the relation of this trauma is not an end in itself, but rather it is designed to encourage reconciliation between America and Vietnam, and specifically to inspire American action on behalf of the Vietnamese. In this way, Hayslip bears witness against her abusers and reveals the systemic nature at the root of her abuse, subtly critiquing both Confucian repression of women in Vietnamese culture and American military policy toward Vietnamese women; rather than stopping here, however, she uses this witness bearing to create a metanarrative designed to heal herself and inspire the same in others, whom she sees as victimized by the war. This is very similar to the way in which American veterans attempted to use their witness bearing not only to expiate their own guilt but also to end the war, as will be discussed in the following chapter. In both situations, healing for war victims can be achieved only through the active response of the public who has heard the witness.

In her first memoir, *When Heaven and Earth Changed Places: A Vietnamese Woman's Journey from War to Peace* (1989), Hayslip recounts her childhood in Ky La, an agricultural village in South Vietnam, her move to and life in the cities Danang and Saigon, and her marriage to an American and subsequent departure from Vietnam. This narrative of escape is interwoven with one of return, as Hayslip also traces her middle-aged journey back to Vietnam, a journey that culminates in a reunion of her family, many of whom she has not seen since she was a young girl. Hayslip clearly intends the narration of her personal story to change her readers' attitude toward the Vietnamese. She presents the reconciliation of her own family as a model for the reconciliation between her two nations. Dedicating her book to "all those who fought for their country, wherever it may be" and also "to those who did not fight—but suffered, wept, raged, bled, and died just the same," she asks her readers to "look into the heart of one you once called enemy. I have witnessed, firsthand, all that you went through. I will try to tell you who your enemy was" (p. xiv).

Thus, Hayslip's memoir is important as a recent example in the genealogy of women's writing in which national and international politics are addressed in terms of the personal, the relational.[36] Within my project, however, Hayslip's writings are most important for their concrete discussion of specific wartime sexual traumas. *When Heaven and Earth Changed Places* contains a litany of sexual violence experienced by Hayslip and other women. In fact, this abuse structures the war-years sections of the memoir; it drove Hayslip as she navigated herself into and out of one sexually dangerous situation after another. While her initial sexual trauma—a vicious double rape—was war-related, many of the other sexual violations and harassment she experienced were not, such as her molestation at a young age by her lecherous, married Vietnamese employer. Hayslip skillfully uses these incidents to reveal the problems endemic to a male-privileged culture. She demonstrates that the Vietnamese culture demanded sexual purity from women yet simultaneously licensed men to harass and violate women; it further commanded women's submission to and silence regarding these abuses. With this, Hayslip skillfully shows why Vietnamese women were especially susceptible to abuse from Americans; their social training had taught them to accept abuse as well as keep silent about it, blaming themselves. By forwarding her sexual violations by Americans with a long string of abuse at the hands of her countrymen, Hayslip shows both cultures' denigration and repression of women.

Even before Hayslip herself became a victim of sexual crime, the threat of rape and sexual assault colored her everyday existence. Her earliest memories included the important lessons her mother taught her about being a "virtuous wife and dutiful daughter-in-law; [and] how to bring [her]self to [her] husband as a virgin" (p. 10). Hayslip speaks of the pains the village women undertook daily to preserve their "virtue:" "My mother and sister mixed red vegetable dye with water and stained the crotches of their pants. They said it would make the soldiers think they had their periods and discourage any ideas of rape. Unfortunately, a few soldiers didn't care what stains were on a woman's pants, but that was every girl's risk in Ky La" (p. 10). The matter-of-fact way Hayslip introduces these preventative measures as part of the village women's routines and her note that this prevention's failure was "every girl's risk" bespeak the terrible frequency of rape and the constant terror in which women were forced to live. Also connoted in this statement is the fact that women could expect no protection from authorities; they were themselves responsible for discouraging inappropriate sexual advances. Women who did not undertake preventative measures were therefore responsible if they were victimized. In addition to watching older women and girls employ defensive tactics, stories of terrible rapes also shaped girls' expectations and fears. When Hayslip was a young child, her mother related a blood-curdling story about neighbors who were killed by French Moroccan soldiers. On bursting into the neighbors' house, the soldiers surprised the woman occupant. "[They] had been disappointed in their search and were pleased to find a victim on which to show their anger. They ripped away the woman's clothes and threw her to the floor. She fought and screamed, of course, but she could hardly resist. Her husband . . . ran in the back door . . . and beheld them raping his wife." After tying the husband to the ground and quartering him with his own hatchet, the Moroccans "went back into the house and waited their turn at the wife. When all were finished," they dismembered her as well (p. 16). Though her mother ostensibly told Hayslip the story so she would recognize the spirits of the neighbors, it was also clearly meant to instruct Hayslip on how to navigate her extremely dangerous world.

Hayslip experienced sexual trauma for the first time at age fifteen. Although she had been a staunch and active supporter of the Viet Cong in her village—even imprisoned by the ARVN three times for her rebel activities—the Viet Cong suspected Hayslip of betraying them during her final imprisonment. Thus, the NLF sentenced her to death; rather than killing her, the two young Viet Cong executioners raped her instead, warning her to keep quiet and leave Ky La immediately. Hayslip's feelings of shame, guilt, and self-hatred after the rape were the same as those of many rape victims, "I knew I was no more than the dirt on which we lay. The war—these men—had finally ground me down to oneness with the soil, from which I could no longer be distinguished as a person. Dishonored, raped, and ruined for any decent man, my soiled little body had become its own grave" (p. 97). Hayslip did not tell her parents about her rape, partly to safeguard their lives, but "also due to shame." She did, however, tell them of her near-execution and the Viet Cong threat to her life, so her mother sent her to Danang, a larger city, to work as a housekeeper for a Vietnamese family.

When her employer in Danang, after a good deal of sexual harassment, molested and attempted to rape her, Hayslip aggressively defended herself against him. Although she remained in the man's employ, she developed coping strategies to avoid him. When her housework suffered for this effort, the boss's wife dismissed her. Upon explaining to her mother the situation with her male boss, Hayslip's mother "commanded [her] never to speak of it. 'What do you want people to think,' she asked, looking at [her daughter] as if everything had been [her] fault, 'that you are a husband tease and a tattler? No. Never anger the people who feed you. We'll go see Uncle Nhu. Maybe he can keep you under control'" (p. 107). In this simple exchange, Hayslip makes readily apparent the fact that Vietnamese culture places responsibility for sexual purity in the hands of women and girls, even as it denies them the ability to protect themselves from those who would exploit them. Rather than blaming the employer for his reprehensible actions, the mother accused her daughter of being a "tease"—blaming the molester's victim—and a "tattler" for speaking of it. This exchange exemplifies how cultural attitudes toward women prevented Vietnamese women from decrying their sexual abuse during the war.

In an attempt to find a new position, Hayslip and her mother traveled to Saigon where they stayed with distant relatives. When Hayslip accompanied the family's teenaged son to the movies, he attempted to molest her. Hayslip angered the boy with her vigorous rebuff, and when he complained of her to his parents, they asked the mother and daughter to leave. After becoming a servant in a wealthy factory owner's home in Saigon, Hayslip fell in love and had an affair with her married, middle-aged employer. However, when the fifteen-year-old Hayslip became pregnant, her mother placed all responsibility again at her young daughter's feet: "[N]ow you've done it! . . . You weren't satisfied with a perfect life in a wonderful house, were you? You had to seduce the husband—make him stray from his wife. Now look what it's got you!" (p. 135). When her mother's attempts to abort the pregnancy failed, the employer's wife sent both mother and daughter back to Danang. On her first night there, when Hayslip went out for a walk by herself, a gang of young Vietnamese teenagers attempted to rape her, though she was saved at the last minute by a military helicopter that flew over and shined its spotlight on the group, just as the boys began stripping Hayslip of her clothes (p. 171). Having learned from her previous experiences, Hayslip said nothing to her mother about the incident. Ignoring her mother's "disapproving look for my mussed-up hair and the missing button on my blouse," Hayslip thought, "'what's the point of cursing rocks that bruise you when you're tumbling down a river?'"

(p. 172). Thus, in one year's time, Hayslip was raped twice, nearly raped twice more, molested, sexually harassed, and impregnated by her much older employer.

After the birth of her son, Hayslip began selling souvenirs on American bases; she would then give the cash to GIs who were willing to purchase cigarettes, liquor, soap, or gum from the PX, which she would sell on the black market to other Vietnamese. Eventually, Hayslip moved her business further out, traveling into the countryside, finding areas and firebases in which smaller groups of American soldiers were active. Although leaving the city and the developed bases held more danger, the business was much more lucrative. During this time, Hayslip constantly defended herself from Americans who assumed she was a prostitute, and once she barely escaped being sodomized by a fellow Vietnamese prisoner when she was jailed for transporting marijuana (p. 188). Her narrative inadvertently attests to the constant sexual danger in which she existed, as, when explaining how she learned to cultivate friendships with certain GIs, she offhandedly mentions, "one [commander] kept me from getting raped inside a tank," without giving further comment to the incident (p. 189).

In the midst of her own story, Hayslip devotes several pages of her narrative to describing the sexual debasement other women experienced because of the war. She explains with horror "a new industry—slave traffic in Vietnamese girls—that was flourishing right under my nose" (p. 223). As young girls and women flooded into the cities from the war-ravaged countryside, they were duped into the employ of older madams who either sold the girls to wealthy clients in the city or exported them to other countries. Hayslip connects cultural expectations of girls and women to be quietly submissive to their willingness to endure such situations. "Most of these poor, ignorant girls made little fuss about being raped and brutalized by their masters—they were used to taking orders from older people and thought that this was just what housekeepers and nannies had to put up with to earn a living . . . For these girls, innocence was not a virtue, but a prison" (p. 224). She also compassionately tells of the women who chose to become prostitutes, suggesting that "[m]any of these girls were widowed by the war or were rape victims like me who despaired of a proper marriage" (p. 224). Sympathetically, she relates the story of one prostitute she knew who "had been eaten up so badly by infections inside that she could no longer tolerate the pain of normal intercourse . . . Still, she had to support her fatherless children, so she became an expert in oral sex until the venereal disease left her face disfigured and unappealing to her customers" (p. 225). Angrily, Hayslip describes the "much worse . . . practice" of using and then killing prostitutes. She witnessed the evidence of this practice one day when a bus she was riding stopped so the passengers could investigate the garbage an American GI truck had just thrown out. In one of the boxes, they found a young woman, stripped naked and mutilated. Based on her appearance, Hayslip figured the woman "was a hooker who had been 'trashed'—used, abused, and dumped—by the servicemen" (p. 226). She does not condemn the women who practiced "flesh peddling"; rather, she feels that for many women, it was a justifiable, necessary way of life, although she has only contempt for the madams who took advantage of unknowing women and girls and the family members who often pimped out their wives, girlfriends, and daughters.

Hayslip's empathy for prositutes did not make her own encounter with selling her body easier, however. For though she had assiduously avoided prostituting herself, when a soldier offered her four hundred American dollars to have sex with two "clean" soldiers, Hayslip relented. She explains,

> I stared at the cash the way a thirsty prisoner stares at water. Four hundred dollars would support my mother, me, and Hung [her son] for over a year—a year I could use finding a better job and making connections or, as a last resort, greasing palms for a paid escape. And to make it, I wouldn't even have to work up a sweat or risk going to jail or getting blown up by a mine or blown away in an ambush. Just lie down and let these two American boys be men. What could they do to me that hadn't been done already? Maybe it was time some men paid me back for what other men had taken. (p. 258)

Hayslip's feelings during the encounter indicated that this physically safer, less strenuous work was not easier, however: "I found myself fighting a sudden urge to scream. The weight of his body and the sudden fullness in mine and the heaviness of the air in the tiny bunker made me feel like I was suffocating—buried alive! The cot began creaking rhythmically and his sweaty huffing in my ear was like shovels of dirty on my face, on the corpse of my father's daughter" (pp. 259–60).

Hayslip's willingness to admit and discuss her prostitution, giving her reasons for her decision to do it and her feelings about it, is one of the vital elements of her writing, for her memoir offers a very different perspective from the typical American perception of Vietnamese women as money-grubbing prostitutes without emotions or values (a belief reinforced by film productions, as will be discussed later). Hayslip's autobiography presents readers with the difficult and complex set of issues that led her into the painful decision to sell her body. For even though she experienced shame from the exchange, in the cash she was offered, Hayslip saw not consumer goods, but the possibility of survival, and even a means of escape for herself and her family. She recognized that the work itself was far less dangerous than her other employment, and finally, the sale of her body was also an act of empowerment, demanding payment for "what other men had taken." Undergirding all other reasons for Hayslip's willingness to engage in this exchange, of course, was her society's perception of her as "ruined for any decent man" because of her previous sexual experience.

As Hayslip continues her story, she reminds readers of Americans' failure to understand the complex situation and contradictory emotions of Vietnamese prostitutes. Big Mike, the soldier who had propositioned Hayslip for the soldiers, responded to Hayslip's assertion that she would never again prostitute herself by saying, "'Okay, Le Ly. You're a good girl. You go home. But I bet a quart of Jack Daniel's [sic] I see you shakin' your booties up here next week. Papa-san gonna drink up that cash chop-chop!' His big American hand pinched my drippy bottom and he walked away toward his jeep" (p. 261). Indulging in many stereotypes, Big Mike believed the cash would be lost quickly to alcohol (instead of carefully saved, as it happens) and that Hayslip, not placing the same high value on the sanctity of her body as American women do, would return to make more "easy" money.

Once Hayslip earned the four hundred dollars, she was able to find safer work, work done in the city so that she could spend more time with her child and her mother. Through an American connection, Hayslip landed work as a nurse's aide at Vietnamese hospital in Danang, making a regular salary that was astonishingly high in her eyes. When one of the Vietnamese administrators began sexually harassing Hayslip, an American friend named Red arranged for her to be transferred elsewhere in the hospital. This began her relationship with Red, a navy medical technician. Though kind at first, Red quickly began remaking Hayslip as a Western woman, demanding she wear short skirts, curled hair, and heavy makeup. He convinced her to quit her work at the hospital because he wanted her to dance at one of the clubs he frequented. When Hayslip checked out the club, however, she was dismayed to find it featured topless dancers. Red wheedled her, "[D]on't disappoint me. I really want to see you up there. These guys . . . see, they think I'm just a runt, a pisshole—some swabbie med tech they can shit on whenever they want! Shit—it's *always* been that way for me! But with you—with you up there on that stage—I'll *be* somebody! *You'll* be somebody!"

When Hayslip refused, Red screamed, "Where do you think you're going? Damn you, woman! You aren't the only gook girl in the world! You hear me—!" (p. 284). Once again, Hayslip's willingness to discuss this embarrassing episode gives the reader a different view of wartime Vietnamese girlfriends, the shadowy creatures who often inhabit American accounts of the war but are given little to no interiority. Told here from the woman's perspective, readers feel Hayslip's shame and anger as they realize along with her that she was only valuable to Red as an ornament or plaything; he openly used her to make himself feel better about his shortcomings, even to the point of degrading her in the eyes of herself and others.

Red proved to be only the first in a line of American boyfriends who appeared to be caring but ultimately had only their own needs and desires in mind. However, through those relationships, Hayslip became more savvy and progressively more enraged at the way women were treated in wartime Vietnam; in her reaction to men's abusiveness, she moved from passivity to action. When one of her American boyfriends, Jim, became jealous and abusive, Hayslip's initial reaction was to blame herself: "I was sure his problem was my fault. A Vietnamese wife, even an unmarried one, was always responsible for the happiness of her man" (p. 301). One night, in a drunken rage, Jim almost strangled Hayslip, stopping at the last minute and reviving her. Instead of enduring this abuse silently, however, Hayslip reported the incident to the MPs the next day, resulting in Jim's deportation.[37]

The confidence Hayslip received from her growing experience with men and Americans reached its peak when she visited the American employment office in Danang. Here an American job counselor demanded Hayslip perform fellatio in exchange for a job. She refused, only to find herself trapped in the locked office, with no apparent means of escape. As Hayslip described it, "something inside me . . . snapped when I saw that little man come at me with his open fly and smug face. I just could not let him—let any of them—get away with it anymore. I would not be their victim, nor—if I had anything to say about it—would any other innocent girl" (p. 310). Her rage at the abuse she and other women experienced at the hands of so many men (the undefined "them" of her statement) finally found its expression. Smashing the glass window of the door with a chair, Hayslip released herself and demanded the first woman worker she found to call the MPs. The offender was arrested, and the office manager personally apologized to Hayslip, ultimately placing her in a good job. Her dizzying victory gave Hayslip a new picture of America; she dreamed of it as a possible place "in this cruel and dangerous world, [where] justice *was* the order of the day, and not just the exception" (p. 310).

In spite of her newfound realization that she must stand up for herself and other mistreated women, Hayslip continued to struggle with the beliefs of her strict upbringing. When an American man, Ed Munro, proposed marriage to her, saying, "I've got a nice house [in America] and I've decided I want a wife to share it with me—a good oriental wife who knows how to take care of her man" (p. 333), Hayslip eventually accepted, despite the fact that she did not love Ed or even find him attractive and despite his racist, sexist expectations that she, as an "oriental" woman, knew "how to take care of her man." However, though this marriage might appear mercenary or degrading, like her act of prostitution, it enabled her to move into a more secure position and began her journey to a successful life in America. This marriage and her escape with Ed to America end the memoir of her early life in Vietnam.

Thus, though the writings and oral accounts by South Vietnamese who experienced or witnessed women's sexual abuse during the war are not numerous, those that do exist corroborate the writings and testimony by American men, which we will see in subsequent chapters. The existing accounts suggest that rape and other sexual abuse during the war was frequent, brutal, and often culminated in death. A knowledge of Vietnamese culture and women's historical position in this society provides a context in which to understand the reasons Vietnamese women were particularly susceptible to sexual abuse and why continuing problems with gender relations and sexual abuse may cause their government to balk at researching or publicizing wartime sexual abuse. The details and context Hayslip's narrative provide especially enable readers to understand why Vietnamese women have been hesitant for social reasons to speak of their abuse. Additionally, her memoir, along with the firsthand accounts by women in *Then the Americans Came*, give Vietnamese women a voice and an interiority to which most Americans have not before been privy. For though Vietnamese girlfriends and prostitutes frequently haunt the pages of American male narratives of the war, any sense of Vietnamese women as true persons with thoughts, emotions, and values is usually missing. Through the testimony of the southern peasants and Hayslip's writing, Americans may appreciate the incredibly horrible situations

Vietnamese women faced during the war and appreciate their strength and heroism in surviving them.

Furthermore, by voicing their trauma, these women suggest that abuse—however effectively silenced—cannot be forgotten. Their anger suggests it should not be. Implicit in the voices of Hess's collection and explicit in Hayslip's memoir is these women's belief that for true healing to occur, a public must be willing to listen to their witness bearing. However, these women do not merely desire pity. Rather, as Hayslip exhorts readers in her epilogue, "Do not fell [sic] sorry for me—I made it; I am okay. Right now, though, there are millions of other poor people around the world . . . who live their lives the way I did in order to survive. Like me, they did not ask for the wars which swallowed them. They ask only for peace . . . and nothing more. I ask only that you open your heart and mind to them, as you have opened it to me by reading this book and do not think that our story is over." She lists the ways in which "[s]ixty-three million souls in Vietnam are still suffering from their 'victory,'" including starvation, birth defects and cancers resulting from Agent Orange and other chemicals, and war-related injuries and illnesses. Hayslip specifically asserts that U.S. international political policy is actively contributing to this continued suffering because of the embargo that was still in place at the time. In her terms, "[t]he circle of vengeance persists" (p. 366).

Hayslip suggests, however, that readers can break this circle of vengeance by listening to and actively working to help victims of war. She ends her book with a call specifically to veterans to return to Vietnam for a humanitarian "tour of duty" to help rebuild Vietnam and finally provides a list of charitable organizations active in Vietnam for those readers who "would like to help." Thus, Hayslip and these other women ask not for pity for themselves as victims, but the formation of a public that will actively seek to resolve the continuing plight of sufferers. Rather than a cathartic, but empty "co-owning" of the trauma suggested by trauma theorists, in these women's formulation true healing occurs for all parties only when the hearing public understands its ownership in the problem and becomes actively involved in the recovery.

3

"Already Bullets"

American Witnesses to Wartime Rape and Sexual Abuse

Although the stereotype of the Vietnam veteran frequently involves his dysfunctional silence about the war, in reality many veterans spoke very publicly about the worst of their experiences. Often the most traumatizing aspects of their war experience were haunting memories of wanton aggression they or their comrades had committed, especially against women. Their reasons for testifying openly about such atrocities were complex. Many veterans saw their testimony as a contribution to ending a war they now felt was unjust and immoral; they hoped to save would-be draftees and volunteers from the war as well as alter government policy. Some wished to open the eyes of the American public, to force the "silent majority" to recognize the Vietnam War for what it was—a "genocide," as they themselves named it.[1] While these political motivations certainly drove the public revelation of atrocities, the catharsis of guilt veterans hoped to derive from witnessing to their personal sins cannot be overstated. In many self-reflective moments during the Winter Soldier Investigation, for example, participating veterans spoke of their wish to expiate the overwhelming guilt they felt by making a public confession and to achieve healing through communion with veterans like themselves.

Therefore, this chapter has two main purposes. The first of these is to demonstrate that there is an abundance of veteran and other eyewitness testimony proving that the sexual mistreatment of Vietnamese women did occur. In fact, this assembled testimony makes evident that the rape and sexual abuse of women was not a rare occurrence but actually took place on such a large scale that many veterans considered it standard operating procedure. The second purpose of this chapter is, in considering the reasons veterans felt compelled to speak about their brutality, to analyze the particular trauma of aggression from which veterans suffered. Unlike popular images of the veteran that emerged in the 1980s, the veterans highlighted in this chapter revealed that it was their aggressive acts against the Vietnamese, whom the military had taught them to violently loathe, that caused much veteran postwar suffering. And, unlike recent notions of "healing" Vietnam veterans through welcome-home parades and the like, these veterans sought expiation through public recognition of their atrocities and crimes. By setting an example, they hoped America and its military would take responsibility for its part in these criminal acts, just as individual veterans were prepared to take personal responsibility.

I will also argue, however, that prominent among veterans' motives for testifying is relief from the mental anguish and trauma of guilt, which is the context out of which the rehabilitation of the veteran, with a focus on his psychic trauma, occurred in later years. This chapter will be especially attuned to the veterans' struggle to understand how they came to commit barbaric acts; they reveal the dehumanizing, misogynist tactics of basic training and the way militarized masculinity created dangerous group dynamics, which demanded that soldiers display loyalty, even in despicable crimes, or be subject to death. Focusing on veterans' perceptions of women and gender relations, I will also demonstrate how the budding women's movement lent its rhetoric to the antiwar movement, giving veterans the language with which to name their damaging understanding of and behavior toward women. Additionally, I will suggest that the mounting vociferousness of the women's movement probably inadvertently helped to squelch publicization of the abuse that women in Vietnam were suffering at the hands of American men, as authorities hesitated to fuel the fires of women's protest.

Beginnings: The Stockholm International War Crimes Tribunal

Some of the earliest veteran testimony occurred at the International War Crimes Tribunal, sponsored by the Bertrand Russell Peace Foundation and held in Stockholm, Sweden, from 2 through 10 May 1967; its sponsors conceived the tribunal as a forum to expose the detrimental consequences of U.S. policy in Vietnam. Presided over by Jean-Paul Sartre, its twenty-one "tribunal members" included such notables as James Baldwin, Simone de Beauvoir, and Peter Weiss. While critics then[2] and more recently[3] decried the tribunal's reliance on North Vietnamese statistics and evidence, the panelists' admitted antiwar stances, their support of the NLF, and the lack of defensive testimony by the United States, the tribunal provides an important point at which to begin an examination of veteran testimony. For this tribunal was held in 1967, before the tide of mainstream American sentiment began to turn against the war (a turn roughly coinciding with the Tet Offensive in January 1968), and thus before the media began publishing many negative views or stories of the war.[4]

The tribunal was designed to establish the illegitimacy and criminality of the American war against Vietnam, and its panelists called Americans and Third World nations to rise up against U.S. policy. As Russell says in his introduction to the Tribunal's transcript:

> This book . . . should be studied thoroughly by anyone who is still in doubt about the role in Vietnam of the United States of America. It is a role which has been disbelieved often in the West, because it is in the nature of imperialism that citizens of the imperial power are always among the last to know—or care—about circumstances in the colonies. It is my belief, therefore, that is in the United States that this book can have its most profound effect . . .
> War crimes are the actions of powers whose arrogance leads them to believe that they are above the law. Might, they argue, is right. The world needs to establish and apply certain criteria in considering inhuman actions by great powers. These should not be the criteria convenient to the victor, as at Nuremberg, but those which enable private citizens to make compelling judgments on the injustices committed by any great power. It was my belief, in calling together the International War Crimes Tribunal, that we could do this, and this book is the record of the Tribunal's considerable success. It serves not only as indictment of the United States by abundant documentation, but establishes the Tribunal as a model for future use.[5]

While the tribunal was politically progressive and led the rising tide of international and American sentiments against the war, it, like the WWII war-crimes trials that preceded it and even those for wars that followed it, was inattentive to the plight of women. While very interested in the war's deleterious effects on civilians, especially from American use of illegal weapons such as white phosphorous, tribunal members did not ask probing questions about how the war and U.S. policy affected civilians in gender-specific ways. In fact, as seen in the transcript's question-answer repartee, questioners often (seemingly deliberately) sidestep invitations to interrogate the brutal sexual treatment of women by American GIs.

For instance, during the testimony of American soldier Peter Martinsen, a former POW interrogator in Vietnam, he brought up American soldiers' faulty perception of all Vietnamese women as prostitutes several times. When questioned by Dave Dellinger—a well-known peace activist—about GIs' knowledge of Vietnamese burial customs, Martinsen replied that he was sure they knew very little if anything about these customs, because "to the soldiers the Vietnamese people are whores to sleep with, servants to supply the cold beer."[6] Rather than inquiring about GIs' misperception of Vietnamese women as "whores," Dellinger instead asked about Vietnamese attitudes toward Americans in American-occupied areas. In his answer, Martinsen returned to the subject of prostitution: "The Vietnamese hate us also because the whole thing is turning into a big brothel . . . Saigon is a large whorehouse. It is. I was there. I saw it . . . We're corrupting the whole country. The money a prostitute in Vietnam can make is three hundred dollars a day, whereas the average wage I believe is thirty to forty dollars a month. How would you feel if your daughter or your sister became a prostitute?" (pp. 441–42). Though Martinsen clearly felt strongly about the exploitation of women, Dellinger ignored these comments on gender-specific damage inflicted by military, instead remarking on Americans' "unconscious arrogance" and "race prejudice." Martinsen's rejoinder again returned to mistreatment of women, "Well, it's not only the race prejudice. There's nothing more obnoxious than a drunk G.I. And there are thousands of drunk G.I.'s [sic] in that country, whistling at the pretty schoolgirls . . . And the students . . . are really a very charming sight. An American G.I. when he arrives there, and probably even when he leaves there, thinks that that woman is a prostitute. He'll proposition to her, lay his hands on her, and expect the Vietnamese to like this" (p. 442). Instead of unpacking Martinsen's analysis that abuse of women stems from Americans' perception of them as nothing more than "whores," Dellinger glibly thanked him, handing the questioning over to other panelists who likewise showed no particular interest in women's suffering. Thus, although Martinsen did not provide direct accounts of rape, such accounts might very possibly have been forthcoming had questioners been inclined to ask for them rather than redirecting the discussion, as Dellinger persistently did.

Other witness testimony underscored Martinsen's suggestive comments on GI relationships to Vietnamese women. Jean Bertolino, a French journalist, spoke at length on prostitution in Saigon, noting that women and girls were driven to the dangerous profession by the wartime economy. He noticed that, even if "freely" chosen, prostitution invited violence toward the women. As one Vietnamese mother told him, "Three of them [GIs] took her [the woman's daughter] to a hotel. The little one did not dare to say anything. They killed her, Monsieur. She was too young; she had a hemorrhage. Filled with panic, the three G.I.'s [sic] enclosed her in a container which they dumped off in the night, here, just across from my house" (pp. 548–49). And as one Vietnamese waiter bitterly told Bertolino, "this situation [widespread prostitution of Vietnamese women to the military forces] is intolerable. Whether they rape or whether they buy our daughters, the result is the same" (p. 549). Another French journalist, Madeleine Riffaud, testified also to the mistreatment of women, particularly the wives of resistance fighters, who were tortured as part of the campaign to coerce them into divorcing their husbands. She noted that of all the torture techniques employed by the South and its allies, they preferred "those tortures which brought about sterility," tortures clearly sexual in nature (p. 556). Less opaquely, Riffaud claimed that "[a]nother characteristic of repressions carried out against women is systematic and collective rape, aimed at lowering them in the eyes of their companions" (p. 558).

Together with the deposition of Tran Thi Van discussed in chapter 2, this testimony reveals that as early as 1967, eyewitnesses reported rape as an unofficial military policy. The evidence also suggests that, had authorities inquired further, much more information on the subject could have been solicited. The Tribunal's refusal to analyze the abuse of women, even when it would have served their agenda—proving the Vietnam War inhumane—demonstrates the persistent tendency spoken of in chapter 1 to ignore women's war-related suffering, except when it is used to mobilize national feelings of vengeance. If only recently feminists vehemently disagreed as to whether rape in the Bosnia-Herzegovina conflict should be seen as part of a larger genocidal project (and thus be prosecuted as a part of the genocide) or prosecuted in its own right,[7] it is not surprising that the 1967 Tribunal did not privilege rape as a peculiar sort of war crime.

If subsuming the costs of war to women into "larger concerns" is not terribly unusual today, ignoring problems specific to women was understandably even more common in the 1960s, even for politically progressive coalitions. For instance, in the United States female peace activists found themselves being exploited by the antiwar movement. Though they made up a majority of members in the draft resistance, "women were playing this most unbelievably subservient role, because that was the only role the women could play, because women couldn't burn draft cards and couldn't go to jail so all they could do was to relate through their men."[8] Enduring "exploitation in the name of some larger justice," many women activists "perceived 'women's issues' as secondary, selfish, divisive, and threatening" to the antiwar cause. Thus, in 1967, many women had not yet recognized the need to focus specifically on "women's issues" and those who had often felt it necessary to subjugate their own feminist interests to larger movement issues. Interestingly, at one leftist conference, Vietnamese women insisted that women had gender-specific matters to discuss, while American women delegates resisted a separate women's meeting. The Vietnamese women, all too aware of the importance of gender in war, gave "a moving presentation of atrocities committed against women and children—torture, rape, and prostitution."[9] Male factions of these American activists groups did not encourage an interest in women's issues; in fact, the rage expressed by their male counterparts when New Left women declared in 1967 "their colonial relationship to men" demanded either the quiescence or ejection of these women.[10]

Such an atmosphere helps explain why a feminist foremother such as de Beauvoir, a Stockholm Tribunal panelist, neglected to investigate more deeply the cost of war to women, perhaps feeling the specificity of such inquiry would detract from rather than support the overall condemnation of the Vietnam War. While from today's vantage point, the tribunal provides interesting insight into the hesitancy of the antiwar movement to embrace women's issues, at the time, whatever its faults might be, it laid crucial groundwork for future Vietnam War hearings and investigations held by both American military and political organizations and by peace activists.

The Winter Soldier Investigation

In April 1967, shortly before the Stockholm Tribunal took place, a group of about one dozen Vietnam veterans gathered with thousands of other protestors in Central Park to demonstrate against the war. In June, this coalition of veterans formed the Vietnam Veterans against the War (VVAW), the protest group responsible for some of the war-years' most memorable and highly inflammatory demonstrations. For example, Operation Dewey Canyon III—the 19–23 April 1971 protest during which seven hundred veterans discarded their combat ribbons and medals on the steps of the Capitol building[11]—continues to loom large in American memory; during the 2004 presidential election, it became a hot topic as pundits of varying political stripes quibbled over candidate John Kerry's involvement in the event. The Winter Soldier Investigation, while much less well known than Dewey Canyon III, is no less important, particularly for anyone interested in wartime atrocities, for its transcripts contain some of the most revealing testimonial accounts given by veterans during the war.

After the My Lai massacre began to make headlines in the fall of 1969, reporters overwhelmed the VVAW with calls, soliciting information and stories that would confirm the reality of such incidents. At the same time, congressional hearings on the war were being conducted, but as Jan Barry—a VVAW founder and an organizer of the Winter Soldier Investigation—told historian Richard Stacewicz, Congress heard "everybody except for people who carried out the policy. What we [the VVAW] suggested was: Why don't you hear from some of the people who have carried out the policy? The general didn't carry out the policy" (p. 234). As an invitation to testify at the hearings did not seem forthcoming, the VVAW planned its own public hearing of veterans of the Vietnam War. Specifically, organizers hoped to show the media that atrocities such as My Lai were not isolated events, but the products of military policy. In response to reporters who asked for the "most gory horror stories you can tell us," the VVAW stance was that atrocities "were done because they were part of a policy to do them. We weren't going to just line people up to tell them horror stories. We were going to . . . demonstrate why these things happened" (p. 235).

To address these issues, the VVAW organized a series of local investigations in thirteen cities in the Northeast and Midwest throughout 1970; however, although these events received local publicity, they did not garner the nationwide attention the VVAW sought. Thus, they organized a major hearing in which one hundred fifty veterans (as well as sixteen civilians) representing most geographic regions, all branches of the military, and a variety of racial, ethnic, and social backgrounds came together to report on the war crimes they had seen and/or participated in during their service in Vietnam. So was born the Winter Soldier Investigation, which took place from 31 January to 2 February 1971. The term *winter soldier* is an inversion of Thomas Paine's famous words from *The Crisis*: "The summer soldier and the sunshine patriot, will, in crisis, shrink from the service of their country."[12] VVAW member Mike McCain, who suggested the term, explains: "We started understanding, as a group of people, [that] it was easier to be a soldier than it was to be a critic of the government, of the state, of the society, but that if we were to be true citizens, that's what we had to do. You can't accept things at face value; you have to be a member of society. You have to argue. You have to decide whether or not something is right or wrong, and then once you've made that decision, act upon it" (Stacewicz, p. 5).

The choice to speak out at the investigation was costly to the veterans who participated. Not only were they publicly exposing their personal culpability in war crimes, but many of the veterans who testified suffered from PTSD, and some experienced the flashbacks and emotional trauma associated with the disorder as they relived situations (p. 234). As Barry Romo, one of the panel moderators, noted, "[I] watched people freak out right and left. This was the first time I had seen post-Vietnam syndrome: delayed stress. Horrible things happened" (p. 239).

Reported Frequency and Types of Gendered Sexual Abuse

In the full transcript of the Winter Soldier Investigation,[13] veterans reported no fewer than twenty-one separate incidents of rape or other types of sexual abuse against women; many stated that the reported incident was only one of many rapes or sexual abuses he[14] witnessed or participated in. Rape was one of the most often reported atrocities, almost as frequently mentioned as abusing prisoners of war, an activity that was not restricted to one gender as was rape (none of the veterans reported male rape). It was mentioned much more frequently than abuse of children, the war's most infamous abuse.

Veterans related varying types of sexual abuse against women over the course of the investigation. Instances range from tormenting and humiliating women by tearing their clothing so as to expose their breasts or by conducting body "searches"—barely obscured rapes—to outright raping done by either single men or groups of soldiers. The worst recount horrific stories of sexual butchery. This section provides a sample of the various levels of sex abuse Vietnamese women endured, as told from the perspective of the veterans who either saw or participated in the abuse. I include often lengthy quotations because most of these stories have never been discussed outside of the investigation, either in popular or scholarly discourse.[15]

Thomas Heidtman, a marine in country from 1966 to 1967, reported the most benign sexual abuse noted in the investigation:

> One [. . .] thing that was more or less like a joke[,] [. . .] and it would get a laugh every time from somebody, was if we were moving through a village and there was a woman

> present. Her clothes, at least the top half of her clothes were just ripped. I've seen that happen and done it several times, probably thirty, forty times I've seen civilians with their clothes just . . . just because they were female and they were old enough for somebody to get a laugh at . . . their clothes—the top of their clothes, at least, would be ripped. Just torn right down. [. . .] [A]nd they would be shoved out into the ditch and we'd just keep going.[16]

Don Dzagulones, part of a military intelligence detachment for the Americal Division who questioned many female prisoners of war and detainees, described a similar type of sex abuse that was as much mental as physical. "[W]e found out that by threatening a woman with having [a] black interrogator rape her, would usually make them talk. So they'd have the woman and her daughter brought in at the same time. We'd send the daughter into a bunker and tell the mother that we were going to send the black interrogator in to rape the daughter if she didn't cooperate and give us information." Dzagulones is quick to note that the black soldier they used as a threat in this psychological torture was "a pacifist" and never physically harmed the women. However, these threats could escalate into physical harm for women, as it did in another incident Dzagulones provided: "Another time they brought in a woman prisoner who also was alleged to be a spy . . . [S]he wouldn't talk . . . So they stripped off her clothing, and they threatened to rape her, which had no effect on her at all. She was very stoic. She just stood there and looked at them defiantly. So they threatened to burn her pubic hairs, and I guess it wasn't done on purpose, I'm sure of that, but they lighted a cigarette lighter and she caught on fire. She went into shock." The interrogators called in medics to treat the woman, who went into a coma. Not wishing to admit the sexual torture that induced her condition, they had the medics admit her to the hospital under the pretense that she had malaria.[17]

Beyond threat and sexual humiliation, outright rapes occurred so frequently that when the veterans testified to them, they sounded almost mundane. For instance, Marine Sgt. Scott Camil disclosed that "[w]hen we went through the villages and searched people the women would have all their clothes taken off and the men would use their penises to probe them to make sure they didn't have anything hidden anywhere and this was raping but it was done as searching."[18] Speaking further about this kind of rape-as-search, an unnamed panelist claimed that "it makes a lasting impression on some guy—some 'zip' [a derogatory term for the Vietnamese]—that's watching his daughter worked over. So we have a better opportunity of keeping him in line by working her over."[19] In addition to revealing the frequency of rape, this testimony also provides an explicit example of how women's bodies—long considered as merely "collateral" to real war participants (men)—are used directly in warfare, a use that continues to be unacknowledged by historians of war and war-crimes investigations.

Veterans' testimony about the rape of village women attests to the systemic nature of the abuse. There are several accounts similar to that given by panel moderator Sgt. Michael Hunter from the First Air Cavalry. At the end of a long litany of illegal actions of which he was a witness or participant, he told of a search operation in which he took part just after the Tet Offensive: "We encountered a large amount of civilian population . . . [A]nd the women . . . were separated. I might say the young women were separated . . . They were told at gunpoint that if they did not submit to the sexual desires of any GI who was there guarding them, they would be shot for running away. And this was best put in the language as best possible for the people that cannot speak Vietnamese and they got the point across because three women submitted to the raping of the GIs."[20] Joe Galbally, who was with the Americal Division from October 1967 to April 1968, reported soldiers regularly using their power to rape Vietnamese girls. He noted that "[the Vietnamese civilians] are aware of what American soldiers do to them so naturally they tried to hide the young girls." But, of course, they were not always successful. During one particular patrol, Galbally's squad "found [a Vietnamese girl] hiding in a bomb shelter . . . She was taken out, raped by six or seven people in front of her family in front of us, and the villagers. This wasn't just one incident; this was just the first one I can remember. I know of 10 or 15 of such incidents at least." Another panelist, Sgt. Ed Murphy, who served in the same squadron as Galbally corroborated his testimony, adding, "At the time most of this happened, our platoon leader was a minister . . . [H]e would condone rapes. Not that he would do them, but he would just turn his head to them because who was he in a mass military policy."[21]

While rapes committed against village women during routine searches appear frequently to have ended as "mere" rapes—the soldiers satisfied by humiliating the women and sexually gratifying themselves—when the soldiers were particularly fearful or thirsty for revenge, rape could give way to murder, as was the case in the rapes that took place during the My Lai massacre. In fact, Jamie Henry, a marine in country from 1967 to 1968, tells a story eerily similar to that of My Lai. After having received orders reminiscent of those given at My Lai to "kill anything that moves," Henry's squad searched a village. As he walked through the village, "I looked toward where the supposed VCS [sic] were, and two men were leading a young girl, approximately 19 years old, very pretty, out of a hootch. She had no clothes on so I assumed she had been raped, which was pretty SOP, and she was thrown onto the pile of the 19 women and children, and five men, around the circle, opened up on full automatic with their M-16s. And that was the end of that."[22]

Similarly, when rapes were committed against suspected NLF or NVA soldiers, they often ended in brutal murder as well.[23] Michael McCusker, a marine, gave the following chilling report:

> [A] squad of nine men . . . went into this village. They were supposed to go after what they called a Viet Cong whore. They went into the village and instead of capturing her, they raped her—every man raped her. As a matter of fact, one man said to me later that it was the first time he had ever made love to a woman with his boots on. The man who led the platoon, or the squad, was actually a private. The squad leader was a sergeant but he was a useless person and he let the private take over his squad. Later he said he took no part in the raid. It was against his morals. So instead of telling his squad not to do it, because they wouldn't listen to him anyway, the sergeant went into another side of the village and just sat and stared bleakly at the ground, feeling sorry for himself. But at any rate, they raped the girl, and then, the last man to make love to her, shot her in the head.[24]

McCusker's language indicates an apparent inability to fully comprehend the heinous nature of these crimes. The phrase "make love" is a horrifying euphemism for the brutal gang rape and murder of this woman, and it points to the military's conflation of love, sex, and violence, which will be discussed at length in chapter 4. Marine David Bishop more briefly mentioned that "four NVA nurses that were captured—were POWs—were raped, tortured and then were completely destroyed—their bodies were destroyed."[25] When Sgt. Camil spoke of the demise of an enemy woman shot by an American sniper, he narrated one of the most perversely violent accounts of the investigation. "When we got up to her she was asking for water. And the Lt. said to kill her. So he ripped off her clothes, they stabbed her in both breasts, they spread-eagled her and shoved an E-tool up her vagina, an entrenching tool, and she was still asking for water. And then they took that out and they used a tree limb and then she was shot."[26]

The sheer animalism to which some soldiers sank was even more apparent in an incident related by Sgt. Joe Bangert. He described how a friend—Bangert reported the man as an ex-major who, at the time of their acquaintance, worked with USAID and the CIA—took him along to observe the ARVN's handling of a village search. After ARVN interrogators captured, questioned, and murdered a woman alleged to be an NVA nurse, Bangert's friend stepped in. He "went over there and ripped [the woman's] clothes off and took a knife and cut, from her vagina almost all the way up, just about up to her breasts and pulled her organs out, completely out of her cavity, and threw them out. Then, he stopped and knelt over and commenced to peel every bit of skin off her body and left her there as a sign for something or other."[27] Though not involving rape, this incident is indicative of the especially heinous sexual treatment reserved for women during the war (and certainly the disembowelment was sexualized, beginning at the vagina and ending at the breasts).

A final example of rape-murder is given by Bishop. His marine unit was part of an allied forces' offensive outside of Da Nang, which resulted in large numbers of killed enemy soldiers. As his unit swept the enemy's bunker system, they came upon four NVA nurses who were still alive. A squad of Republic of Korea (ROK) marines asked if they could have charge of the nurses. Not caring about the ROK's reputation for brutality toward women,[28] the American unit handed over the prisoners for the sake of expediency. Bishop reported, "[W]e were still in the area when the ROK Marines started tying them down to the ground. They tied their hands to the ground, they spread-eagled them; they raped all four. There was like maybe ten or twenty ROK Marines involved. They tortured them, they sliced off their breasts, they used machetes and cut off parts of their fingers and things like this. When that was over, they took pop-up flares (which are aluminum canisters you hit with your hand; it'll shoot maybe 100–200 feet in the air)—they stuck them up their vaginas—all four of them—and they blew the top of their heads off."[29] Although this horrific incident of sexualized violence was not committed by Americans, it demonstrated the pattern of brutality Vietnamese women suffered under the allied forces. Extrapolating outward from the rapes many of these one hundred fifty veterans witnessed with their own eyes (remembering their reminders that the rapes they related were only single instances of repeated actions), a horrifying picture of sexualized violence in Vietnam becomes clear. We must suppose that rape was widely condoned—or, at the very least, widely tolerated—by the U.S. military and that often these rapes culminated in heinous murders.

"Already Bullets": The Roots of the Military's Sexual Violence

During the investigation, veterans did not merely recount horrifying stories. Instead, they struggled to explain how they—typical, young American men—were capable of such brutality. The most common culprit to which veterans pointed was racism. Recognizing American culture's deeply entrenched racism, they understood that American soldiers had absorbed and transported these racist attitudes to Vietnam, including soldiers of color, who acted out against the Vietnamese the same racism they themselves experienced at home. Veterans' recognition of racism was due in large part to the civil rights movement which had been active throughout the 1960s; many minority members of the VVAW were also participants in the black power or Chicano movements. With their attunement to racial issues, several veterans of color at the investigation demanded a panel on racism alone. As Romo (who was an officer in the Americal Division) told Stacewicz, "[W]e had a third world revolt. I was the only Hispanic there, and [I] united with the only Native American and the blacks . . . We held the panel on what racism was to the Vietnamese . . . but also the question of racism among servicemen in the military. This was the first revolt against a sort of a more liberal antiwar view" (p. 239).

Although most panelists were aware of racism's pre-existence in American society, many report that racism was heightened during their military training. Jim Weber, a sergeant in the Americal Division, pointed to the vicious dehumanization of a racially "other" enemy in military training:

> [The army's advanced infantry training] is where [. . .] I started to hate, hate anything that wasn't exactly like me. Anything that wasn't a fighting machine. Gooks. You've heard that mentioned here for three days, but I don't think you really know what it means unless you know how much hate is instilled in one person, how much, how much really guilt, I mean . . . like if you're not white and 21, you know, forget it. And this is what they do. [. . .] They turn you into a fighting machine and it's, it's so, it's so hideous some of the things. I mean we've gone into barracks and we've had

> like pictures of . . . well, they weren't pictures, they were like cartoons, with slant eyes, you know.
>
> Everything was a slant eye and these little hats on the top, you know. And these were the people you were hating. They were positioned right above the gun racks, you know. No uniform or anything, just, just simply the profile of one, or maybe the face, full face of another.[30]

Weber's description points to the military's dangerous conflation of a race with a national enemy. As in earlier American depictions of the Japanese in World War II, America's new enemy had "no uniform"; instead, it was the entire Asian race. The racism instilled in the soldiers' civilian life and focused by their military training reached new levels of enmity when they arrived in war-torn Vietnam. While in country, as Bangert testifies, soldiers did not think of the Vietnamese "as human beings, they're 'gooks.' [. . .] [T]hey're not human, they're objects."[31]

Soldiers frequently cited racism-enabled dehumanization of the Vietnamese as the cause of their abuse of civilians. For instance, marine corporal William Hatton told a story that did not involve physical harm to the Vietnamese but that demonstrated the soldiers' utter disregard for the plight of Vietnamese civilians, who were often malnourished and in various stages of starvation. "There used to be a game we played—we'd pour liquid garbage off the end of our truck to make 'em crawl for it. The mama-sans would come up with half-cut fifty gallon drums and they'd try to fill it up. They'd get pork chops and sloppy rice and mystery meat or wop slop, or whatever we had for chow, and put it in there and we'd let 'em walk so far and then we'd tip it over, spill it on the ground, and watch them scrape the dirt in there. Anything to dehumanize them."[32] Many soldiers suggested that the combination of racism, which resulted in a complete devaluation of Vietnamese life, and the loss of normal cultural values in wartime led to the terrible acts against women. With the view of all Vietnamese as inferior beings, it is not surprising that many veterans did not recognize the gender-specific maltreatment women received. Their attribution of women's abuse to the effects of racism and the loss of a moral compass is exemplified by Bangert's reply to the question of why women seemed to be treated especially badly: "I think that in regards to women in Vietnam, first of all, you get this feeling sometimes when you're over there that you don't even think of their sex. This is really disgusting. You don't even think of them as human beings, they're 'gooks.'"[33]

After several mentions of rape, audience members questioned panelists specifically about the brutality against women: "Is rape and other sexual brutalities to women—brutality involving the vagina in particular—is that a usual feature of people on tour in Vietnam?" Christopher Simpson, a marine corporal, answered the question, "Me myself, I think it's pretty usual over there. Cause you'll be out in the bush and you'll meet women out on the trails. And the marines over there, just like the army and the Navy, are human. But they just don't go about it the right way—they might stick a rifle in a woman's head and say, 'Take your clothes off.' That's the way it's done over there. Cause they're not treated as human beings over there, they're treated as dirt."[34] This statement, while at least acknowledging the fact that the GIs' treatment of Vietnamese women was reprehensible, reveals the widespread but faulty assumption that men must have sex.[35] When he says, "Marines . . . are human," Simpson demonstrated his belief in the impossibility of soldiers' remaining abstinent during war. Although he felt soldiers should use legitimate, less-coercive means of obtaining sexual satisfaction, this assumption about men's "sexual nature" naturalized by extension even the sexual coercion of women.

Moving beyond naturalizations of rape, a few veterans began to make a larger connection between the sexism in America in the sixties and seventies and the atrocities committed in Vietnam—often seeing racism and sexism combining in a particularly lethal form. Japanese-American Scott Shimabukuro, a corporal in the Third Marine Division, explicitly notes the parallel between the treatment of Vietnamese and American women: "It's the same way right back here in the United States . . . The female, according to the way that the males have been brought up, is inferior. Like, they are inferior, period, you know; and yet we still go to bed with them because we have certain needs that have to be satisfied. And she's a female in Vietnam, whether she's subhuman or not, she's got the body, she's got the right build, she's got the proper things to do it, you know."[36] Shimabukuro clearly recognized the particular racial discrimination Vietnamese women suffered, for he earlier observed that Asian women in general were thought of as "sexual objects," a perception the military continues to reinforce even today by sending its soldiers to Asian countries to be serviced by Asian prostitutes during R&R.[37] However, he also saw soldiers' brutal treatment of Vietnamese women as owing in large part to American male views of women as generally "inferior," though necessary as sexual partners.

When an audience member asked, "In terms of practice does that mean that women were treated especially rudely?"[38] Bangert responded by referring to the disembowelment story: "Back to this specific instance where I talk about the disembowelment of the women—I think the person involved was a freaked out sexist, if that's what you're trying to get at." Bangert's interesting reference to the soldier as a "sexist" indicates that by 1971, the women's movement had made sufficient inroads that its rhetoric had seeped into this veteran's vocabulary. Moreover, this linguistic borrowing offers the suggestion that the women's movement, even as it found it necessary to break away from the antiwar movement to voice its own issues, contributed important conceptualizations to the veterans' antiwar movement. As this testimony indicates, veterans found feminist critiques of patriarchal society useful in naming the damaging attitudes toward women that were inherent in American masculine culture and encouraged by the military. Thus, moving from the silence and apparent disinterest in women's suffering seen in the Stockholm Tribunal, only four years later audience members and panelists at the WSI were much more attentive to and critical of these matters, though these critiques would become even more developed in later veteran analysis. This rapid change offers the possibility that the women's movement and the veteran's antiwar movement, at least, were more compatible and less competitive than previous histories of the two have suggested. While within the scope of work completed for this project, I cannot offer more than possibilities, it seems probable that further research might reveal more positive confluences between the two groups than thought before.

In any case, by the time of the WSI, soldiers were beginning to see in fairly sophisticated ways the connections between a sexist culture and the military's demand for a certain form of masculinity that implicitly demanded destruction of women, a destruction endorsed by military training and policy. For example, Michael Farrell, who was in the army's Ninth Infantry Division, reported that his platoon sergeant "told [the platoon. . .] 'If there's a woman in a hootch, lift up her dress, you know, and tell by her sex; if it's a male, kill him; and if it's a female, rape her.' You know, like this man, this was his third war. He's rather proud of the fact that he was in his third war. Served in World War II, Korea and Vietnam."[39] Farrell's emphasis of the sergeant's extended military service implied that war itself, as well as the military's training and policy, has a brutalizing effect on people over long periods of time; this example also suggested the extension of the military's mistreatment of women beyond the Vietnam War. One panelist, when asked if servicemen were actually encouraged to rape women, not only noted the military's overt antiwoman policy but also pointed to the psychological ideology underlying this policy.

> Yes, in ITR [Infantry Training Regiment] in the Marine Corps . . . [t]hey have a class on when you interrogate a POW

> or a villager what to look for—where they hide things. They stress over and over that a woman has more available places to hide things like maps or anything than a male. So it took about twenty minutes to cover where to search for a male suspect, and about an hour on a female. It was like everyone was getting into it pretty heavy like, . . . wishful-thinking, you know. *But it seems to me that the philosophy over there is like somehow or another we're more afraid of females than we are of males, because, I don't know why, but the female was always like you never knew where you stood, so you went overboard in your job with her in all your daily actions. You doubled whatever you would do for a male.* Because we always heard these stories that, like, the fiercest fighters were the females over there. *You know, we didn't want to be embarrassed by getting our asses kicked by a bunch of females.*[40]

Not only evidentiary of the fact that soldiers' "probing" of Vietnamese women was military policy, this testimony also provided an incisive look into the psychology of basic training and its reliance on the destruction of the feminine as necessary to proper masculinity, with fear of women as a byproduct. As Richard Moser puts it, "[b]oot camp has been the military's central socializing experience. In boot camp, the fighter spirit was powerfully communicated to the new recruit by example, through training, and in ritual."[41] A large part of the training was comprised of "strident and persistent appeals to sexual identity." Sexist and homophobic hate speech was used to train and discipline soldiers. Women provided a negative example and common "other" for the servicemen who came from widely varying socioeconomic levels, races, and ethnicities. As one Air Force veteran recalled, "If you screwed up—your name became some woman's body part." In boot camp, the sexual strategy portrayed "conventional feminine stereotypes as the polar opposite of the fighter spirit." Even the recruits' mother, wives, and girlfriends were stereotyped as "whores and lesbians" (p. 26). Thus, a properly militarized masculinity was achieved by denying any positive connection between male and female, and in fact, demanding a disavowal of anything considered feminine. This rhetorical use of sexuality was supercharged by the actual suppression of sexual activity during the training period. Many soldiers saw links between this suppression and the terrible violence enacted by soldiers, as one writer in an underground GI paper put it, "The suppression of natural sexual gratification leads to various kinds of substitute gratifications. Natural aggression becomes brutal sadism" (qtd. in Moser, p. 28). The negative use of women to achieve a particular kind of masculinity was not only an end itself, but misogyny provided a starting point for other forms of domination as well, primarily racism and the general dehumanization of the Asian enemy.

The panelist who spoke about the ITR class recognized the way the military inculcated its lessons about women. At the same time the military denied any commonality between men and women, it simultaneously cast woman as a mysterious and powerful unknown. Thus, just as the recruits repressed the feminine in themselves as part of their military training, so in Vietnam they annihilated women where possible as a means to check the power of this unknown. The employment of women by the NLF and NVA added a physical reality to the symbolic threat posed by women. The GIs' knowledge of women combatants encouraged their brutal hatred, for while any loss to the enemy would be humiliating, loss to a woman of an inferior race and sex would be doubly so and in fact would shake the very grounds on which soldiers' masculinity was based—their superiority to women. Veterans suggested that even men who would never condone such abuse in civilian life were convinced by the military's misogynist ideology or felt powerless to fight this ideology, even when it was expressed in a policy of rape. As Sgt. Murphy, mentioned earlier as the corroborating witness for a gang rape, noted, when his platoon leader first arrived in Vietnam, "he was a pretty well high-character man because he was the minister. By the time he got killed he was condoning everything that was going on because it was a part of policy. Nobody told you that it's wrong. This hell changed him around."

The supposed danger posed by female enemies to servicemen's masculinity was reinforced by military directives for media coverage, which were formulated to protect servicemen's psyches from such blows. Larry Rottman, a first lieutenant who worked for the army's Public Information Office, testified that, "If the [newspaper] story emphasized the bravery or determination of women guerrillas, it was, of course, killed. If, on the other hand, it made a point of how VC were hurting so bad from U.S. presence that they were forced to recruit women (who supposedly were not as good fighters), the story would pass." He brought an example of a story the clearance office had killed:

> "Sweeping the ambush site, the GIs found that two of the dead guerrillas were packing automatic weapons but their real surprise was the enemy point man, who was actually a point girl. She was leading the VC when the ambush was sprung and died with a 45 caliber pistol in her hand. This clash was

> but one of several in recent weeks which involved female VC. In one case, a U.S. patrol was attacked by a guerrilla unit led by a submachine gun toting girl who one U.S. soldier described as 'very attractive, but a bad shot.'" Across the bottom of this press release it says, "not cleared for release, MACOI." This is a Xeroxed copy of it. Attached to that is a censor sheet from the U.S. Infantry Information Office, United States Army of Vietnam, signed by _____ _____, Chief of the Clearance Branch, PID, and it says "Remarks: Not cleared for release per MACOI."[42]

Thus, influenced by the powerful social movements rocking the United States in the early seventies, veterans perceived the sexual brutalities against Vietnamese women to be caused by racism, sexism, or a combination of both. As typical American men, they saw these problematic attitudes beginning early in their lives; however, they also clearly realized how the military made use of both perceptions of the lower worth of certain people (nonwhites—Asians in this case—and women) to create a certain kind of fighting man.

Perhaps because they were so recently enmeshed in the military's system, most veterans did not fully comprehend the ways militarized masculinity, with its emphasis on gender differentiation through bellicosity, began in childhood and was encouraged by state and cultural apparatuses. Coming from a far different vantage point, the analysis of sociologist–peace activist Sid Peck manages a much more complex analysis, which indicted the U.S. socioeconomic system. A participant of the panel entitled "What Are We Doing to Ourselves?" Peck sought to disprove the idea, expressed by many soldiers, that basic training alone was responsible for what veterans termed their "dehumanization." Rather, he suggested that far from beginning in boot camp,

> the programming to be a bullet and a bomb, begins in [the] working class household. That's where the dehumanization process initiates, because if you come out of a working class background family . . . you come into a situation where your father, as the provider for that family, is in fact a very powerless figure.
>
> Your family itself is a very powerless kin unit . . . And so the one dominant characterization . . . in a working class area, is a . . . profound powerlessness. Of not being able to really determine your own future in your own way. To that extent you're constantly involved in an effort to prove oth-

> erwise. To prove that you really are something . . . That you really represent some sense of power. Often times this [results in] . . . a pattern of intense male chauvinism . . . that focuses primarily on penis power. That's where you become powerful, through your penis. By literally not only expressing your dehumanization in a profound way, but by brutalizing other persons, primarily women in your neighborhood. Just as your old man brutalized your mother. And so you grow up in a household, and in a neighborhood [. . .] that is fundamentally oppressive. Yet you're trapped and the only way you can get out of it, in addition to this kind of penis power, is through a sort of entertainment route. You know, like you can join the Golden Gloves . . . Or you become an all-star, all-city quarterback in football, which I was, and at each moment you have to prove and demonstrate your male prowess and your male power and your masculinity, which involves brutalizing other persons. That's reinforced fundamentally in the basic socializing agency in the working class area, namely the working class school . . . Where can you break out to? You can't be a man hero; you can't be a football hero; you can't be the leading outstanding boxer; you join the service.[43]

Peck further suggested that part of the psychic struggle veterans faced was a realization that the people against whom they were being asked to fight were fundamentally like themselves—they were "fighting people who are struggling for a certain kind of dignity of person, fighting a people who were struggling against a similar kind of oppressiveness." He ended his lengthy testimony by suggesting, "It is not a question of becoming somehow dehumanized as though you left the States as a humanized person and somehow you become dehumanized and now we have to put you back to where you were . . . [A]ll of us, each in our own way, have been brutalized and dehumanized and we're already bullets before we go into the military."[44] The transcript indicates that Peck's analysis received no comment from the audience or other panel members. Perhaps its sweeping scope or its deep pessimism, as he repeatedly characterized the working class as powerless, seemed a dampening voice in what was otherwise an optimistic endeavor to transform American military and foreign policy. However, Peck's analysis is an important antecedent to critiques veterans would make almost a decade later in literary works. At this later time, more veterans would concur with Peck that the brutal excesses of militarized masculinity were not primarily the result of war, but that concepts of masculinity experienced by American boys—especially those of the working class—had already dehumanized and brutalized them, preparing the way for violent enactments of masculinity in war.

"Victim and Executioner": The Roots of the Veteran-as-Victim

Because it offers such an extensive range of eyewitness testimony concerning the brutal treatment of women, the Winter Soldier Investigation must be paramount in any study of the sexual abuse of women in the Vietnam War. Beyond this, the investigation offers intriguing insight into the coming erasure of women's abuse from the history and rhetoric of the war. Although rape and sexual abuse held a place of prominence in the investigation, an analysis of veterans' reasons for testifying reveals preparation for the rehabilitation of the veteran as victim and the submersion of women's trauma into the trauma experienced by veterans. At the same time it spawned these crippling representations, however, the investigation, with its demonstration of the veterans' desire for a public hearing of their crimes and experiences, also suggests a workable format for veteran healing on which future healing might be based.

Robert J. Lifton, the renowned trauma scholar, was deeply involved in the veterans' movement both during and after the war. He was a cofounder of the "rap group"[45] movement and met with one of the original rap groups regularly over a period of two years (1970–72). Lifton had opportunity to speak to about four hundred veterans, and he spent 80 hours interviewing individuals and some one 150 hours in rap group sessions; he published his findings from these contacts in *Home from the War: Vietnam Veterans, Neither Victims nor Executioners* in 1973.[46] Because of his extensive personal contact with veterans, he was asked to testify on the panel, What Are We Doing to Ourselves? Unlike Peck, who in his Althusserian critique stressed that every soldier is always already part of the military's system of brutality because of the U.S. socioeconomic system, Lifton agreed with many veteran witnesses that basic training was the greatest cause of brutality in Vietnam: "You must remember that what is characteristic of this kind of process [thought reform, which Lifton argued was present in basic training] is that a man is made to feel extremely guilty, as if he doesn't exist at all, can't exist, and is threatened with terrible harm unless he takes a very narrow, and in this case, very brutalized pattern, adopts it as his own, internalizes it, and then expresses it. I think basic training has to be looked at very severely in this light."[47] Never noticing the links between culturally endorsed forms of masculinity and the policies and attitudes of basic training, Lifton instead stressed the feelings of guilt experienced by the recruit. He suggested soldiers had no choice but to internalize the military's "brutalized pattern . . . as his own." Thus, he decontextualized the military's problematic ideology, by denouncing the "process." His interest in the training's methodologies as inherently traumatizing denied the damage that the military's misogyny itself did to men.

Lifton believed that the guilt suffered by soldiers during and after the war was so strong that it approached the level of trauma experienced by victims of the soldiers' brutality. He expanded on the traumatizing nature of guilt in his discussion of the "burden of atrocity."

> I would stress very strongly, the GI in Vietnam becomes both victim and executioner . . . In [keeping with] the burden of atrocity, . . . the veteran becomes enormously sensitive to the way in which he's probed or questioned by others in the society at large . . . [I]n rap sessions, a lot of vets said, "Well, I just can't stand it when people ask me what I did over there, whether I killed anybody." . . . [T]he reason why vets can't stand being asked this question is because they see themselves being accused of having been a monster in some way over there, of having been something less than human. The problem is so great because they inwardly tend to accuse themselves of having been this, and it's one reason why it's so important for vets in making their recovery and undergoing their process of renewal . . . that they understand how they were forced by the situation to act in a way . . . It has to do with military training . . . ; it also has to do with the extreme situation of Vietnam which itself creates the aberrant behavior, rather than with some particular trait that particular vets have in order to then lend them to do these things. They carried with them also a tremendous burden of violence, and every session we have with vets has, at its center, the issue of violence.[48]

Blaming military training and "the extreme situation of Vietnam . . . itself" for "forc[ing]" the GI to act a certain way, Lifton's critique removed agency from veterans; this was the first step in transforming the veteran from "executioner" to "victim." Peck's analysis suggested that, though interpellated in a system larger than themselves that encouraged American men to prove their masculinity in violent ways, soldiers still bore responsibility for their acts because they had bought into this system. Furthermore, this responsibility extended to all Americans who maintained this system, not just those who had the misfortune of going to war. Contrary to Peck's conclusion, in Lifton's assay of the situation, the veterans were almost totally without blame for their brutality because they were forced to it, and in fact, they were ultimately victims of this brutality because of the psychic trauma it caused them. Though he correctly noted that aggression was itself traumatizing, because of his denial of veteran agency, Lifton conflated the veteran's aggression-caused trauma with victimization.

Though certainly the veteran *was* a victim of an oppressive, culturally imposed concept of gender difference and of the military's brutal training techniques, he could not be a *victim* of his own brutal actions. Lifton's conflation of the guilt caused by soldiers' actions with their victimization by a cultural and military system thus underwrites the erasure of these soldiers' true victims—Vietnamese women. Moreover, this early conflation sets the pattern for the rehabilitation of the veteran as a victim. Ultimately, the definition of guilt as a kind of victimization allowed not just veterans but America itself to transform its national guilt from the war to victimization. Though he laudably recognized the trauma of aggression, Lifton's incorporation of this trauma into the veteran's victimization as *proof* of his victim status collapsed his potentially nuanced understanding into the simplistic veteran-as-victim representation that still persists. In this, Lifton, who has remained influential in academic discussions of trauma and Vietnam veterans, is a forerunner of subsequent trauma theorists who would jettison any memory that veterans' trauma was sometimes induced by aggressive acts, instead focusing on them solely as victims.

In their testimonies, veterans themselves struggled between demanding their own and others' accountability for American actions and desiring sympathy and understanding as well as the healing they hoped it might bring. William Bezanson testified that "I was tired of living with the nightmares [. . .] The people that I, myself, messed up. The people I've seen my buddies mess up and then the next day they're killed . . . But I just got tired of living with my nightmares and I think *by relating I can share them with you*, you know, and, and, *it takes kind of the guilt off me*, in a way. And maybe it'll stop, like my younger brother, or, or some of your younger brothers or sisters, or your children, from going over there and then having to come home and live with these same nightmares."[49] Although Bezanson explained that he had nightmares because of brutality he committed, so he presumably wished to end such atrocities, he articulated that he would like to stop the *guilt* that he and other veterans felt because of the acts they committed. What he most wanted to prevent were not future atrocities against the Vietnamese, but future nightmares—further guilt—for Americans. In this way, Bezanson's testimony, even the entire investigation, was predictive of the way in which the memory of what caused much veteran and American guilt—atrocities and the social systems of which veterans were truly victims—would be lost through the rhetoric of victimization.

This process of victimization also occurs in the closing remarks of Don Duncan, a sergeant of the Special Forces. Although he begins by suggesting, as Peck did,

> Whatever it was that was in these men, that allowed them to do the things they did, is in all of us. We start taking it in . . . from the day we are born in this country. The men did not become racists when they entered the service . . . It was taught to them . . . The idea that the United States has a God-given right to go into any country and take out its raw materials at an advantage to ourselves is not something that they learned in Vietnam. They learned it in our schools. They learned it from their mothers, fathers, their sisters and their brothers, their uncles. They learned it from all of us.

Thus, Duncan firmly situates the overarching cause of the war, defined here as neoimperialism, and the cause of the particular brutalities of the war, which he attributed to racism, within U.S. culture. He pointed out that this violence is both naturalized ("They learned it from all of us") and state-sanctioned ("They learned it in our schools"). However, from this fairly radical critique of the U.S. state and culture, Duncan turned to focus on the veteran and his plight, lamenting,

> We did a terrible thing to a lot of men in Vietnam and we're still doing it. *I don't know who the ultimate victim in Vietnam will be.* Will it be those who went from the United States to fight in it or the Vietnamese that tried to resist? I do know this, having met and talked with many Vietnamese who have gone through worse hardships than anyone in this room who has been here these three days, that they, at least, do not seem to have lost their humanity in the process. But I fear that many of us, if we don't shorten up and get the message out, we will have lost our humanity beyond redemption.[50]

Here Duncan was clearly suggesting that American veterans might turn out to be the biggest casualty of the war because they might "lo[se] [their] humanity beyond redemption." The Vietnamese, who, he acknowledged, suffered much greater physical hardship, did not suffer the mental anguish of the Americans.[51] Thus, even as he attested to the brutalities suffered by the Vietnamese, Duncan positioned the veteran—the American—as the greatest victim of all.

My aim here is not to suggest that it was unethical for the veterans and Lifton to hope and seek for an assuagement of the guilt from which they suffered. On the contrary, I wholeheartedly agree with Duncan's sentiments later in his closing statements, "I don't want anybody here to carry away a feeling of guilt with them. I want them to carry away the realization of what you have done, and I have done, and why we did it. And I want us all to do something with that." Though guilt is not a useful emotion in itself, he suggested that this guilt might motivate soldiers to take responsibility for atrocities they committed as well as understand the broader societal impulses behind their actions; their guilt could be put to a laudable use—namely, stopping the war. Thus, acknowledgment and analysis of guilt can be tools of personal agency and cultural change. In demonstrating this, the investigation offers a wonderful example of a healing forum for veterans. All that is missing is a public willing to listen to such a witnessing.[52]

However, even as the investigation stands as an example of healing confession, at important self-reflective moments, veterans revealed that, for many of them, their desire to end the war was rooted in a sense of guilt and wish for atonement. In this veterans privileged their own guilt and suffering, even to the point of suggesting the Vietnamese ultimately endured less pain than the Americans because the Vietnamese fought for a just cause. At these moments the veterans themselves modeled the representation of veterans as the ultimate victims, a representation encouraged by theorists such as Cathy Caruth, who would later subsume and use the trauma of the victimized to attest to the trauma of the aggressor. This representation of veteran as victim was ultimately embraced by Americans to the point that veteran guilt was forgotten completely. Thus, in the testimony of the WSI—concerned almost solely with atrocities committed against the Vietnamese—one also finds the seeds of the national focus on American trauma to the exclusion of Vietnamese trauma. Today, if Americans think of the Vietnamese at all, they are, as Bezanson suggested, merely "the nightmares" veterans live with. They are not real people, real victims, but terrible memories of "[t]he people that [the veterans] . . . messed up." The memory of

Vietnamese victims attests not to their own suffering but to the suffering of their victimizers, who live guilt-ridden.

Other War-Years Testimony

In this section, I will discuss three other sources of veteran testimony on rape given while the war was still in progress, including the proceeds of a congressional hearing, the testimony procured during the My Lai investigation and the Calley court martial, and Daniel Lang's report on the army's investigation into the "incident on Hill 192." This testimony augments the evidence indicating the widespread incidence of rape that the WSI provided. As in the Stockholm Tribunal and the investigation, the audiences' responses (or lack thereof) to this other testimony reveal America's apparent indifference toward war rape and its devaluation of Vietnamese women. The specific contexts of these (non)responses suggests that they were colored by the audiences' desire to suppress evidence that would enhance American women's claims that patriarchal societies, specifically American culture, are inherently oppressive to women.

In response to the WSI and in conjunction with Dewey Canyon III, Senator George McGovern of South Dakota organized an ad hoc congressional hearing for the VVAW. In his report on the meeting, dated 17 May 1971, McGovern stated that "[t]hose of us who were able to attend those hearings learned about specific events that we had not known earlier and saw, at first hand, the effect of the war on young Americans who participate in it."[53] In his opening remarks to the meeting, McGovern commended all the men who arrived at the capital to demonstrate during the week, suggesting that "they . . . manifested . . . the very highest form of patriotism, which is the willingness to place love of one's country above any personal inconvenience, and to manifest whatever courage is necessary to stand by the best ideals of this nation, and to call our country to a higher standard."

As a witness, Sgt. Camil, who earlier testified at the WSI, elaborated upon the "raping done as searching" mentioned earlier. He avowed before the congressional hearing,

> Raping of women was a very common thing. When women were searched . . . [t]hey would be stripped naked, and kind of a game was made out of it. Like, men would put their fingers up their vaginas, supposedly searching for articles. And they would say, "I think maybe my penis is a little longer, and I will try with that and see if there is anything there." The

> general attitude was, we are over here helping these people. "The least they could do was lay a little leg on us." People would say, "Let's go out and get (?)," and they would go out and rape them, then shoot them. (p. E4466)

The attitude that Vietnamese women ought to "lay a little leg" on American GIs in exchange for their trouble points to another cause of the widespread rape during the war: a sense of sexual entitlement linked to soldiers' belief in American exceptionalism—the belief that America's wars are just, heroic, and desired by the people "for whom" they are fought.

Soldiers' disillusionment with American exceptionalism in Vietnam combined with the militarily endorsed objectification and devaluation of women to form a dangerous reaction, as elaborated in the testimony of army veteran Jim Neilson, who conducted a poll among returning veterans. One of his questions—"The South Vietnamese people seem most interested in which of the following"—was meant to elicit the soldiers' views of how invested the South Vietnamese were in winning the war against the North (p. E4472). Based on the responses, Neilson suggested that GIs were primarily resentful of risking their lives for the freedom of a people who seemed to be mainly interested in earning money from the soldiers. He claims one GI's pithy response sums up this resentment: "The men can't fight and the women can't ———" (presumably the censored word is "fuck"). Neilson paraphrased this comment at the hearing: "'The men can't fight and the women can't—'do their thing'" (p. E4471). This comment constructs Vietnamese women as merely (inadequate) sexual objects; Neilson's paraphrasing of the comment only makes this construction more clear.[54] He converts the word "fuck," too obscene for Congress's ears, to the phrase "do their thing." Although Neilson means this phrasing to be less objectionable, it even more firmly constricts the function of Vietnamese women to the sexual sphere. If this was indicative of American GIs' general attitude, as Neilson suggested, it is no surprise that rape was a widespread occurrence: Vietnamese women had one function, which was to sexually gratify men. Following this logic, men who raped Vietnamese women were only demanding that women fulfill their function, a demand that was the GIs' by right because they were fighting the war for the Vietnamese.

As occurred in the Stockholm Tribunal, when the floor was opened to the audience, they questioned Camil and Neilson further about burning villages, killing civilians, and the treatment of returning veterans, but no one wondered about the sexual mistreatment of women. No congressperson commented on the assumption by Neilson's interviewee or Camil's feeling that Vietnamese women "owed" the American soldiers sexual favors. While their silence does not necessarily indicate agreement, it opens several possibilities: that the audience agreed with the soldiers' assumptions to a certain extent, that they were unable to see the problematic nature of such assumptions about women, or that they were so uncomfortable with the implications of the soldiers' testimony that they simply could not think how to address it. Taking into account the historical moment, it seems likely to me that Congress's ignoring of such inflammatory testimony indicates their unwillingness to address this testimony specifically in terms of gender. For, had Congress publicized such information by acting on it, surely the women's movement would have seized on this as further evidence of American male chauvinism and its authorization by the military and tacitly by the government.[55] This silence regarding gendered violence is intriguing, then, for it may have had less to do with insensitivity to women's issues than a hypersensitivity, indicating Congress's political anxiety that broaching such issues would only fuel the fire of the women's movement, which was making huge strides at this historical moment.

The findings of the investigations by Congress and the U.S. Army into the My Lai massacre provide further evidence that rape was a constant and widespread crime. Even more horrifying, the investigation findings particularly reveal that the danger of being raped was not confined to women but extended to very young girls. Yet, in spite of these ghastly findings, no changes in military policy were demanded. Rather, the government and the military satisfied themselves with the conviction of one officer—William Calley—for murder, rather than punishing all the men who committed these rapes and the wanton killing. Calley has long been called a scapegoat by his defenders; while I find their politics abhorrent, his apologists are correct in labeling him a scapegoat. He was the only person or entity punished in a crime that was far greater than he, though this does not mitigate Calley's personal culpability for the role he played. Indeed, he deserved a much harsher sentence than the one he received.[56] Convicting only one man of these crimes, however, effectively denied the army's complicity in these crimes vis-à-vis its policy, a policy the collected testimony overwhelmingly revealed.

Today, when Americans mention My Lai as shorthand for the atrocities committed in Vietnam, they are referencing the mass murder of civilians—not the extensive raping that also occurred. This demonstrates yet again how completely violence against women has been erased from the history of the war, for the rapes committed as part of the massacre were the linchpin in the prosecution's case against Calley, as the lawyers suggested the extensive raping proved the lieutenant's utter lack of control over his men. When asked whether he thought rape was a widespread practice in Vietnam, Michael Bernhardt, one of the soldiers from the company responsible for the massacre, said, "I thought it was . . . It was predictable. In other words, if I saw a woman, I'd say, 'Well, it won't be too long.' That's how widespread it was."[57] Bernhardt also recalled the gang rape of a Vietnamese woman by three soldiers, which was unconnected to the My Lai incident. When a Vietnamese interpreter threatened to report the soldiers, they planned to kill the interpreter. After Bernhardt reported the plot to his commander, one of the men was disciplined with loss of rank for conspiring to commit murder; no one was punished for the rape.[58] Thus, Bernhardt painted a careful picture of continuing and unpunished sexual violence as precursor to the gruesome events at My Lai. For during the killing and mayhem at My Lai, many soldiers witnessed and/or participated in raping women at gunpoint. As part of his defense, Calley reported that when he caught one of his men raping a woman, he ordered him "to get his pants back up and get over to where he was supposed to be" (Olson and Roberts, p. 22). Varnado Simpson, a participant in the slaughter, brought up the gang rape and murder of a girl in his testimony about the various killings. He testified, "I saw Wright, Hutto, Hudson, Rucker . . . , and Mower go into a hut and rape a 17 or 18 year old girl. I watched from the door. When they all got done, they all took their weapons, M-60s, M-16's, and caliber .45 pistols and fired into the girl until she was dead. Her face was just blown away and her brains were just everywhere" (p. 89).

Rape was so often mentioned during the My Lai investigations that prosecutors compiled a list of rape victims and summarized the rapes. The investigators concluded that at least twenty Vietnamese women and girls were raped. However, it is possible the true number of rapes was much higher. Many of the murdered women identified as rape victims were examined for sexual abuse only because they showed outward signs of being raped such as nudity or torn clothing. It is conceivable that some attackers did not leave outward evidence or that some women had opportunity to redress before they were killed and thus were never examined for proof of rape. Perhaps the list's most horrifying revelation is the youth of many victims. Almost half of the twenty known rape victims were under fifteen. Seven of them were thirteen or younger; the youngest was ten (pp. 99–102).

Historians James S. Olson and Randy Roberts, who gathered and prepared primary documents for their history of My Lai, point out the importance of rape when determining whether My Lai was truly an atrocity. For since the events at My Lai first became known to the American public, a startling number of people have defended the division's actions at My Lai "on the grounds that Vietnam was a 'different' kind of war, that because American soldiers often could not distinguish between civilians and enemy troops, they had to attack non-combatant Vietnamese to protect themselves" (p. 76). Others criticized the soldiers and the press who publicized the atrocity; as one Indiana interviewee said in November 1969, "Things like that happen in war. They always have and they always will . . . It's bad enough to have to kill people without telling everybody about it . . . This sort of thing should be kept classified" (pp. 180–1). Of course, the rape of so many women and girls at My Lai greatly hampers the former argument, for rape is never an act of self-defense and thus never "necessary." The second argument assumes atrocity is inevitable, thereby excusing both rape and gratuitous murder. Examining both rationalizations reveals important societal attitudes about rape, particularly the rape of racially, ethnically other women. Doubtless the Indiana man who argued that atrocities like My Lai "should be kept classified" would not believe rape were inevitable if American women had been raped and murdered by an invading army. This type of willful ignorance proved to be indicative of Americans' future refusal to recognize or remember the suffering of the Vietnamese in the war.

Perhaps most interesting—and troubling—about the investigations of the rapes that occurred at My Lai and their use in the courts-martial is the fact that the rapes themselves were never prosecuted. And, though war rape was not internationally prosecuted until the 1990s, it was a litigable offense within the American military justice system and, in fact, carries the highest penalty. The Uniform Code of Military Justice states that "any person . . . who commits an act of sexual intercourse, by force and without consent, is guilty of rape and shall be punished by death or such other punishment as a court-martial may direct."[59] The Peers inquiry reported that the crimes "visited on the inhabitants of Son My [another label for My Lai] Village included individual and group acts of murder, rape, sodomy, maiming, assault on noncombatants, and the mistreatment and killing of detainees."[60] However, Calley, the only soldier convicted in connection with the rape-massacre, was found guilty only of the premeditated murder of twenty-two civilians. No soldier was brought up on charges of rape, demonstrating once again the government and the public's unwillingness to deal with American GIs' abuse of women.

One might argue that the rape of twenty women and girls pales in comparison to the slaughter of these women and at least five hundred to six hundred more persons. However, as Olson and Roberts indicate, prosecutors ought to have pursued rape convictions if for no other reason than to disprove the defense that all the soldiers were merely following orders in ransacking the village and slaughtering the inhabitants. Certainly they were not ordered to rape the women, as Calley himself demonstrated when he instructed the soldier to "get his pants back up." Thus, prosecution for the rapes would not only have gained "justice" for the women, but evidence of and convictions for rape would have enabled cases against individual soldiers in the larger matter of the massacre. The prosecution's neglecting to pursue rape convictions provides further evidence of the nation's denial of women's abuse in a perhaps unconscious attempt to underplay a potentially explosive issue. For the gathering forces of the women's liberation movement had recently gained "tremendous media notice" with events such as the demonstration at the fall 1968 Miss America pageant.[61] A nationally publicized trial of American soldiers for rape would have lent further credence to American women's complaint of sexism's oppressiveness and perhaps have encouraged less radicalized women to join the new movement.

A final aspect of the My Lai trials that has bearing on future representations of the war and its victims is the cult-hero status that Calley achieved within some segments of society. During and after his conviction, various veteran groups and individuals lobbied for parole, pardon, or clemency. Olson and Roberts explain that "[m]any Americans—especially in the South, Midwest, and West—viewed Calley as just another victim of My Lai, not as a war criminal" (p. 179). William Wilson, one of the original army investigators into the My Lai atrocity, wrote that he remembered "being startled when the public seemed to make a hero out of Rusty Calley, or at least a victim. It sure didn't look that way from up close."[62] The fact that the public could possibly conceive of Calley—who had callously ordered the mass murder of hundreds of civilians, personally slaughtering over one hundred people, including children and infants, himself—as a victim speaks to Americans' overwhelming desire to turn American aggressors into victims. His transformation in the public imagination from mass murderer to victimized, innocent officer is a grotesque antecedent to the similar transformation of all Vietnam veterans into victims that occurred in the 1980s. Calley's "victimization" demonstrates that the potential and precedent for such redefinition and revisionism have long been a part of American culture.

The final testimony of rape I will examine is that given by "Sven Eriksson" to reporter Daniel Lang. Eriksson, a fictional name assumed for protection, was an army veteran who informed authorities about the actions of his reconnaissance squad, which kidnapped, raped, and murdered a young Vietnamese woman. After telling his story to many different army officials, Eriksson finally set in motion an investigation of the crime, and the four other members of his squad were eventually court-martialed and convicted of rape, murder, or both. Lang published a story in the *New Yorker* (18 October 1969) based on his interviews and the investigation reports and courts-martial transcripts; a book form of the report, entitled *Casualties of War,* also appeared in 1969. The "incident at Hill 192," as it was known to the army, was one of the most widely known atrocities involving rape.

The basic events are as follows: five men, known by the fictional names Tony Meserve, Ralph Clark, Rafael Diaz, Manuel Diaz, and Eriksson comprised an elite reconnaissance squad, which was sent out alone on a five-day mission. Before the mission, Meserve, a sergeant and the squad leader, revealed his plan to kidnap a girl, "avail themselves of her body" for five days, and then murder her to avoid any legal complications.[63] True to his word, Meserve directed the squad to detour through a village on the first day of the mission, kidnapping the teenaged Phan Ti Mao, who had been sleeping at home with her parents and sister. After a forced march of several hours, the men set up a camp and, with the exception of Eriksson, proceeded to rape Mao.

Eriksson's recollection of the rape provides important insights into how received notions of militarized masculinity had deadly consequences for women and how it also subtly coerced men into committing horrendous acts. In Kathy J. Phillips' *Manipulating Masculinity,* she argues that societies, such as Cold War American culture that strongly emphasized gender divisions in the nuclear family and public life and even more especially the American military, "which arbitrarily label a number of purely human traits 'feminine' possess a tactic useful to war-making, for men are bound to detect some of these human traits in themselves—and then worry that they have strayed into a feminine, inferior realm. Placed in a constantly renewed insecurity about their status, men must scramble to amass 'proofs' of masculinity."[64] Meserve and other squad members positioned the rape of Mao—a physical and symbolic domination of the feminine—as just such a "proof." For when Eriksson refused to join the gang rape, the others specifically impugned his masculinity, calling him a "queer" and a "chicken." Both of these epithets suggested Eriksson's masculine inadequacy in areas that Phillips argues are essential to modern American masculinity: bellicosity and heterosexuality.[65] Furthermore, the squad perceived of Eriksson's refusal to participate in the macabre bonding ritual as dangerous to their group cohesion; for in refusing to rape the girl, he also disavowed the squad's united domination of women and the Vietnamese, upon which their vision of brotherhood-through-violence was based. Eriksson's refusal to participate shook the ground on which the squad and the military's assumptions about masculinity were based by suggesting a less violent approach to manhood. Meserve found Eriksson's nonparticipation so threatening in fact, that he warned the soldier that "[u]nless Eriksson went along with the others, . . . he would run the risk of being reported 'a friendly casualty,'" meaning he would be "accidentally" killed by someone in the squad (Lang, p. 35).

While Eriksson's resolve not to harm the girl remained strong, his revelations demonstrate how the group dynamics of militarized masculinity are particularly persuasive in exacting violent behavior from "normal" American men. For Rafael "testified that he could not have withstood the epithets he had heard Meserve heap on Eriksson," and he explicitly said it was fear of such derision that caused him to join the rape (p. 35). Further, Manuel justified his participation in the rape with his certain knowledge that "if he had not gone into the hootch he would have risked becoming an outcast" (p. 99). Thus, this story reveals the dark side of the much ballyhooed wartime brotherhood: its violent, oppressive demands for conformity. These demands were demonstrated again the next day when Mao was found to be quite sick and the squad encountered enemy troops; Meserve decided she needed to be disposed of quickly. Similarly to his attempt to force total participation in the rape, Meserve ordered Eriksson and both of the Diazes to kill Mao, though he ultimately allowed Clark to stab her several times, and then ordered everyone in the squad to fire at her, at which time she was finally killed, the shared criminal violence ensuring their silence.

When the squad returned to their base, Eriksson immediately reported what happened to his commanding officer, who told him not to "buck the system" and to leave the matter alone (p. 56). Eriksson then broke the chain of command, reporting the incident to several other officers; however, although the original squad of men was broken up and Eriksson relocated to preserve his safety, the army refused to conduct an investigation. Finally, at his new post Eriksson spoke to a chaplain who managed to open an inquiry. All four of the men were eventually court-martialed on charges of rape and murder. Clark, the soldier who stabbed Mao, was given a life sentence for rape and premeditated murder; Rafael Diaz received an eight-year sentence for rape and unpremeditated murder; Manuel Diaz was sentenced to fifteen years for the crime of rape. Bafflingly, Meserve, the mastermind of the entire plot, was found innocent of the charge of rape and sentenced to ten years for unpremeditated murder (p. 101). When the men were transferred to the United States, however, their cases were all reviewed and greatly commuted. Manuel was acquitted entirely and received an honorable discharge and back pay; Clark's life sentence was reduced to eight years, as was Meserve's; Rafael's sentence was commuted to four years (pp. 112–13).

After reading the testimony of the WSI, the actual story of Mao's gang rape and murder is only startling in its premeditation. However, Eriksson's difficult struggle to bring the rapist-murderers to account for their crime further attests to the little consideration the Vietnamese, and particularly Vietnamese women, received from the American military, its justice system, and even the American public. For surely, if Lang's story had prodded Americans to protest the easy treatment of these convicted felons, they could have forced military courts to treat such cases more seriously, and even more important, forced a change in the abusive military attitudes that condoned such behavior. However, no such uproar occurred. Also shocking is the resentment of which Eriksson found himself the object for his reporting of the crime. Bitterness and vindictiveness from the men against whom he led the investigation were to be expected, but other GIs also repeatedly reproved Eriksson for his actions. He recollected, "One M.P. . . . told me he could have understood it if I'd gone to bat for a G.I. who was murdered, but how could I do it for a Vietnamese? But he was very tolerant about it. He said it was only human to make mistakes" (p. 104). Astonishingly, the MP believed it was Eriksson—rather than his squad who raped and murdered a woman—who made a mistake in judgment.

The materials presented in this chapter repeatedly reveal irrefutable evidence that the rape of Vietnamese women and girls was a problem of epidemic proportions during the war. Though obviously every soldier stationed in Vietnam—or even most—did not commit rape, the testimonies of men who witnessed or participated in rape and sexual abuse are far too numerous and from too many different periods and branches of the military to suggest that the incidents they describe are isolated. Moreover, the soldiers themselves desperately desire, with their testimony, to show how rape was itself both a symptom and a result of the military's overly permissive misogyny both in its racist policies in Vietnam and in its sexist training and propaganda. Some who spoke out were even beginning to see that the military's sexism and racism did not originate with the military but were deeply rooted in American culture. Too, the audiences' reactions to these testimonies consistently reveal America's unwillingness to inquire about women's sexual suffering, either because the public did not believe rape and sexual abuse to be a legitimate "atrocity" worthy of punishment or further inquiry, or because the authorities found the issues potentially too explosive. When presented in investigations or hearings, stories of rape elicited only silence and a persistent turning of the subject to a different portion of the witness's testimony. Whether this bespeaks a deep embarrassment and emotional inability to discuss a too-terrible subject or a simple disregard for the suffering of women—stemming from sexist, racist attitudes or from the myth that rape is inevitable because soldiers must fulfill their sexual urges—is impossible to say.

Although there is no definitive answer, the evidence suggests that as the sixties gave way to the seventies and the women's movement matured, audiences became more capable of recognizing the particular suffering of women and also the roots of their abuse in sexist American culture. The antiwar veterans' use of feminist language in 1971 to describe the destructive male attitudes toward women that were present in their prewar lives and were used by the military demonstrated that the critique and rhetoric of the women's movement contributed importantly to enabling these new understandings. Paradoxically, even as the women's movement enabled this critique, authorities surely supposed that publicly recognizing, publicizing, and prosecuting the sexual abuse of Vietnamese women by American men would add legitimate fuel, not just to the antiwar movement but also to the claims and demands of the women's movement, a movement the state wished to control and subdue. This squelching of unwanted testimony is an early example of national culture's persistent tendency to marginalize unwanted testimony and its subtle pressuring of witnesses to revise their stories into more acceptable forms.

Whatever the reason for ignoring or disregarding veterans' testimony about rape, in all of these moments of testimony, we find another similarity—a focus on the veteran himself and his emotional suffering caused by the acts he and/or his comrades committed in Vietnam.[66] Certainly this is understandable in the case of the Winter Soldier Investigation, when the veterans paid a great price to testify—admitting their personal sins and those of their friends in an extremely public forum, reliving nightmares they had tried to forget, and facing investigation and harassment from the Nixon administration.[67] Less understandable is the public conferral of victim status to the men in Calley's company, men who only confessed to their crimes when criminal investigations were begun. But these extremely different cases reveal America's habitual (and apparently incurable) drive to perceive its own soldiers as innocent, even when they were caught with bloody hands. I further suggest that these early instances of "veteran victimization" form the embryonic stage of the fully rehabilitated veteran of the eighties. If the veteran could be sympathetically understood as a victim even as he stood explaining how he had raped and killed Vietnamese women and girls because they "owed him" for fighting their war, how much more easily could Americans conceive of him as purely a victim in the eighties when the public had conveniently forgotten such crimes against women—remembering only that in this guerilla war soldiers sometimes killed civilians because "they had to."

4

Naming Themselves

Sexual Abuse in Vietnam Veterans' Antiwar Literature

In the last chapter, I analyzed veteran testimony about the rape and sexual abuse of Vietnamese women during the war. This testimony was given during the war and endangered veteran witnesses for several reasons: they testified at legal risk to themselves and their standing within the community; relived painful experiences that they would rather have forgotten; and opened themselves to harassment from the Nixon administration, which sought to discredit demonstrators who opposed the war. Because they spoke in the midst of the war, it was difficult for the Winter Soldier veterans and other war-years' witnesses to discern the larger causes of the atrocities that they witnessed. They recognized that their military training seemed to play a role, and some suggested that racist attitudes at home played a part in dehumanizing the Vietnamese and thus making them targets for war crimes. A small minority, apparently influenced by the rhetoric of the growing women's movement, quietly suggested that sexism—extant in society and stressed in basic training—might be a contributing factor in their treatment of women.

Overall, though, it was understandably difficult for veterans to make larger, causal connections between the complex ways in which militarized masculinity in American culture came together with military training to produce atrocities. At the Winter Soldier Investigation, Sid Peck, a sociologist who was not a participant in the war, did have the distance and vocabulary to recognize the connection between concepts of working-class masculinity and atrocities, and he eloquently pointed not just to military training as the culprit, but also to school curricula and spectator sports as more subtle contributors to war atrocities. His testimony was received without much comment, perhaps because the audience was only beginning to realize the ways in which patriarchal society produced masculine and feminine roles in American culture and the far-reaching impact of such roles.

Within the rich literature that sprang up from their experiences, the connections between class and gender that Peck made were exactly the connections certain veterans noticed in the postwar decades. Having at least six years distance from the end of American involvement in the war, these veterans had gained enough perspective to begin to unravel causes and effects. Moreover, their motivation to write was somewhat different from that of the veterans who gave public testimony. The war they wrote about was over: they did not have to denounce its immorality in order to stop it; rather, they explored their wartime actions in an attempt to "name" their experience. Larry Heinemann, one of the leading Vietnam War novelists, writes in his recent memoir, *Black Virgin Mountain* (2005), that he, unlike the stereotypical "silent" veteran, "could not shut up about what I had seen, what I had done [in the war], and what I had become. I told anyone who asked, and without the polite dashes, the tasteful euphemisms, or the discreet ellipses. The power to name is extraordinary . . . I wanted to name myself . . . and be precise; not a victim, certainly not a hero, just a man trying to deal with an uncommonly grotesque circumstance and come out the other end of it in one piece."[1]

Veteran writing does not just witness to horrors lived through, merely preserving survivor memories. It attempts to work through the writers' own guilty participation in these horrors. As Heinemann says about his own feelings, "all these years since, I cannot get around the fact that I was not simply a witness, but an integral, even dedicated, party to a very wrong thing" (p. 37). Thus, as I will argue in this chapter, much of the most thoughtful veteran writing was created not to pose the veteran as a victim or to rehabilitate him but to analyze how and in what ways he often became a perpetrator of atrocities. A careful examination of such literature proves the inadequacy of popular and most academic understandings of veteran trauma. Following the lead of trauma theorist Ann Cvetkovich, my analysis will highlight the cultural and historical specificities of American soldiers' social locations. I carefully analyze the frequently traumatizing social systems of which soldiers were already participants and sometimes victims, rather than erasing these systems in favor of a view of national subjectivity that denies difference and confers a blanket victim status to all participants in the war.

Most particularly, I attend to veterans' discussions of how growing up male in Cold War America taught them, often violently, that a militarized, "tough guy" masculinity was required to be a man and a good citizen. From the example of their World War II–veteran fathers, and, equally influentially, from Hollywood war films starring Audie Murphy and especially John Wayne, American boys were taught that true masculinity was best achieved through participation in war. Encouraged by John F. Kennedy's rousing exhortation, "Ask not what your country can do for you,"[2] American boys who had grown up fighting "the Krauts and Japs" in their backyards enthusiastically volunteered for military service in the sixties. Even as the Vietnam War's unpopularity grew, many men nonetheless signed on with the military despite their misgivings about the policies and morality of the war.[3] In addition to the glamour and excitement of war, veterans most often cite as reasons for their service their cultural beliefs about the correctness of military duty and the essentialness of the war experience to one's masculinity; using as evidence the novels of Larry Heinemann, I will show that this was especially true for members of the working class.

In the overwhelming and disorientingly harsh environment of basic training, recruits were molded into soldiers and, by definition, into men. This transformation from "soft" civilians into soldier-men was effected by a destruction of the soldier's premilitary identity—equated with the feminine—and its replacement with a hardness and aggression designated as true masculinity. Though veterans marveled at the extreme levels to which woman hating was taken in basic training, they also recognized it as only an exaggeration of what was already present in masculine formation in American society. Here I use as evidence Gustav Hasford's *The Short-Timers* and W. D. Ehrhart's *Vietnam-Perkasie*. The destruction of any quality considered feminine within the recruits leads eventually to a general devaluation of women, especially those who were racially "other." The narratives examined in this chapter demonstrate a direct link between these attitudes about the feminine and the horrifying sexual atrocities committed against Vietnamese women. Heinemann's novels further suggest that the traumas of the class system at home often fed into the rage toward and violence acted out against women. As Michael Bernhardt, the My Lai whistleblower, told Susan Faludi about the men who committed the rapes and mass murder at My Lai, "These guys were lost *before* we got [to Vietnam] . . . They didn't need Vietnam to set them off. They were already that violent . . . We didn't need Vietnam to create a My Lai. We had social problems *here* that created that."[4] Moreover, because such acts resulted from the masculine identities the men had assumed, they could not be contained to the theater of war; instead, the attitudes enflamed by the military found an ugly outlet in American soldiers' relationships with women after the war. These relationships were often further strained by the challenge to the authority of masculinity posed by the women's movement in the later war years;

the works of Heinemann and Ehrhart hint at the multiplicity of men's responses toward this challenge.

A study of such literature, then, highlights for readers the specificities of the systemic traumas of which American soldiers were victims. I mean by this the trauma of growing up in a culture that demanded of boys and young men an aggressive and violent militarized masculinity, a masculinity that often entailed male initiation and "rebirth" in basic training, complex group dynamics requiring men to participate in sexual atrocities in Vietnam or face potentially deadly retribution, and the perpetration of terrible aggression against other human beings. Rather than suggesting, as most writing on veteran trauma does, that veterans' problems were caused solely by combat and were of a medical nature requiring only proper psychiatric care, I will instead argue that veteran trauma was a result of complex and unequal social systems. As such, true acknowledgment of veteran trauma (and the atrocities they inflicted in Vietnam) requires not only clinical treatment but also societal and systemic change to alter American concepts of masculinity. Furthermore, and perhaps most provocatively, I argue that veterans have not and cannot heal from their trauma until new publics are created, publics truly willing to hear veteran testimony about the war and the causes of the atrocities there. Rather than reincorporating Vietnam veterans as a symbol of wounded masculinity, as Susan Jeffords suggests happened in the early eighties, this new public instead must recognize the destruction of women implicit to such a concept of masculinity and so realize its cancerous nature.

Expanding on Jeffords' work in *The Remasculinization of America: Gender and the Vietnam War* (1989), I aim to recenter this type of veteran literature, alongside the testimony of veterans and other witnesses from the war years, so that it cannot be overlooked in refigurings of the Vietnam War (and simultaneously of American masculinity). I am interested here in refining Jeffords' analysis of postwar veteran representation by pointing out how these works *do* put forward the pernicious excesses of militarized masculinity. In the next chapter, I will demonstrate that such literature has been ignored, misread, or transformed into safe, filmic representations that purge these excesses. Ultimately, I will suggest that this transformation—and its attendant remasculinization—can be reversed if a new public underwrites veterans' literary and pubic confessions.

Veteran Literature in the Postwar Decades

Much of the Vietnam War writing published in the late seventies and the eighties included oral accounts and war novels in the tradition of World

War II realism-naturalism (i.e., James Jones and Norman Mailer). Such writing, even while attesting to war's brutality and based on the truism "war is hell," glamorized war and military life. This type of Vietnam War literature is exemplified by the novels *Fields of Fire* (James Webb, 1978) and *The Thirteenth Valley* (John Del Vecchio, 1982). With their highly sympathetic soldier characters and focus on soldiers' individual heroics and brotherly devotion, such novels ignore the politics of the war itself and create very negative portraits of the peace movement. Though they disparage the government's treatment of American GIs in the Vietnam War, these narratives never critique the foreign policy and ideals of American exceptionalism that sent young Americans to Vietnam. Even more, these novels particularly work to show the war's loss as *not* the fault of American soldiers, who are depicted as courageous soldiers and sympathetic victims. Rather, they suggest that the war was lost only because of internal social bickering in the United States (i.e., the problems voiced by the black power, peace, and women's movements) and the weakness and corruption of the federal government and politicians, who were unwilling to "do what it took" to win the war by invading North Vietnam or using nuclear weapons.[5]

These works grow out of the American war novel tradition of such authors as Crane, Hemingway, Mailer, and Jones. Drawing on their predecessors' use of naturalism-realism, these Vietnam War authors ultimately realize the same profound loss of innocence in war, the power and beauty of soldierly brotherhood, and the individual's insignificance in the greater game of war. They perceived their war as different from earlier authors' only in terms of the specific location, people, objectives, and new technologies. The Vietnam War realist-novels certainly do not criticize war in general. On the contrary, through their valorization of the actions of individual soldiers, they continue the glamorization of war that was so popular in the post–WWII period. As Webb voices through his protagonist, Lt. Robert E. Lee Hodges, "Man's noblest moment is the one spent on the fields of fire. I believe that."[6] The *Philadelphia Inquirer*'s review of the novel suggests that "Webb has rehabilitated the idea of the American hero—not John Wayne, to be sure, but every man, caught up in circumstances beyond his control, surviving the blood, dreck and absurdity with dignity and even a certain élan."[7]

As Thomas Meyers argues in *Walking Point: American Narratives of Vietnam,* this type of novel attempts to "use the realistic mode much like a neutral camera" and "abdicate[s] the tasks of larger historical vision and cultural connection."[8] Critic Don Rignalda adds to this argument that such realistic novels, which have been very popular, "unconsciously *masquerade* as neutral cameras. Because the reader is so habituated to mimetic conventions, he too is unconscious of how these texts violently impose the order of linearity, causality, and closure upon [war's] disorder and randomness."[9] In order to create the feel of a "neutral camera," these novelists strictly adhere to even the minutest facts. And, as the novels are written by veterans, people accept them as entirely truthful and authentic—without bias. For instance, reviewers praised Del Vecchio's novel particularly for its "experiential veracity, its rendering of the feel of ground combat" (Meyers, p. 56). Not only are these realistic novels overstuffed with facts, figures, and details to lend to their aura of authority and documentary realism,[10] but they also frequently contain maps of Vietnam and glossaries to explain the unfamiliar language of "the grunts" to uninitiated readers. These extra materials suggest a specialized knowledge to which only the veteran is privileged but that he may bestow—to an extent—upon readers; additionally, these supplements associate the novels they accompany with the textbooks and other nonfiction in which such appendices are typically found. By attaching these explanatory materials, writers endow their novels with the historical authority and authenticity of supposedly neutral, academic histories. Writers employing the rhetorical and aesthetic strategies of realism do so for a very precise reason: to (re)write the Vietnam War in a conservatively revisionist light for American audiences while maintaining the guise of neutrality. At the 1984 Vietnam Writers Conference, Del Vecchio explained that he wrote *The Thirteenth Valley* "to set the record straight." Rignalda notes that the realist author saw his novel "as a corrective to the blatant distortions of the allegedly nihilistic, often 'unmapped,' film *Apocalypse Now*. Del Vecchio contend[ed] that America did know what it was doing in Vietnam and that it was doing the right and necessary thing. Ho Chi Minh was a bloodthirsty, despotic assassin. Americans did not—with few exceptions—commit atrocities" (p. 24). Thus, Del Vecchio and other realists see themselves as waging literary battles over the final "meaning" of the Vietnam War within national American culture.

What critics like Rignalda and Meyers overlook is that these realistic works do more than restore myths about the glory of war and rewrite the Vietnam War as noble and just; giving needed attention to gender relations in such literature, Jeffords argues that their reframing of the Vietnam War ultimately enables a rewriting of masculinity. She notes that, according to these revisionist novels and the similarly veined Vietnam films of the early eighties, the United States lost the war only because of the peace movement (typified by women and long-haired men) and the weak and duplicitous, and therefore feminine, U.S. government. The nation itself, in these depictions, was a victim of a feminized government and equally feminized internal division, and its victimization was symbolized by that of the Vietnam veteran. In positing men and nationalized masculinity as victims of feminized forces, these works perform what Jeffords calls a "remasculinizing" of American culture, in which representations of the war enabled an expansion and redefinition of a "masculinity that presents itself as separate from and independent of an oppressed feminine."[11] Once the victimization of veterans had been established via this reframing, their victimization was used "to bolster a call for the regeneration of these victims—particularly white men—for a restitution of their 'rights' and a return of their [masculine] identity," which had been "stolen" by the advancements of the women's liberation movement (p. 127). Thus, *Time* magazine was quite right to declare that these novels and films facilitated "a very literal and significant transaction" in which "[—]in the American imagination[—]the Viet Nam veteran, erstwhile psychotic, cripple and loser, has been given back his manhood" (qtd. in Jeffords, p. 127).

Jeffords assumes all genres and mediums participate equally in this project of remasculinization; thus, in her otherwise excellent analysis of Vietnam War writing and film, she overlooks another type of Vietnam War narrative, one which I call "antiwar literature" and focus on here. This critical school of Vietnam War literature is composed of a small though highly regarded group of authors, among them the novelists Heinemann, Steven Wright, Gustav Hasford, Jack Fuller, Tim O'Brien, and Peter Straub, as well as poet and memoirist W. D. Ehrhart. With the exception of Straub, all served in the Vietnam War just as the writers of the realist novels did. While I concur with Jeffords' assessment that the revisionist cultural productions have won out in the American imagination, one must not discount the antiwar literature. In fact, the American public's ignoring of these works is further evidence of the willfulness of America's remasculinization. This antiwar literature does not work to rehabilitate the Vietnam War or glorify the concept of war in general; rather, it reveals the horrific psychic and physical human costs that underlie all war. Specifically, antiwar literature about Vietnam belies ideals of war as necessary to masculine identity. Though its writers are veterans, in their interest in revealing the obscene truth about the Vietnam War and the beliefs and cultural values that enabled the atrocities there, they forgo heroicizing American soldiers, even to the extent that they suggest their own complicity in crimes of war.

Heinemann's angry response to Del Vecchio's earlier quoted remarks at the Writer's Conference speaks to the aims of antiwar writers: "The war was evil and mean, and there was no redeeming . . . nothing redeeming about it, and don't let anyone tell you there was! We went there for *evil* reasons and we performed *evil*, and *millions* of people are fucked up because of it!" (qtd. in Rignalda, p. 24). Instead of justifying and rehabilitating the war, this critical literature forwards the reprehensible tactics employed by the American military, tactics that brutalized its soldiers and condoned atrocity. Not begging forgiveness for these acts, these writers artfully demonstrate the complex cultural systems and ideology that ultimately led to atrocious acts in the war. Moreover, just as Heinemann accepts responsibility for his own part in the war in his outburst at the conference—utilizing the pronoun "we" rather than deflecting responsibility with the third-person—so this type of writing requires readers to recognize their own potential complicity in the atrocities of the war via their participation in oppressive cultural systems and their willingness to ignore the results of such systems. While the realist genre of Vietnam War novels, in order to suggest that the sacrifice of American GIs was meaningful, apologizes for the policies of the war, critical narratives unrelentingly demonstrate Heinemann's analysis that there is "no redeeming" the Vietnam War. As part of their attempt at understanding the horror of the war without redeeming it, this strain of writing often uses the abuse of women as evidence of the ultimate indefensibleness of the war. Rather than the American wives, sweethearts, and mothers of the realist-naturalist Vietnam War genre, Vietnamese women—who are revealed as victims of violent, militarized masculinity—more frequently populate the critical novel. Far outside the realm of the American family, they are prostitutes, rape victims, and lovers to be abandoned when the soldier's tour is finished.

While the works of the antiwar authors mentioned here are quite different from each other, they share certain formal and structural characteristics, which clearly differentiate them from the realistic mode. As Lucas Carpenter points out, they display "many of the central concerns and qualities of postmodern content and style, among them relativism, diversity, parody, alterity, anti-hegemony, fabulation, self-reflexivity, and metafiction."[12] Because of these attributes, their works are commonly classified as postmodernist. Fredric Jameson suggests that the postmodernist style is widely employed by Vietnam War novelists because "[t]his first terrible postmodernist war cannot be told in any of the traditional paradigms of the war novel or movie—indeed, that breakdown of all previous narrative paradigms is, along with the breakdown of any shared language through which a veteran might convey such experience, among the principle subjects of [such books] and may be said to open up the place of a whole new reflexivity."[13]

These postmodernist works subvert the simplistic understandings of the war the realist-naturalist novels attempt to impart. In his novel, *The*

Things They Carried, O'Brien's narrator fights at the level of metanarrative against the very authority that realist novelists such as Webb cultivate with their reliance on facts, details, and pseudoscholarly appendices. He suggests that in a "true" war story, "[a]bsolute occurrence is irrelevant. A thing may happen and be a total lie; another thing may not happen and be truer than the truth."[14] Further, he rejects the realist tendency toward the glorification of war and its heroes, instead saying,

> A true war story is never moral. It does not instruct, nor encourage virtue, nor suggest models of proper human behavior, nor restrain men from doing the things men have always done. If a story seems moral, do not believe it. If at the end of a war story you feel uplifted, or if you feel that some small bit of rectitude has been salvaged from the larger waste, then you have been made the victim of a very old and terrible lie. There is no rectitude whatsoever. There is no virtue. As a first rule of thumb, therefore, you can tell a true war story by its absolute and uncompromising allegiance to obscenity and evil. (p. 76)

In this metafictional meditation that echoes Wilfred Owen, O'Brien eloquently voices the postmodern understanding of the Vietnam War that underlies the strategies of many antiwar writers. Thus, although I do not agree with Jameson's oversimplification of the war and the literature that sprang from it, I will argue that the theoretical underpinnings of post-structuralism and their outgrowth in postmodern culture, which suggest the difficulty or impossibility of true communication and the inability to neutrally narrate history, enabled veteran writers to find a different structure and method for narrating their stories, one that allowed them to critique the war rather than to reframe it conservatively.

Gustav Hasford's *The Short-Timers*

Years before O'Brien wrote his manifesto, "How to Tell a True War Story," other authors had begun to publish postmodern accounts of the war. In 1979, after shopping the book with publishers for three years, Gustav Hasford published *The Short-Timers*, a brutally laconic novel that popular critics met with mixed emotions. One *Newsweek* reviewer enthusiastically called it "the best work of fiction about the Vietnam war I've read,"[15] and a reviewer for *Kirkus Reviews* hailed the novel as "mark[ing] a real advance in Vietnam war literature."[16] Other readers were not so receptive to Hasford's critical vision of the Vietnam War and the military, however. Not surprisingly, the *New Republic*'s review excoriated the novel, saying, "It is 154 pages long, and on what feels like 150 of those pages there are bloody and artistically implausible killings administered by whatever means of obliteration Gustav Hasford's obsessed imagination can contrive. That, unfortunately, is all Hasford's imagination can do." The reviewer lambastes Hasford's "mannequin figures" who die "cardboard deaths."[17] Similarly, the *Los Angeles Times* suggested that "the reader, more than [Hasford's] characters, becomes the victim of overkill. In his attempt to remind us of our days of the past imperfect, Hasford commits the ultimate war book crime: He destroys his chapters in order to save them."[18]

Hasford's tripartite novel traces the progress of the protagonist, Joker, from new recruit in basic training to hardened killer in Vietnam during the time of the Tet Offensive. Unlike soldiers populating the realist-naturalist novels, Hasford's characters are not given detailed back stories; readers never know their psychological motivations and ambitions. In fact, readers do not even learn most of the characters' real names—Joker's compatriots include T.H.E. Rock, Rafter Man, Animal Mother, Cowboy, and Mr. Shortround.[19] They are, as the *New Republic* reviewer accused, something of "mannequin" figures. However, rather than demonstrating Hasford's lack of artistry, this is a strategic choice. Instead of encouraging reader empathy, his cardboard characters provide blank figures upon which, without the distraction of realistic emotional entanglements, Hasford writes large the grotesque consequences of war. These "mannequins" are far from loveable. Joker sees and portrays vibrantly what he and the other characters have become, not noble warriors, but sadistic monsters—"werewolves," as the novel calls them. Hasford uses machine, Nazi, and holocaust imagery to connect explicitly fascist/Nazi aims and means and the American war machine and policy. Joker memorably refers to Parris Island as a "suburban death camp" and himself as a "young Dr. Goebbels."[20] Oscillating between paradoxical images of the marine recruits as death camp inmates and the U.S. military as the Nazi regime, Joker makes it clear that he believes the young marines are both victims of but also believers in an ideology that enables them to participate in the genocidal warfare. He does not attempt to rehabilitate U.S. attitudes, purposes, or methods in Vietnam. Rather, Joker expresses the hypocrisy of America's war. He explains his role as a combat reporter in a series of rewritten clichés, "I've fought to make the world safe for hypocrisy. We have met the enemy and he is us. War is good business—invest your son. Viet Nam means never having to say you're sorry. *Arbeit Macht Frei*— . . . I write that the Nam is an Asian Eldorado populated by a cute, primitive but determined people. War is a noisy breakfast food. War is fun to eat. War can give you better checkups. War cures cancer—permanently" (p. 50).

In addition to its one-dimensional characters, the novel also makes reference to fantastic beasts, monsters, and events: the marines frequently bare their "werewolf" fangs, a vampire officer makes an appearance, an invisible tank kills a marine, and rifles speak in women's voices. In addition to these narrative strategies that quickly separate *The Short-Timers* from the realist-naturalist American tradition of the war novel, Hasford is quintessentially postmodern and implicitly critical of the tradition of war novel realism in his elliptical prose and his refusal to explain away fantastic incidents, to provide easy morals, or to give closure to his story. *The Short-Timers* is particularly instructive for my purposes because it successfully reveals the connections among military training's dependence on the denial of the feminine, the abuse of women in country, and the destructive consequences of mixing sex and violence.

The Short-Timers is somewhat different from other Vietnam War novels in that the first section of the novel is entirely concerned with basic training; its extended development suggests that the trauma Joker suffers in basic training is crucial to understanding the events that occur during the war. From the beginning of their training on Parris Island, Private Joker and the rest of his class are subjected to gendered and homophobic hate speech, as in the opening spiel of Sergeant Gerheim, the drill instructor: "*If* you ladies leave my island, . . . you will be a minister of death, praying for war. And proud. Until that day you are pukes, you are scumbags, you are the lowest form of life on Earth. You are not even human. You people are nothing but a lot of little pieces of amphibian shit" (p. 4). Throughout the rest of his time with the recruits, the DI continues to call them "ladies," "pussies," and "queers." Nonhuman name-calling and gendered hate speech are meant to be equally derogatory; in this world, women and homosexuals are subhuman, "amphibian shit." During basic training, not only does Gerheim repeatedly compare the recruits unfavorably to women whenever possible, but the comparisons he makes are usually sexually charged. In one memorable metaphor, as the recruits do push-ups, Gerheim tells them, "You maggots are huffing and puffing the way your momma did the first time your old man put the meat to her" (p. 5). Here the recruits are not merely "ladies." Instead of telling them they are filling the roles of their fathers as military men, Gerheim instead positions the recruits as women being penetrated by their fathers. Within American ideals of masculinity, however, real men are the penetrators, not the penetrated. By humiliatingly positioning them as the penetrated, Gerheim destroys any empathy in his recruits for women or what is understood as the woman's role. In this way, he achieves the goal of basic training—to make the recruits into real men. And within the world of the military, "man" is synonymous with killer. Thus, when the recruits graduate, "salty . . . [and] ready to eat their own guts and then ask for seconds" (p. 17), the instructor tells them, "You people are no longer maggots. Today you are Marines" (p. 22).

The Short-Timers thus reveals that basic training requires the recruits to suppress and hate everything within themselves that is feminine, a hatred resulting in a general devaluation of the feminine. As O'Brien notes in his memoir, *If I Die in a Combat Zone* (1973), in basic training, "women are dinks [one of the many racial slurs applied to the Vietnamese and other Asians]. Women are villains. They are creatures akin to Communists and yellow-skinned people and hippies."[21] Christian G. Appy, in *Working-Class War: American Combat Soldiers and Vietnam* (1993), extrapolates from his interviews with approximately one hundred veterans that in basic training, "[f]ailure as a soldier constituted failure as a man and left the recruit with a status of a woman . . . Women and gays were referred to interchangeably as the epitome of all that is cowardly, passive, untrustworthy, unclean, and undisciplined."[22] As the testimony from chapter 3 demonstrated, because the military reviles women and all that is nonmasculine, it systematically dehumanized women along gendered lines just as it did the Vietnamese along racist lines.

Within the scenario set up in basic training, then, the physical and sexual abuse of women is not just a casual or natural consequence of military training, but a structural one. Woman is the necessary "other," which must be repressed within man—overcome and ultimately destroyed—at all costs to keep the feminine from infecting American soldiers.[23] Sexualized abuse, which not only hurts the individual women who are abused but functions to symbolically represent both woman's penetrability and man's ability to penetrate and dominate her, is the quintessential expression of masculinity's need to destroy woman, since sexual abuse both literally and symbolically represses the feminine. This is why, as army deserter John Picciano testified, "[a] perfectly regular guy could come into the Army, and before he knew it, he was doing things he'd never done before . . . Talking about what it would be like to gang together and take the bus-terminal café waitress out in the alley."[24] The verbal abuse of women modeled in basic training ultimately authorized women's physical, sexual abuse as well. In fact, sexual abuse, which involves intimate contact with women is perhaps the final litmus test for a soldier's manhood. As Eve Kosofsky Sedgwick notes, "Only women have the power to make men less than men within this [framework]. At the same time, to be fully a man requires having obtained the instrumental use of a woman, having *risked* transformation by her."[25] That these men have withstood sexual contact with women and have come away unfeminized solidifies their masculinity.

Important to my argument here is the fact that the novel does not present this repression of the feminine as damaging only to women. Rather, I argue that over the course of the narrative, Hasford suggests that "the feminine" is essential to a man's humanity. As are all signs associated with femininity or weakness (which are synonymous), crying is an activity the recruits are forbidden during basic training. Leonard Pratt is a slow, sloppy recruit who suffers brutal abuse at the hands of Gerheim throughout his training. After Leonard almost drowns in his eighteenth attempt to master a physical training obstacle and is brought back to consciousness, he openly weeps. Joker narrates his punishment: "Sergeant Gerheim fits a Trojan rubber over the mouth of a canteen and throws the canteen at Leonard. The canteen hits Leonard on the side of the head. Sergeant Gerheim bellows, 'Marines *do not* cry!' Leonard is ordered to nurse on the canteen every day after chow" (p. 12). This humiliating punishment not only infantilizes him, but also positions Leonard as a woman/homosexual; clearly it is designed to destroy any "womanliness" or "childishness" within him. However, this repression of femininity in the form of crying is later represented as a loss. When Rafter Man, one of Joker's friends, is killed in country, Joker kneels next to him, noting, "I want to cry, but I can't cry—I'm too tough" (p. 109). This inability to cry, which is a common trope in Vietnam War literature of all kinds, importantly indicates that Joker has lost an integral part of himself. Additionally, an earlier episode involved the decision of Joker's "Spirit" to abandon his "Mind" and "Body." In a passage narrated discomfitingly in the second person, Joker protests against Spirit's abandonment, "NO! You try to explain . . . that part of you is missing in action . . . you don't want your missing part to be left behind. But you cannot speak" (p. 88). Rather than valorizing male "toughness," this passage together with Joker's inability to cry speaks to the terrible theft of spirituality and emotional openness—associated with the feminine—soldiers experience in basic training and war. Moreover, Spirit's abandonment of Joker symbolizes the underrecognized trauma of aggression stemming from a soldier's brutal acts. For, as Joker repeats throughout the novel, "What you do, you become" (p. 112). He finds it is impossible to participate in the aggression of war without being fundamentally affected by his actions, and he clearly finds this change undesirable, deeply psychologically damaging.

In addition to revealing how the feminine must be devalued in the creation of a militarized masculinity, the novel's first section also introduces the barter of women between men, a system that further demonstrates the defining of maleness and masculinity through and in opposition to the bodies of women. When the recruits first arrive on the island, Gerheim tells Joker, "I like you. You can come over to my house and fuck my sister" (p. 4). Joker has pleased Gerheim by making him laugh, and for this, Gerheim gifts him sexual permission to his sister. The recruits' adoption of such thinking through the course of their training becomes clear when Joker narrates, "For the hundredth time, I tell Cowboy that I want to slip my tube steak into his sister so what will he take in trade? For the hundredth time, Cowboy replies, 'What do you have?'" (p. 17). The repetition of "hundredth time" emphasizes that this sister-trade talk has become a longstanding ritual between the two men. The running joke continues throughout the book; when Joker and Cowboy meet up again in Vietnam, mentioning Cowboy's sister is part of their reunion protocol (p. 33). She gets a final mention at the end of the novel, just before Cowboy leaves to kill his squad members who have been wounded by a sniper.[26] As Cowboy—who plans to commit suicide momentarily—gives Joker last minute instructions on how to lead the squad, Joker asks, "What about you Cowboy? I mean, if you get yourself wasted who will introduce me to your sister?" Cowboy, with an expressionless face, replies, "I don't have a sister. I thought you knew that" (p. 149).

The barter of Cowboy's sister is particularly interesting for two reasons. First, as Katherine Kinney notes in her essay "Women, War, and the Pacific," traditionally within the war novel, "[w]omen enter the narrative of war and nation under male coverture, as either mothers, wives, or sweethearts. Sisters and daughters are the domestic excess of such narratives and thus offer . . . writers literal and symbolic positions of counternarrative."[27] The fact that Cowboy is willing to exchange his sister supports the correctness of Kinney's suggestion that daughters represent a "domestic excess," and indeed Hasford's novel is unusual in that this sister is mentioned more often than mothers and sweethearts. Thus, Cowboy's "sister" opens a counternarrative to the role women usually play in Vietnam War novels. Rather than supportively nurturing her husband, lover, or son, she functions as a metaphorical object of exchange between Cowboy and Joker. In such, Hasford suggests another role for women within masculine culture: woman as a conduit for homosocial bonding, by which I mean the formation of bonds for the production and maintenance of male power.

The function of Cowboy's "sister" as bonding mechanism is her second interesting aspect. For surely this sister functions as Sedgwick suggests the dark lady does in Shakespeare's sonnets. "The Sonnets present a male-male love that . . . is set firmly within a structure of institutionalized social relations that are carried out via women: marriage, name, family, loyalty to progenitors and to posterity, all depend on the youth's making a particular use of women" (p. 35). Thus, when Gerheim offers his sister to Joker as a reward for proper masculine behavior, he is conferring some of his authority to the younger man. The exchange of sisters also provides the recruits/soldiers an acceptable means of expressing and working out their own desire for one another in the extremely homophobic environment of the military. While the use of one man's female relative by another man represents a transfer or sharing of power, it is also a conduit for otherwise inexpressible male-male erotic desire. In this way, men can symbolically act out their desire for each other while safely maintaining the bounds of properly masculine heterosexuality.

In his presentation of the barter of women, Hasford questions this construction, rather than simply describing unquestioningly the way men have long used women to relate to each other, assuming that such a use is natural. Cowboy's final, quiet admission that his "sister" is fictional, which significantly ends his and Joker's last intimate conversation, implicitly demands that Joker accept the knowledge he already possesses—that this sister, who is both their erotic connection and a buffer for this dangerous desire, is nonexistent. Cowboy and Joker's desire for each other is laid bare, with nothing in between to protect them. However, Hasford clearly sets up the ultimate realization of this desire as what enables, perhaps even demands, that Joker execute Cowboy. For, at the end of the scene, though Cowboy had planned to kill himself after shooting his fallen soldiers, the sniper wounds him so that he cannot. Instead, Joker must carry out Cowboy's intentions by shooting his friend. Through this progression of events, Hasford suggests that the new self-knowledge the men have about their desire requires a destruction of their now dangerous relationship by death, for the maintenance of militarized masculinity and male power rests on its ability to normalize male-male desire via women. Thus, rather than suggesting, as war narratives typically do, that the men are fighting heroically to protect their women at home as well as the feminized nation, Hasford's novel presents women's importance to the military and war primarily in terms of exchange between men. By underscoring this usually hidden use of women, he opens it to interrogation; in this way, Hasford provides evidence for feminists' claim that patriarchally imposed heterosexuality can best be discussed in terms of various forms of traffic in women. In *The Short-Timers*, women are exchangeable property whose primary purpose is to seal the bonds of men with men (Sedgwick, p. 26).

A final destructive use of women by the military to which Hasford points in *The Short-Timers* is the deliberate confusion of women and rifles, sex and killing. As Joker narrates, "during our sixth week [of basic], Sergeant Gerheim orders us to double-time around the squad bay with our penises in our left hands and our weapons in our right hands, singing: *This is my rifle, this is my gun; one is for fighting and one is for fun.*" Further, Gerheim orders the recruits to give their rifles women's names, saying, "This is the only pussy you people are going to get. Your days of finger-banging ol' Mary Jane Rottencrotch through her pretty pink panties are over. You're married to *this* piece, this weapon of iron and wood, and you *will* be faithful" (p. 11). As Appy points out, "While the ostensible point [of such exercises] is to distinguish between sex and violence, applying the language of weaponry to both does more to associate the two behaviors than to divide them" (p. 102). The rifle and the penis are somehow the same, as are killing and sex.[28]

Hasford reveals the destructiveness of such a linkage in Leonard Pratt's murder of Gerheim. On their final night in basic training, after lights out, Leonard frightens Joker by speaking to his rifle, which, as ordered by Gerheim, he has named Charlene. Leonard tenderly hugs and then engages in a one-sided lover's quarrel with "Charlene": "Okay, okay. I *love* you! . . . I've given you the best months of my life. And now you— . . . I LOVE YOU! DON'T YOU UNDERSTAND?" As he field-strips his rifle, Leonard tells Joker, "This is the first time I've ever seen her naked." He extols Charlene's "pretty" and "beautiful" parts. Hasford reveals the destructiveness of the sex-death confusion, however, when Gerheim, awakened by Leonard's shouts, confronts the monsters he has created. For when the sergeant orders Leonard to relinquish his weapon, the recruit shouts, "NO! YOU CAN'T HAVE HER! SHE'S MINE! YOU HEAR ME? SHE'S MINE! I LOVE HER!" and later, after shooting Gerheim, Leonard says, "Did you see the way he looked at her? Did you? I knew what he was thinking . . . That fat pig and his dirty—" (pp. 25, 26). Thus, Gerheim's murder is figured as a result of Leonard's jealous lust for Charlene. Further, after threatening to kill the other recruits, "[Leonard's] grin changes to a look of surprise and then to confusion and then to terror as Leonard's weapon moves up and back and then Leonard takes the black metal barrel in his mouth. 'NO!

Not—'" and shoots himself (p. 27). In this sequence, with opaqueness typical of the novel, Hasford refrains from explanation. When presented with such a situation, readers of a realist novel would assume Leonard has experienced a psychotic break; within the magical realism of *The Short-Timers*, however, readers must entertain the possibility that Leonard is *not* insane and that the training has given Charlene a mind of her own, a possibility supported by the fact that other recruits, including Joker, also have heard their rifles speak (pp. 18, 23). The incident clearly demonstrates early in the novel the danger of merging woman with weapon, sex with death.

The devastating consequences of the sex-violence linkage to women is shown in the portions of the novel that take place in Vietnam. When Joker meets up with Cowboy in Vietnam, he hears Animal Mother, one of Cowboy's squad members, telling his friends, "Man, I almost got me some eatin' pussy." Another soldier explains, "Mother was chasing a little gook girl with his dick hanging out . . . She was just a baby . . . thirteen or fourteen." Animal rebuts his comrade's obvious disgust with the comment, "If she's old enough to bleed she's old enough to butcher." Animal then reminisces to Cowboy, "[R]emember when we . . . blew away that NVA rifle squad? You remember that little gook bitch that was guiding them? She was a lot younger than the one I saw today . . . I didn't get to fuck that one either. But that's okay. That's okay. I shot her motherfucking face off" (pp. 76–78). With Mother's alteration of the aphorism, "If she's old enough to bleed, she's old enough for me," which itself justifies sex with an underage female, sex and butchery become equivalents. Although he apparently would have preferred to rape these girls, he found brutally murdering them to be an acceptable substitute. Thus, Hasford reveals the ultimate consequence of the military's method of relating sex and violence; it is a linkage that is deadly for women, whose deaths are sexually gratifying in themselves.

Indeed, according to Animal Mother's logic, Joker himself rapes a woman, though he does not have sex with her. In the novel's second section, an unseen sniper picks off several men from Cowboy's squad, which Joker and Rafter Man are accompanying. After Rafter Man mortally wounds, but does not kill, the sniper, who turns out to be a young girl, Joker protests that the soldiers cannot leave the girl in such a condition. Realizing that no one else is willing to kill her from such a personal range, Joker narrates, "I look at the sniper. She whimpers . . . I look into her eyes . . . She sees me. She recognizes me—I am the one who will end her life. We share a bloody intimacy. As I lift my grease gun she is praying in French. *Bang*. One round enters the sniper's left eye and as the bullet exits it tears off the back of her head" (p. 101).

Animal Mother's earlier suggestion that killing and death are equivalent seems relevant as Joker describes the knowledge he and the girl share as a "bloody intimacy." And, as Jeffords points out, Joker has in actuality "shot her motherfucking face off" just as Animal Mother did with his intended rape victims (p. 176). Understanding the erotic nature of Joker's murder of the sniper is essential to registering the more subtle meaning of Joker's killing of Cowboy at the end of the novel. For as sex and death become increasingly linked through the novel's progression of murders, one finally cannot deny Joker's killing of Cowboy as an erotic consummation of their relationship, though sublimated through violence.

Working-Class Interests: The Novels of Larry Heinemann

Close Quarters

Although quite different formally from *The Short-Timers*, the Vietnam-centered novels of Larry Heinemann are equally critical of both the war and the atrocities committed in it, as well as pointing to the American societal attitudes that made these atrocities possible. Heinemann's first novel, *Close Quarters*, which he began writing in 1968, was published in 1977. Like Hasford's novel, *Close Quarters* does not render the war in clear detail with the eye of a "neutral camera." Rather, Heinemann unapologetically throws his reader into the disorientingly chaotic world of the Vietnam War; neglecting to provide appositive explanations, explanatory glossaries, or maps, he leaves readers on their own to make sense of the war's "ugly, deadly music."[29] Readers comprehend meaning only as the narrator, the newly arrived Corporal Philip Dosier, processes his experiences within the army's mechanized infantry division.

The book is a grueling read; more often than it narrates harrowing firefights it details the soul-killing, backbreaking drudgery required of the infantry soldiers, a device that sets out early Heinemann's interest in the working-class experience. In one interview, Heinemann said as he was working on his own novel, he found himself impressed by Herman Melville's detailed description of the "work" of whale hunting in *Moby Dick.* He thought, "I'll hang the story on the work, the same as Melville. It struck me that folks back here not only did not know what it was like to be in an Army barracks, but also knew nothing about the war as work."[30] This focus on "the war as work" precludes firefights, search and destroy missions, and ambushes from appearing glorious or even exciting. Rather, they constitute a dirty and dangerous continuation of the soldiers' more mundane duties. Elaborating on his purpose in enclosing battle scenes within menial labor, Heinemann also points to the unavoidable trauma of aggression: "In every sort of work there is a literal physical satisfaction that comes over you when a job's well done, a personal pride. But if you're an infantryman, your job is to kill people. 'Close and engage' the lifers call it. I've heard historians refer to it as 'state sanctioned murder.' But it's still murder. And how can you possibly have any good feeling about that?"[31] Presenting military duty as equal parts drudgery and traumatic action, Heinemann checks any tendency to see war as patriotic, noble, or fulfilling.

The trauma of soldiers' murderous toil in war is clear by the end of the narrative, but Heinemann's portrayal of the changes wrought by the war as deeply negative and psychologically injurious is not unusual. What sets his writing apart from literature such as Philip Caputo's *A Rumor of War* (1977) or Ron Kovic's autobiography is his reliance upon women, and men's treatment of them, to gauge the changes in his male characters. These other authors typically situate their stories within an all-male world, untouched by women. In Heinemann's early novel, however, women are an important physical presence during the war, and he reveals connections between Vietnamese and American women, exposing generalized American male concepts of women. These connections contradict the proposition that the abuse of Vietnamese women during the war was merely a function of racism; Heinemann shows it to be a complex mixture that, though certainly inflected by racism, was also founded on the masculine assumption of women as other and primarily sex objects rather than as human beings.

Throughout *Close Quarters*, women are consistently referred to and defined in relation to their sexuality. The Vietnamese women in the novel are even given names expressive of the GIs' assessment of their sexual value. For instance, one of the main female characters, Claymore Face, is called so because of the pox scars covering her face and neck. Cross, one of Dosier's workmates, introduces Claymore Face as "the greatest piece of ass this side of the Saigon River. She ain't much ta look at but she puts out like crazy. Just put a paper bag over her head" (p. 35). Rather than a person like themselves, for the soldiers, this woman exists simply to provide a sexual service they require. Their derogatory naming of her based on how well she fulfills this need, which encapsulates their entire understanding of her, denies her basic humanity. She is simply "the platoon punchboard," who has "the *ugliest* cunt for a hundred clicks" (p. 65). Similarly, a prepubescent Vietnamese girl who peddles drinks to the soldiers is called "No-tits." Again, this name reveals the lens through which the soldiers see the girl. Though she is only a young girl with an undeveloped body, they cannot conceive of her apart from her sexual function and name her for a perceived deficiency. Never does Claymore Face or No-tits give her real name (and, of course, they are not asked by the soldiers), so readers are uncomfortably forced to occupy the soldiers' subject-position, thinking of the women by these derogatory names. Though unpleasant for readers, Heinemann skillfully requires readers to recognize the dehumanizing masculine gaze.

This pattern of thinking of women only in relation to sexual function is highlighted in the synecdochical use of women's genitalia to refer to individual women. A Vietnamese woman—the unofficial girlfriend of Quinn, Dosier's good friend—is called "just Quinn's free pussy" (p. 96), and once after sweeping through a village, one soldier remarks, "Man! Did you see tha' pussy down by Charlie Papa Echo? Lot a meat on tha' one" (p. 101). This synecdoche reduces all women to the function of sexual gratification for men. The objectification of women, which dehumanizes them for the men, endangers them physically as well. Dosier narrates how his GI friend Rayburn, when he "catches [his wife] messing around with a couple [of] Davenport cops[,] . . . does her in with a butcher knife" (p. 103). Another time, Dosier receives a letter from a friend back home that details how a woman they know had a party, "got fucked up on Chivas Regal and gang-banged the dudes who didn't bring dates, which was very polite of her." Dosier and friends find this situation amusing, "grinning the whole time," even when the letter goes on to reveal that the woman's husband "beat the shit out of her" (p. 134). Not only do readers see Vietnamese women being disrespected and abused by American men, but American women as well. Thus, Heinemann suggests that this problematic treatment of women goes deeper than mere racism or bad behavior incited by the "fog of war." Rather, he points to culturally accepted (even prized) forms of masculinity that framed women and femininity in terms of sexuality. In fact, the women's movement of the sixties and seventies was itself catalyzed by these very attitudes, which women activists experienced in various social movements. As one woman complained, even in the supposedly progressive New Left, sexual politics permitted "[a] man [to] bring a woman into an organization by sleeping with her and remove her by ceasing to do so. A man [could] purge a woman for no other reason than that he ha[d] tired of her . . . and that purge [was] accepted without a ripple."[32]

Not only does Heinemann put forth Dosier's treatment of women as a descriptive indicator of the state of gender relations in Vietnam, but his treatment of women also acts as a barometer of how the war negatively affects him. When Dosier first arrives in country, and Claymore Face asks him, "You like short-time?" Dosier politely responds,

"No, no thank you, not this morning" (p. 35). While his friends avail themselves of the prostitute's services, Dosier averts his gaze, looking everywhere but at the work the woman conducts (p. 36). However, about two-thirds of the way through the novel, the protagonist reveals that he "finally went to her" himself "when the ache and boredom got to be too much," though he shows revulsion for Claymore Face by listing with disgust the services she is willing to provide for a paltry sum: "She would do anything for a fiver—fuck regular, ass-fuck, titty-fuck, lick your asshole, suck, fuck with the crook of her elbow if that's what got you off—any-fucking-thing" (p. 191). Thus, he has gone from being ashamed and critical of the soldiers who take advantage of the prostitute to exploiting her himself. Yet, even as he uses her, he reviles the woman herself. In this way, his attitude toward Claymore Face parallels his own feelings for himself and the changes that come over him as his complicity in the war affects him.

Claymore Face does not represent only herself; in the novel, Dosier's relationship to her is reflective of his attitude toward all Vietnamese women. When, as part of his slide toward depravity, Dosier begins "hustling Claymore Face, freak-sideshow fashion, to the fucken new guys," he tells one disappointed GI, "M'man, she's as good as it gets 'round here" (pp. 258, 259). And the full scale of Dosier's hatred for Vietnamese women is apparent in the final scene in which Claymore Face appears, shortly before Dosier leaves Vietnam. Unfolding as the novel's most horrifying scene, Dosier systematically describes in graphic and cruel detail how he and his friends gang rape Claymore Face. Dosier and Quinn set up a makeshift bed in their vehicle for the prostitute, and she conducts her business there. Dosier narrates that several of the soldiers sat "around the crew hatch with our legs dangling in . . . watching Claymore Face fuck some new guy . . . We looked down, bug-eyed, clapping and shouting encouragement." The men were so impressed with the job Claymore Face did that they threw money down for her.

> We asked the dude to move his head so we could throw the money at her face, and she blinked and squinted when they hit the mark, as though she was looking up at a monsoon rain . . . Claymore Face jumped up and scrambled around, snatching up the money, bare-ass—her jugs just jiggling, like somebody was slapping them with open-handed slaps, her meaty, sweaty thighs smeared with cum. The fucken new guy sat back on the bench . . . watching her climbing around and grunting. He watched us laughing and pointing to her upturned ass cheeks, and shouting . . . When she had

all the crumpled bills she could hold, she stood up in the crew hatch among that circle of legs and crotches, smiling that God-awful-ugly no-tooth smile of hers, hugging the money to her chest.

"Hey, sweetheart. That money ain't for free," I said, . . . "No, no, negative, no. You all got to suck me off. Matter a strict fact, you got to suck everybody." I unbuttoned my fly and eased out ol' Deadeye and pointed at him with my eyes and a sawing motion of my hand. She made a face and giggled, lowered her head and shook her shoulders, acting dumb and dufus, as though she thought I was kidding. But when I made a show of reaching down and unsnapping the flap of my forty-five holster she jerked her head up and stiffened, like somebody had kicked her dead in the ass when she was asleep and told her to move on. She dropped her money on her clothes and stepped between my legs and put her lips down over the tip, free-handed. She sucked in her cheeks and slobbered and licked some and glanced up at me, as much to say, "Okay. All right. I'm going. I'm *going*" . . . When I came she popped me out of her mouth and looked around, and there were six more dangling out over the crew hatch. She went from cock to cock, among the giggling and jostling and dudes poking her in the back, and by the time she came around to Deadeye again her lips and chin and neck were smeared with spit and cum. I was hard again and everybody was hard again, so I told her to go around one more time.

We just sat in that circle while Claymore Face went the rounds again, her eyes darting from gun to gun. And that fucking new guy sat inside all the while. "You guys are fucked up," he kept saying. "You dudes are crazy, you're nuts!" He went to Sergeant Corso and the El-tee and some other dudes in the platoon, but nobody paid any attention to him until Stepik finally told him not to be such a fucking Boy Scout.

After that Claymore Face didn't come around much, and nobody much cared. (pp. 259–61)

I quote this passage at length because the language and details in Dosier's narrative reveal the men's horrific cruelty, but they also paint Claymore Face, a prostitute, in a sympathetic light, unlike most popular representations of Vietnamese prostitutes. It is impossible to read this passage and not understand, like the new guy, that it is not Claymore Face, but Dosier and the other soldiers who "are fucked up." Heinemann horrifically demonstrates that the military's construction of women as entirely other and creatures made for sexual pleasure, as demonstrated earlier in the novel, ultimately leads to the soldiers' complete dehumanization of and destructive violence toward Claymore Face.

Moreover, Heinemann seconds the Winter Soldiers' claim that the problem of hatred and violence toward women was a systemic problem, for Sgt. Corso and the lieutenant's ignoring of the situation and their dismissal of the new guy as a "Boy Scout" reveal the army's unwillingness to correct such behavior and thus its tacit approval. And, again reinforcing the testimony of the Winter Soldiers, Heinemann uses Dosier's participation in this act to reveal that the trauma of war comes not only from exposure to combat but also from the atrocities soldiers commit. Dosier ponders his moral degeneracy a few pages after the rape, "The war works on you until you become part of it, and then you start working on it instead of it working on you, and you get deep-down mean . . . I dug free-fire zones because we could kill anything that moved, and all I wanted to do was kill and kill and burn and rape and pillage until there was nothing left" (pp. 278–79). With the rape lingering in reader's minds as the last notable event of Dosier's war experiences, it seems directly linked to the profound psychological trauma and alienation he experiences on returning home. In the final pages of the novel, Dosier bleakly describes his internal landscape, "I have traveled to a place where the dead live above the ground in rows and bunches. Time has gone somewhere without me. This is not my country, not my time. My skin is drawn tight around my eyes. My clothes smell of blood. I bleed inside. I am water. I am stone. I am swift-running water, made from snow. I am stone, chipped from giant granite boulders, small shards, jagged and sharp-edged, sliding . . . I have not come home . . . I have gone ahead, gone back. There is glass between us, we cannot speak" (p. 307).

In this early novel, although Heinemann intuitively senses the connections between the brutality against women in the war and against women at home as he weaves together the mistreatment of American and Vietnamese women in his narrative, neither he nor his narrator fully comprehends the ways in which extant American male attitudes about women authorize such treatment, both at home and in war. However, the novel importantly admits the soldier not just as an innocent victim but also as an aggressor himself. *Close Quarters* explores the soldier's aggressive rage as both a symptom of and causal agent in the complex trauma war creates. Heinemann did not abandon these concerns with time, but brought them to fruition in his second, more complex novel—*Paco's Story.*

Paco's Story

The public received *Paco's Story*, published in 1986, warmly and with critical approbation; it won the National Book Award in 1987. Unlike *Close Quarters*, Heinemann's second book is set in the United States and is concerned with the return of a Vietnam veteran, Paco Sullivan. Paco is the lone survivor of a terrible accident in which his company was bombarded by American artillery. In fact, the novel is narrated by the street-wise, fast-talking collective ghost of Paco's decimated company. Littered with parenthetical asides and obscenity, the narrative addresses itself to the reader, whom it calls "James." Heinemann explains in the foreword to later editions of his novel that "[t]he 'James' comes from the custom of street folks engaging total strangers by calling them 'Jim' or 'Jack' . . . in a jivey sort of way."[33] Just as someone on the street most likely would feel about being accosted as "James," the reader of *Paco's Story* tends to find this mode of address irritating. The narrative framework is similar to that of *The Rime of the Ancient Mariner* in which the mariner discourses with an unwilling listener (whose point of view the reader shares), one for whom it is imperative to hear the story. So also, through the course of *Paco's Story*, it becomes clear that Heinemann believes that his American readers all share a portion of the blame for the events of the Vietnam War, the scars from which Paco wears like an albatross. The narrator demands that readers recognize their complicity through his story. In this later novel, which brings the war home, concepts are mature that were only nascent in *Close Quarters*. Heinemann draws complex connections among America's class system, gender relations, the brutalities of the war, and possibilities for veteran healing.

From the forward, which explains the working-class origins of the address "James," the book announces itself as of the working class, as are both Paco and the narrator. The narration catches up with Paco as his bus ticket expires outside Boone, Texas, where he secures a job washing dishes at the Texas Lunch. As in *Close Quarters*, *Paco's Story* also emphasizes war-as-work, this time connecting it more explicitly with work in nonmilitary life. In the first chapter, when the narrator reviews some relevant facts from Paco's tour in Vietnam, he emphasizes the labor involved in "humping"—the walking infantrymen did. "A body never gets used to humping, James. When the word comes, you saddle your rucksack on your back . . . and begin by putting one foot in front of the other. After a good little while you've got two sharp pains as straight as a die from your shoulders to your kidneys, but there's nothing to do for it but grit your teeth a little harder and keep humping" (p. 9). Paco's harsh manual labor at the Texas Lunch is not dissimilar from the painful humping of the war, and after a long day, "Paco's back is plenty warm with pain and sore as hell, his legs ache and his face tingles, and he's ready for his medication" (p. 115). Far from the romanticized male manual labor of Henry David Thoreau and Jack Kerouac—more traditional to American writing—labor in Heinemann's universe is portrayed as stinking, grinding, and soul killing.

The novel accentuates the generational effects of working-class identity. Skillfully connecting the various situations in which identity is created through labor, Heinemann also focuses on the working-class childhood of Gallagher, one of Paco's squad members. Gallagher narrates the physically treacherous and dream-shattering drudgery his father endured as a Chicago city bus driver. "I remember he used to come home nights ass-whipped tired, just *draggin'* his ass" (p. 120). After removing his ragged clothing, Gallagher's "old man would stand in front of that closet—'putting away his work,' he called it. . . . And every once in a while he'd stand there . . . for a *long* time . . . stinking of fuel oil and diesel fumes, and this look of pale and exhausted astonishment would come over him, like he just woke up and couldn't bring himself to believe where he was and what he was looking at . . . My old man busted his ass all his life, and all's he got out of it was beat-up hands, bad eyes, and a bend in his back" (p. 124). Not only has the American dream, in which hard work pays off with social and economic advancement, been chimerical, but manual labor has been physically destructive as well. Gallagher recalls that some nights, his father would "crouch nearly double, his head in his hands, half blinded by headaches, squeezing his scalp for all he was worth, with those cold, rawed-up fingers of his, and his eyes'd be red and milky, shining—and sometimes those fuckin' headaches went on all night; years later he told me he could feel his face droop like a gob of warmed wax" (p. 124). Rooted in a thoroughly working-class perspective, the narrative portrays labor as an unfulfilling—even degrading—necessary evil in the life of such people.

Heinemann is not alone in connecting the working-class experience of war's labor and menial labor in the United States,[34] for historian Appy notes that "[f]rom 1961 to 1972, an average of 14,000 American workers died every year from industrial accidents; the same number of soldiers died in Vietnam during 1968, the year of highest U.S. casualties . . . Combat may be more harrowing and dangerous than even the toughest civilian jobs, but in class terms there were important commonalities between the two" (p. 7). Both writers suggest that the continuity between the physical labor in nonmilitary society and that of the military prepared working-class men to be soldiers. Implicitly operant in the psychology of Heinemann's working-class soldiers is the military's claim that it provides opportunities and a means to move up in the social system; with its emphasis on labor in both spheres, however, the novel suggests that that the military offered working-class men similarly dangerous, back-breaking employment with very little room for advancement.

Beyond showing how the U.S. class system supports itself by the working class's labor even as it promises them false hope of escape through hard work and consumerism, Heinemann also reveals some of the more insidious consequences of such a system, such as masculine ideals based on violence and the oppression of those less powerful and the generational nature of systemic trauma. Gallagher and his brothers are victims of their father's physical and mental oppression. Gallagher describes with detail the coin-changing belt his father wore, using this symbol to connect the abuse he suffered as a boy to his father's working-class masculinity:

> [T]hat was the belt we got our lickin's with, you understand? I remember many a night curled up as tight as a fist under my covers, listening to one or another of my brothers getting a whipping—them hopping around downstairs on all fours like a damn crab—my old man stompin' after them, shoving furniture aside and thrashing at them with that fuckin' belt—bellowing, *screaming* angry. Shit, bub! You could stuff a blanket and an afghan and a pillow apiece into your ears and you could *still* hear that goddamned belt rip and whistle through the air. My brothers and me got scars from that fuckin' buckle. (p. 123)

Not only witnessing his father's slow psychological and physical destruction over the years, the son becomes the fearful victim of his father's simmering rage from his "dream deferred." However, far from merely resulting in child abuse—tragic in itself—his father's life is the context in which Gallagher grows into an adult male and, like his father, abuses those less empowered.

Importantly, it is Gallagher who spearheads the rape of the Viet Cong woman, mentioned in the preface. When first captured, the woman is treated respectably, even given a meal. However, the kindness shown to the woman—in contrast to the cruelty and harshness of his own life—incites Gallagher's rage, culminating in the woman's gang rape. For the narrator notes that Gallagher, after balefully watching the woman eat, "had had enough. The next thing you know, James, he had her by the hair and was swearing up a storm, hauling her this way and that (the spit bubbles at the corners of his mouth slurring his words)" (p. 175). Gallagher ties up the woman and rapes her, as do the other soldiers in the company. "And when everyone had had as many turns as he wanted . . . , as many turns as he could stand, Gallagher took the girl out behind that . . . hooch, yanking her this way and that by the whole head of her hair . . . He had a hold of her the way you'd grab some shrimpy little fucker by the throat—motherfuck-you-up street-mean and businesslike—and he slammed her against the wall and hoisted her up until her gnarled toes barely touched the ground" (pp. 181–82). Gallagher then shoots the girl, and "Paco remembers the spray of blood, the splatter of brick and bone chips on Gallagher and Jonesy and *every*one, as thick as freckles, and how it sparkled . . . He remembers the brown bloodstains down the fronts of our trousers for days afterward; remembers Gallagher turning to the rest of us, still holding her scalp . . . We looked at her and at ourselves . . . and knew that this was a moment of evil, that we would never live the same" (pp. 183–84).

By placing a passage that depicts one of the most gruesome rapes of Vietnam War literature just after readers have been informed of Gallagher's traumatic childhood, Heinemann makes it clear that this rape is a logical outgrowth of the trauma of the working-class oppression of which Gallagher and the other soldiers are a product. Just as the child Gallagher was abused by his father, so he has grown into an abuser who seeks out the less powerful on whom he can violently display his masculinity. Conditioned in basic training to hold women as the ultimate enemy because of their paradoxically threatening weakness, the Vietnamese woman is the ideal victim. As a Viet Cong fighter, she is especially threatening, as the very idea of a successful woman soldier upsets the carefully learned definition of soldier as "man."[35] Rape demonstrates Gallagher's dominance, shores up his power as a man, and is physically and psychologically demeaning to the woman. The narrator emphasizes the gendered force of Gallagher's treatment of the prisoner, noting, "You've got to understand, James, that if the zip had been a man we would have punched on him, then killed him right then and there and left him for dead" (p. 177). So, Heinemann carefully points out that it is the prisoner's status as a *woman* that incites Gallagher and the others to commit extended torture and gang rape. Paco's remembrance of Gallagher's holding the woman the way a schoolyard bully would "grab some shrimpy little fucker by the throat" clearly pits Gallagher as an abuser seeking to assure himself through violence of his own empowerment and agency. The tangled complexities of the multiple and contradictory systems at work in the United States—specifically gender relationships that privileged the masculine over the feminine and a class system that disempowered working-class men, prompting them to adhere even more strongly to violent masculinity as a means to power—have long been noted and commented on in relation to the Vietnam War. Picciano explicitly made the connection between the militarized masculinity of the army and American ideals of gender and sexuality when he remembered his working-class childhood, specifically "the gangs closing in on Sal Companella, the neighborhood's budding fag." He concluded that "[t]he military was just an exaggeration, a caricature, of all that had gone before," in his experience of the masculinism and heterosexism of American culture (p. 83). By prefacing the woman's rape with the long descriptions of Gallagher's childhood and his father, Heinemann asks readers to realize what Peck and Picciano earlier explained: the oppressiveness of the working-class situation encouraged the formation of violent masculinity as a means of disavowing a perceived lack of agency and value to society. And this violent masculinity played itself out on the bodies of the less empowered—sometimes men, sometimes children, but primarily women.

As he tentatively did in *Close Quarters*, Heinemann more forcefully demonstrates in *Paco's Story* that the revulsion for the feminine does not have consequences only for the Vietnamese women, for the hatred of women follows the military men home. Jesse, another Vietnam veteran who passes through town, launches into a viciously misogynistic diatribe against a hypothetical woman:

> "Been waiting for one of those mouthy, snappy-looking little girlies from some rinky-dink college to waltz up and say"—and his voice rises into a fey falsetto, squeaking as though he's rehearsed it—"'You one of them *vet'rans*, ain'cha? Killed all them mothers and babies. Raped all them women, di'n'cha'—*I only got two hands, lady!*—'Don't touch me, *so* nasty,' as the fella says, 'I ain't putting out for you, *buster*, not so much as a handshake!' Okay by me, girlie," Jesse says, . . . "And when this happens—this conversation with this here girlie—I'm gonna grab her up by the collar of her sailor suit (or whatever the fuck they're parading around in these days), slap her around a couple times, flip her a goddamned dime . . . and say, 'Here . . . give me a ring in a couple of years when you grow up.'" (p. 156)

In this passage, Jesse envisions an encounter based on what he believes American women must think of the Vietnam veterans. He imagines that this woman will be self-righteously disgusted by him and his supposed activities in Vietnam. Jesse's description of "grab[bing] her up by the collar" and "slap[ping] her around" echoes the way Gallagher violated the Viet Cong girl, and their similarly violent reactions to the different women reveal the gendered lines of their rage and hatred. And, just as Gallagher's working-class, masculine identity plays a role in his abuse of the prisoner, so class tension is an important factor in Jesse's hypothetical encounter. Jesse is envious of her having the means to attend college, though he denies his envy by belittling the college as "rinky-dink." He believes the woman's privileged, middle-class identity informs her scorn for him, which she expresses by denying him sexual gratification, and by extension, power over her. This denial in turn fuels the rage of his masculine identity and justifies his abuse. While he does not rape her, Jesse—like Animal Mother and Joker in *The Short-Timers*—finds an acceptable substitute for consensual sex in "slap[ping] her around." Unlike Hasford, however, Heinemann emphasizes that gendered violence is also induced by conflicting systems of class and sexual hierarchy.

Paco, too, can only conceive of sex as an enactment of violent masculinity. Just before the memory of the rape in Vietnam overtakes him, he eavesdrops on his neighbor Cathy having sex with her boyfriend. Paco fantasizes about forcefully occupying the other man's place. Though his fantasized encounter is a rape, or rapelike at the very least, the narrator paradoxically depicts Paco's fantasy as a wish for redemption. The narrator tells us that Paco is "just a man like the rest of us, James, who wants to fuck away all that pain and redeem his body. By fucking he wants to ameliorate the stinging ache of those dozens and dozens of swirled-up and curled-round, purple scars . . . He wants to discover a livable peace" (p. 174). Kinney persuasively argues that, in keeping with a long line of male war literature—most importantly Ernest Hemingway's *Farewell to Arms*, in which Frederic Henry searches for a "separate peace"[36]—Paco hopes for a healing sexual encounter (*Friendly Fire*, p. 171). However, his inability to relate to women as anything other than a stage on which to violently enact his masculinity precludes any kind of redemptive relationship. For as he lies longing for this redeeming encounter, the memory of the gang rape violently, insistently invades Paco's consciousness. Almost as though he is himself being raped, Paco unwillingly "remembers the rape of the VC girl, and the dreams he has had of the rape. He winces and squirms; his whole body jerks, but he cannot choose but remember" (p. 174). Heinemann's rapelike description of Paco's unwanted memories emphasizes the traumatizing nature, not of combat, but of masculine aggression.

Paco recognizes the hopelessness of his desire for a redemptive sexual encounter, when, snooping in Cathy's diary, he reads of a dream she has had about him. In her dream, Cathy is eager to take Paco into her bed. However, while having sex, Cathy becomes repulsed by Paco. When he climaxes, Paco "begins to peel the scars off as if they were a mask . . . Like you'd see someone pull up dried spaghetti from a kitchen table . . . and [Cathy] think[s] [she] hear[s] screams, as if each scar is a scream" (p. 208). Paco begins laying his scars on Cathy's body, "[a]nd when each scar touches [her], [she] feel[s] the suffocating burn, hear[s] the scream" (p. 209). Unlike Paco's "livable peace," Cathy's rewriting of Paco's fantasy "ma[kes] [her] skin crawl." She recognizes what Paco wants from her—a body on which to place his burdens, to unload his psychological scars—and she finds the idea revolting and suffocating, another kind of rape. When Paco reads his dream from Cathy's perspective, he "[s]uddenly . . . feels as if he's met his wraith" (p. 209). Seeing himself through her eyes as a man violently forcing upon her the terrible memories of the brutalities he has committed, Paco recognizes that his use of both Cathy and the Viet Cong women is the same—to rebuild, restore his masculinity.

Cathy's unwilling relationship to Paco has often been read simply as "a record of the non-veteran's inability to understand or feel the pain of those who fought in the war" (Jeffords, p. 71). Her refusal to bear Paco's scars might be read more productively as American society's silencing of unwanted testimony of trauma. With the revelation of the gang rape, readers recognize that Paco's trauma is caused by his participation in this atrocity; however, within the novel, it is clear that if he were to explain the horrific act at the root of his pain, the townspeople would only despise Paco more. Heinemann suggests that an important prerequisite for a healing public, then, is a recognition that veterans were not solitary psychopaths, but that the systems by which they were molded within American culture enabled them to commit atrocities in Vietnam. Moreover, Cathy's inability to endure a sexual/love relationship as a stage for masculine unburdening does not necessarily indicate a lack on her part, but rather a suggestion that veterans must recognize that a healing audience for male confession needs to be composed of "not-lovers"—a public that is not a girlfriend or wife.

Gender and class relations are the matrix through which the abuses of the war and the public rejection of veterans are explored in Heinemann's novel. The novel's interest in the impossibility of the veteran's reintegration into society suggests that merely seeing the veteran as a traumatized individual is not the answer to his problems. Paco and the other veterans like him are not mere trauma victims, but victimizers as well, and, with Paco's quietly leaving town at the novel's conclusion, Heinemann questions whether it *is* possible or even desirable to reintegrate individuals who have committed such horrific crimes. However, the novel does require that readers recognize the larger connections between Paco and the other soldiers' actions in Vietnam and their understanding of women generally. So, at the same time he appears to question any reintegration of the veteran, Heinemann also suggests that jettisoning the veteran from society, as a scapegoat for America's role in Vietnam, would be to deny the problem rather than to address it.

The Memoirs of W. D. Ehrhart: The War Comes Home

To conclude this chapter, I will now turn to two of W. D. Ehrhart's memoirs, *Vietnam-Perkasie: A Combat Marine Memoir* (1983) and *Passing Time: Memoir of a Vietnam Veteran against the War* (1986). Though Ehrhart, who volunteered for the marines at seventeen and saw combat while in country,[37] is best known for his poetry, his memoirs are also highly praised and frequently taught. Ehrhart's memoirs are particularly relevant to my project because of the priority he gives to gender relations as he gropes for explanations as to his own behavior toward women. Throughout these two memoirs, and especially in *Passing Time*, he repeatedly relates his experiences with women in Vietnam to his troubled interactions with women in the United States. Ehrhart suggests that the abusive attitudes toward women that manifested themselves in Vietnam did not remain there but followed him home, infecting his relations with American women. Similarly to Heinemann's novels, the greatest trauma that haunts Ehrhart from his war experience is his abuse of women. He clearly sees himself not simply as a victim of lost ideals, poor military planning and equipping, or the brutal trauma of combat but as a victimizer who must come to terms with the darkest aspect of himself and his society.

Vietnam-Perkasie begins with Ehrhart's high school career and runs just through the young soldier's return from his service in Vietnam. Beginning his memoir with a record of his basic training, Ehrhart contextualizes his troubled relations to women in Vietnam and after as being at least partly a result of the military's exploitation of women as the psychological and physical "other" of men and soldiers. This exploitation begins with a sexualization of the entire context of basic training. Ehrhart recalls his drill instructor's terrifying berating of the newly arrived recruits, "Keep your head and eyes front, piggy! . . . What're you lookin' at, sweetpea?! You eye-fuckin' me, sweetpea?! You wanna fuck me, scum?! Z'at it, shitbag?! You queer, piggy?! Fuck the deck, piggy! Down, piggy, hit the deck! Push-ups! One! Two! Three! . . . Lemme hear you squeal, piggy! *Squeal*, goddamn you!!" (p. 13). In this brief address, the drill instructor specifically casts suspicion on the masculinity of the unfortunate recruit by questioning his heterosexuality. Further, in the world of basic training, even the simplest actions are endowed with a sexual meaning and motivation, as eye contact is redefined as "eye-fuckin," and pushups are converted to "[f]uck[ing] the deck."

When the DI looks at one man's photograph of his sweetheart, he barks, "She looks like a whore, puke" (p. 13). The man replies, "No, sir," and the following exchange ensues:

> "You callin' me a liar?!"
>
> "No, sir."
>
> "I can't hear you, piggy!"
>
> "No, Sir!"
>
> "She looks like a whore!"
>
> "Yessir!"
>
> "She's probably fucking your father right now."
>
> "YESSIR!" (p. 14)

This dialogue provides a fascinating insight into the psychology and means of the military's use of anger toward women to mobilize its soldiers. Demonizing the recruit's girlfriend on the basis of her sexuality is a particularly effective method for inciting anger at women, for calling her a whore implies a lack on her boyfriend's part as well, since the woman supposedly seeks sexual fulfillment elsewhere. Though at first the recruit denies the DI's claims, because of the basic training system that demands unquestioning agreement with whatever the instructor says, the recruit must eventually give in, agreeing that his sweetheart does look like a whore. The DI then further humiliates the recruit by suggesting that she is even "fucking" the recruit's father. Again, the recruit must agree. Anger toward the DI for putting the recruit in such a humiliating position seems natural, but readers must also suspect that the recruit feels a twinge of anger at his girlfriend as well, who, even if she has committed no infidelities, has at least been the unwitting cause of his shame. Thus, the recruit's ire, which is raised by the DI's name-calling and is initially directed at him, ultimately comes to rest on the woman in question. Following this structure, as the recruits are humiliatingly referred to as "girls" and "pussies" throughout their training, their anger at being called these names shifts from the instructors who berate them to women generally. For it is the recruits' prior association with the nonmilitary world and feminine softness that allows the DIs to position them as women.

Furthermore, basic training included many references to "Jody," "[a] legendary figure in military culture, . . . a civilian who steals girlfriends and wives while soldiers are away fighting wars." As Appy explains, "Promoting animosity toward draft evaders and Jodies (sometimes presented as the same figure) was a backhanded way to build support for the war in Vietnam. Somehow fighting in Vietnam would be a way to get back at those . . . who had not shared the abuse of basic training, those who could sit home and . . . steal girlfriends" (p. 106). Implicit in the idea of Jody as a draft evader was his privileged socioeconomic status, which enabled him to avoid military service. Thus, besides aiding DIs in tearing down the recruits' sense of self, abusing women and Jodies subtly suggested participation in the war was a means to strike back at these "disempowering" groups.

The effectiveness of basic training's rhetoric on Ehrhart becomes clear when he receives a "Dear John" letter from his girlfriend, Jenny. Ehrhart is understandably hurt by Jenny's rejection of him, especially after "[e]ight fucking months" of "[l]ong letters. Passionate letters . . . A perfect chain, like a rosary, a lifeline . . . Gone just like that" (p. 132). However, his automatic response to Jenny's rebuff, which in actuality results from her changing view on the war's morality, is to accuse her of infidelity with a Jody: "Niles Mancini. You ever hear a fuckin' name like that? Niles Mancini. She went to the prom with him last spring . . . Fuckin' rich kid, you know? . . . 'We're just friends,' she says, 'don't worry. I love you no shit, GI.' . . . I ever get home, I'll kill that son-of-a-bitch. I ain't kidding . . . That bitch! I'll fuckin' kill 'em both, I swear to God" (p. 136). Aside from threatening mortal violence, this passage is revealing of military attitudes toward women, for Ehrhart's language figures Jenny as a prostitute. When she speaks in Ehrhart's monologue—"We're just friends . . . don't worry. I love you no shit, GI"—her diction changes from that of an American schoolgirl to a Vietnamese sex worker. The pidgin English and jargon is vocabulary used by women such as Claymore Face in *Close Quarters.* Thus, in his mimicry of Jenny's thoughts, Ehrhart conflates the American girl (whom he believes is unfaithful) and Vietnamese prostitutes. This collapse justifies for him his belief that Jenny is an unfaithful whore—she is like a prostitute—and simultaneously authorizes his anger toward Vietnamese women, who remind him of his unfaithful girlfriend.

Throughout the memoir, women's failure to bolster Ehrhart's masculinity enables his abusive relations to them. One woman, whom he does not abuse, but whose inability to fulfill his desires haunts him, is a young Danish woman named Dorrit von Hellemond, whom he meets during his R&R in Hong Kong (p. 161). She's the first "real girl" Ehrhart has talked to "in a thousand years," and he instantly falls in love with her, describing her as a "magical faery queene" (p. 160). Dorrit provides Ehrhart with the redemptive green world Paco could only imagine, and at the end of his R&R, Ehrhart seriously considers deserting. Dorrit talks him out of the proposition, however, which Ehrhart later sees as another failure of women (p. 170). Back in-country, his memories of his "Danish faery queene" sustain him as he looks forward to seeing her again. His hopes come to an end, however, when he reads in the military newspaper that Dorrit has been killed in a "brutal sex murder" in Hong Kong. Dorrit was raped, tortured, and murdered (p. 239). The suspect in the killing is described as Caucasian, with the clear suggestion that her killer was an American GI. Dorrit's death not only represents for Ehrhart the insanity of the war itself, but by dying, even the most perfect woman abandons him.

Dorrit's inability to console him leads Ehrhart to an interaction with a Vietnamese woman that is ultimately even more traumatizing to him, as it implicitly links him to the men who abused and murdered Dorrit. During the Tet Offensive, one of Ehrhart's buddies tells him, "We found a whore over at the University. She'll take us all on—and it won't cost us a single piastre. All she wants is food," only "one meal per fuck" (p. 263). Though records of visiting prostitutes are commonplace in Vietnam War literature—even in memoirs—Ehrhart's lack of matter-of-factness or bravado differentiates his experience. Rather, he notes that "When my turn came, . . . I didn't know what to say or where to begin. 'Chow Co,' I said . . . She just grunted softly, and fumbled for my belt buckle . . . I hadn't had much experience at this sort of thing—but even I knew that the woman's awkwardness and stiff body suggested either inexperience or deep hatred. 'Probably both,' I thought. My stomach felt sick" (p. 264). After he has finished, Ehrhart tells the other men, "I don't think she was a whore," to which another soldier answers, "So what?" With a sensitivity to the woman's situation, the memoirist makes it clear that this woman sold her body, not out of greed or lack of sexual mores, but because she—and most likely her family—was hungry. He immediately feels guilty, and he revisits this moment in which he contributes to the woman's degradation repeatedly in his future writing. Yet, when the incident occurred, Ehrhart chose to participate, demonstrating the complex group pressure that is part of the psychology of aggression. He had inculcated enough of the racist and sexist teachings of the military and felt a pressure to belong to the group—the rest of whom displayed no qualms about their exploitation—so that he had sex with the woman despite his misgivings, despite her obvious hatred.

Ehrhart's troubled relations to women only just begin with his war experience. When he imagines his homecoming, he cherishes the fantasy of buying a coke for a "round-eyed" American girl in the airport. However, when he tries to enact this dream, the girl he asks is afraid of him and refuses his offer. Ehrhart is deeply angered and hurt, and he mutters to himself about the "Goddamn bitch." Then Ehrhart "realized that [he] had been sitting there for some time thinking not about the woman [in the airport], but about Jenny" (p. 277). As Kalí Tal suggests, Ehrhart's "conflation of the two women, and his anger at them, is indicative of the common tendency of [trauma] survivors to seek a justification, an outside enemy upon which they can heap the blame and condemnation that they fear they themselves deserve."[38] For Ehrhart, women function paradoxically as both this outside enemy and as possible saviors. Even as he realizes the deep anger he harbors for Jenny, he desperately longs to see her. But when Jenny later refuses to see him, Ehrhart heaps abuse on her: "I'm over there getting' my ass shot at every goddamned day, and you're back here spreadin' your legs for every rich draft-dodger that comes down the pike. You goddamned whore!" (p. 289). Thus, Ehrhart has learned well the DI's instruction. He now thinks of his girlfriend as the "whore" the DI once suggested all their sweethearts were and of all the men who did not fight as potential cuckolders. Furthermore, despite the fact that he was raised in a middle-class household (he was a minister's son), Ehrhart reveals an identification with the working class when he positions the "draft-dodger" as "rich," and his positioning of himself as less-than "rich" feeds into his injured sense of masculinity.

In the bleak final paragraph of this memoir, Ehrhart ruminates on the various women he has known. "I thought of Dorrit von Hellemond . . . I thought of the woman in the gun pit in Hue . . . I called Jenny from a pay phone and begged her and begged her to love me . . . I went back to the base and masturbated in the shower, passing out beneath the warm stream of water before I finished" (p. 311). In this passage, as he does throughout his memoirs, Ehrhart reveals the confusion created by an ideology which posits women as the spiritual saviors of men, as Catherine Barkley and Dorrit the "faery queene," and yet as their masculine enemy, who by their infidelity, hold the power to destroy their masculinity. And though he has interacted differently with these women, Ehrhart makes clear the detrimental consequences of a militarized masculinity they have all suffered.

In *Passing Time*, Ehrhart makes more explicit the connections between the women of his war experience and the American women he meets later. This second memoir is written in a back-and-forth structure, making use of a frame-story "present" in which Ehrhart resides on a ship at sea, telling the story of his past to his friend Roger. He describes his movements after his tour in Vietnam ended, focusing on his matriculation at Swarthmore College. Although the transition to college life is difficult for him, Ehrhart navigates it successfully, making new friends and eventually throwing himself into the antiwar movement. One aspect of his life that remains as troubled as before, however, is his relation to women. Though Ehrhart quickly finds himself involved in a serious relationship with a woman named Pam, he discovers that she does not—cannot—truly comprehend his war experience. When Pam and her friend ask the naïve question, "What's the worst thing you ever did?" Ehrhart tells them about the woman in Hue. "One night up in Hue City, . . . a bunch of the scouts gang-banged some refugee . . . We paid her with C rations. She wasn't a prostitute, I don't think—she was just starving, probably had a couple of kids to feed." When the women react in horror, Ehrhart responds violently, "Christ, . . . you don't wanna know, don't ask . . . Look, it's not like we raped her. She got what she came for . . . Worse things can happen to a person." However, Ehrhart, the memoirist, reflects, "But we *had* raped her—or might as well have: homeless, devastated, perhaps the rest of her family dead" (p. 53). When Pam continues to cry, Ehrhart denies that the event happened: "You've felt these hands in action, kid . . . Are these the hands of a man who could do something like that?" Pam is comforted by these words, but the reader is left with the disquieting knowledge that the hands in which Pam finds comfort are, in fact, "the hands of a man who could do something like that."

Ehrhart's anger toward women does not end when he becomes engaged to Pam, however; as with Dorrit, his fiancé's failure to "fix" him only provokes his rage. In one incident, an irrationally angry Ehrhart threatens to "break [Pam's] fucking neck" (p. 61). When Pam, terrified, confronts him about this mistreatment, Ehrhart berates her further, ending his tirade by bringing up her past sexual activities, though they are irrelevant to their current argument. "Christ, Pam, that old boyfriend of yours—you suck him off, you let him eat you out, you even ass-fuck the guy! And then you tell me you're still a virgin! . . . How sick is that?

And you're asking me who *I* am?" After the fight, Ehrhart "felt angry and ashamed and cheated . . . What kind of person could gang-fuck some poor starving refugee in the middle of war? . . . What the hell had happened to me over there?" (p. 62). Thus, Ehrhart attacks Pam on the basis of her sexuality in an attempt to prove that she is deserving of his violence, indicating that he continues to think of women primarily in terms of their power to destroy his manhood. However, this outburst culminates in Ehrhart's traumatic memory of his own unjustifiable sexual violence—the "gang-fuck." His linkage of these two inexcusable violences reveals the fallacy of the military's suggestion that women deserve such abuse. Further, it is clear that Ehrhart's PTSD, of which such outbursts are a symptom, is directly related to his memories of the "gang-fuck," traumatic as a moment of terrible aggression.

Ehrhart's uncontrolled anger becomes more violent as time passes and eventually escalates to physical abuse. After he has hit Pam with a closed fist for a second time, Ehrhart reads in her face the fear and anger of the Vietnamese he once tormented. "Pam's eyes were the same eyes I'd seen in a thousand faces in a hundred villages, staring up at me in mute hatred as I towered over her, my whole body still cocked, ready to explode again. And this time there was no rifle, no uniform, no Sergeant Taggart barking orders, no mines, no snipers, no grenade ready to explode, no juggernaut momentum of vast military bureaucracy out of control and bogged down in human quicksand, not a single excuse with which to defend myself. So this is what you are, I thought" (p. 87). Treating women at home with the same anger and brutality he earlier unleashed on the Vietnamese, Ehrhart recognizes the falsity of the platitude that soldiers only act badly because they are under the terrible, deadly pressure of combat. The turning of this violence toward Pam also reveals that women, who were singled out in training as the ultimate enemy and then, failing to provide redemption at home, become the *de facto* target for this cultivated aggression.

Moreover, Ehrhart's perception of women's failure at supporting him was surely strengthened by knowledge of the burgeoning women's movement, which was just beginning to assert its own voice through political demonstration and consciousness raising exercises that asked women and American culture to recognize and rectify its oppression of women. Thus, when Pam, encouraged by women's changing attitudes toward gender roles and their relation to men, refuses to endure Ehrhart's physical abuse and breaks off their relationship, he sees this as further evidence of women's hostility toward men. For even though he recognizes why Pam left him, Ehrhart continues blaming women for his psychological problems, even to the point of blaming Dorrit for her murder: "I did not care to trust anyone the way I had trusted Jenny or Pam. Even Dorrit, my beautiful Danish faerie queene, had failed me in the end, persuading me that I had to go back to Vietnam and then dying a horrible death in a back alley" (p. 129). Yet, while he continually thinks of himself as victim of women, Ehrhart recognizes his own cruelty toward the same women. *Passing Time* catalogs a long line of women Ehrhart emotionally or physically wounds; he notes that the eyes of a later girlfriend "were the same eyes I'd seen the day I'd tried to knock Pam Casey's head off, the same eyes I'd seen on the faces of the Vietnamese peasants whose lives I'd routinely made so miserable . . . Was there no end to what I was capable of?" (p. 254). Again, Ehrhart makes clear that his treatment of this last woman, like Pam, is not fundamentally different, but merely a more recent incarnation of his abuse of the Vietnamese.

Further, Ehrhart, like the authors discussed earlier, connects the violence and trauma "produced" in war with the everyday violences of Cold War American society, which often required participation in violent forms of masculinity from its male children. He recalls that the shooting of several bound Vietnamese prisoners of war reminded him of a day when he "was about nine years old and for no reason [he] could understand, Jerry Dougherty had begun punching [him] in the face over and over again, taunting [Ehrhart] to fight, and [he] didn't know how and was too frightened even to try to defend [him]self, and so [he'd] just stood there crying while the other boys stood around . . . laughing" (p. 221). As he grew older, brutality and fighting back were increasingly seen and rewarded as indicators of masculinity. He completes his remembrances by thinking of the Vietnamese he has killed, most of whom are old men and women. The juxtaposition of these incidents suggests that the slayings, though far different in scale and severity from childhood bullying, are only the fruition of the everyday physical violence perpetrated on and expected of American boys.

In response to his epiphany that the violence of his boyhood, let loose and exponentially exploded in Vietnam, has poisoned his ability to relate peacefully to women, Ehrhart withdraws from society. After graduating from Swarthmore, he takes to the sea, which he finds "utterly free from time and sorrow and memory" (p. 272). At sea, he educates himself, writes letters to his congressmen, and talks with Roger about what he has learned about his country and himself through his experiences. But his withdrawal is not permanent; he is "just resting up. Sort of collecting [his] reserves" (p. 275). Rather than demanding redemption from a woman, Ehrhart finds that isolation and inward reflection provide him the opportunity to recuperate himself.

At this stage of his journey, Ehrhart has discovered that he cannot have fulfilling relationships with women while maintaining the military's picture of them as somehow responsible for his problems. Thus, the self-knowledgeable Ehrhart of *Passing Time* is very different from the Ehrhart at the end of *Vietnam-Perkasie,* who, remembering all his failed relationships and blaming women for his problems, tries to wash away his pain in that ultimate scene of unrealized sexual fulfillment. This later Ehrhart nakedly reveals the reprehensible acts he committed during and after the war in order to show that, through his actions, others—particularly women—have been the ultimate victims of the war. Together, the memoirs extend a vicious trajectory from basic training, which itself draws on ideals of masculinity already extant in American culture, to the destruction and oppression of women in Vietnam and after, revealing abuse of women not as mere collateral damage, but as a necessary type of aggression cultivated by the military. Furthermore, as memoirs, these narratives function as a kind of written testimony, a testimony that molds an audience who must recognize the linkages of violence Ehrhart illustrates.

In this chapter, I have analyzed a range of literary works—from autobiographical novels in the realism-naturalism strain to highly stylized, postmodern novels, to profoundly personal memoirs. In contrast to Jeffords, I have argued that an important set of veteran antiwar literature exists, which does not contribute to the national process of remasculinization that occurred in the eighties. The works of Hasford, Heinemann, and Ehrhart particularly work *against* the project of remasculinization by pointing out the violent excesses of the aggressive masculinity encouraged in American culture and further shaped by the military into a particularly violent misogyny. Rather than reifying such concepts of masculinity, these veterans suggest they are highly destructive to women and ultimately a contributing factor in male soldiers' trauma. The works I have studied here are not only highly regarded within the field of Vietnam War studies—celebrated as some of the best works of their genres—but they also all share a particular sensitivity to the toll the Vietnam War took on Vietnamese women. These writers share the drive of which Heinemann spoke to name for themselves their experience in the war; they repeatedly show Vietnam veterans as something quite other than "victim[s], certainly not . . . hero[s]." That is, these works suggest that the soldier is a victim-victimizer and that American soldiers' violences in Vietnam and after were a product of intricately interrelated social systems.

If veterans were merely victims, as national rhetoric would have them, one has merely to pity them and criticize the forces that victimized these young soldiers. However, to see veterans equally as aggressors demands that readers analyze how social forces, while they victimized soldiers, came also to work within and through them as soldiers violently enacted their masculinity upon women. By implication, this literature questions more basically whether the price of producing soldiers is worth the spoils of war in terms of human suffering—both mental and physical—and systemic social problems. Further, these authors ask their audience to recognize the forces and narratives at work in American society that encourage young men to become a party of the military system and that then enable them to internalize the masculinist message of basic training—a message that urges them to view the feminine as the ultimate enemy, both within and without.

Rather than iconizing the veteran's experience as pure "trauma," which erases important differences between the trauma victims suffer and the trauma aggressors suffer, these writers suggest that the American public must recognize that veteran trauma often results not only from the trauma enacted upon the soldiers but from their perpetration of aggression. The Vietnam veteran's trauma cannot be collapsed with that of the rape survivor or the Holocaust survivor. To call him a victim not only denies the soldier's culpability, but it also denies a large part of the veteran's trauma, which stems from the disjunction between the demands of his conscience and his aggressive actions that violate this conscience.

As veterans in the Winter Soldier Investigation suggested earlier, these writers imply that in order for veterans to experience healing from their war trauma, the public must recognize the entirety of the veterans' war experience. Moving beyond earlier veteran testimony that often simply bore witness to atrocities, these writers explore the complex causes of atrocities against women in Vietnam. In doing so, they demand that a public's healing recognition encompass not just the heinous acts soldiers committed, but most particularly the destructive national narratives of gender and class division that prepared American boys to commit these atrocities. Recognition of these malignant national narratives requires the American public to see, through its support of such narratives, its own part in the atrocities of the war and the misogyny inherent in militarized forms of masculinity, as well as its responsibility to change these narratives.

5

Victimized Veterans and Disappearing Women

The Vietnam War Film

If numerous oral accounts testify to the fact of rape and sexual abuse in the war, and later literary works confirm this testimony and explore the reasons for and the complications of woman abuse, how is it that rape and sexual abuse came to be glossed over and erased from the Vietnam War as it is commonly understood within the United States? Clearly the literature does not propitiate veteran and American guilt; on the contrary, it confesses it. Instead, the more ubiquitous visual media provide the redemption of the Vietnam veteran, and by proxy America. Visual media—specifically Hollywood films—are the primary vehicle of forgetting violence against women in Vietnam.

In this chapter, after giving a brief overview of the history of Vietnam War film from the war years through contemporary times, I will then compare several of the literary works discussed earlier with film adaptations of them, including Stanley Kubrick's *Full Metal Jacket* (Hasford's *The Short-Timers*), Brian De Palma's *Casualties of War* (Lang's report), and Oliver Stone's *Heaven and Earth* (Hayslip's memoirs), as well as his *Platoon.* I will show how, though the literary works they adapt are explicitly concerned with and propose reasons for sexual violence toward women, this concern has been dropped entirely (*Jacket*), contained (*Causalities*), and appropriated (*Heaven*) in such a way as to deradicalize it. I will also discuss rape and sexual violence as a structuring absence in other Hollywood representations of the war; in these films, Vietnamese women are absent altogether or propositioning sex workers who con naive GIs, and Vietnamese victims have been replaced by American victims, most notably POW/MIAs. I will speculate as to why the transference to visual media enables, perhaps even requires, a disappearance of the Vietnamese woman's trauma. The trope of "friendly fire" as described by Katherine Kinney will bear forcefully on this discussion, as the absence of violence against women allows the Vietnam War to be portrayed as a bloody and destructive fight between Americans, and ultimately it allows only American male trauma to be spoken and validated, obscuring the cultural and military attitudes that condoned sexual violence against Vietnamese women.

Of course, I am not arguing that visual media producers collectively conspired to erase the violence done to women; rather, I will show that, as a market-driven industry, in their effort to produce dramas to which audiences would respond, they subtly converted narratives that focused on violence to Vietnamese women to avoid offending audiences. In doing so, these films erased violence toward women, which enabled them to appropriate the language of trauma for the veteran and by extension the nation. This was both uncontested and sustained by other producers of national culture, for Hollywood's depiction of male victimization was also part of the tendency in the eighties toward "remasculinization," Susan Jeffords' descriptor of the cultural move to reclaim and reexalt (white) militarized masculinity against the preceding decade's advancement of women by positioning Vietnam veterans as victims. Erasing evidence of militarized masculinity's violent excesses and its traumatizing prescriptions, which had been highlighted by veteran literature and testimony, Hollywood films instead vilified Vietnamese women and posed American men as the true victims.

Hollywood's Wars: Beginnings

Before launching into a history of the Vietnam War in film, it is important to understand Hollywood's historical place in the American war machine, for film has long been integral in shaping Americans' attitudes toward and understanding of wars. Before and during World War II, Hollywood cooperated with the Office of War Information (OWI)—the government liaison to the media—to produce films that, while positively influencing audiences toward the war effort, would not obviously propagandize. The ideal war film would introduce the government's messages casually and naturally with ordinary language.[1] OWI and Hollywood's relationship, though sometimes antagonistic and ultimately disintegrating, was extremely fruitful.

One strain of the hundreds of war films Hollywood churned out that has particular bearing on the Vietnam War was that dealing with the Japanese enemy. Disregarding OWI's encouragement to forgo "hate pictures," which portrayed the enemy as embodying all evil, Hollywood depicted the Japanese almost exclusively as what Koppes and Black term "the beast in the jungle" (p. 248). While German soldiers were often presented as good and decent people separate from the Nazi leadership, the Japanese were characterized almost exclusively in terms of racial difference—a faceless mob of stereotyped Asians. While OWI deplored such pictures ("we are fighting a system not a race," they reminded the studios [p. 250]), as Tom Engelhardt points out, Hollywood merely reflected popular attitudes. "A poll of [American] servicemen revealed that 38–48 percent of soldiers agreed with the statement 'I would really like to kill a Japanese soldier'; only 5–9 percent [agreed] when it came to Germans."[2] The geography of the war enforced a differentiation of European and Asian enemies. While in the European theater, battles took place in cities and villages—in civilization—the war in the Pacific often took place in the wilderness, specifically in the jungle. As Koppes and Black note, "[t]here is a long tradition in the West of identifying the wilderness with the absence of civilization—indeed, as a place of evil, where the hard-won norms of civilization give way to savagery. In civilized warfare the rules are understood, but there are no rules in the wilderness" (p. 253).

Hollywood's combat films had enormous influence on boys of the "Vietnam generation," those born in the forties and fifties who came of age during the Vietnam War. First acting as motivational tools, combat films promised and encouraged boys toward the experience of masculine heroism in war. As historian Christian G. Appy notes, "It is hard to exaggerate the extent to which young boys growing up in the 1950s and early 1960s were captivated by fantasies of warfare." They grew up "fighting an imaginary version of World War II" in their backyards.[3] Though their fathers' real experiences in World War II influenced many young boys in this imaginary warfare, even more were molded by Hollywood war productions. Almost any Vietnam veteran memoir will mention the influence of Hollywood war films on American boys' understanding of war as a masculine rite of passage. The remembrances of Ron Kovic in his 1976 memoir, *Born on the Fourth of July*, are typical: "Every Saturday afternoon we'd all go down to the movies in the shopping center and watch . . . war movies with John Wayne and Audie Murphy . . . I'll never forget Audie Murphy in 'To Hell and Back.' . . . He was so brave I had chills running up and down my back, wishing it were me up there . . . It was the greatest movie I ever saw in my life."[4] The appeal of combat films extended beyond white boys of the middle class, despite the overwhelmingly negative representation of people of color in such films. Vietnam veteran Larry Matsumoto, a Japanese American, recalls,

"I didn't really have cultural heroes growing up as a kid, except TV heroes like John Wayne and Gene Autry. I always believed that the good guys were American soldiers, fighting for the country, being loyal and courageous. To this day, I still watch Westerns. These are the romantic heroes that are ingrained in me."[5]

As any survey of such memoirs will reveal, John Wayne was a particularly potent emblem of war's glory and the ultimate bearer of the codes of masculinity for young boys growing up in Cold War America. As the narrator of Larry Heinemann's *Close Quarters* reflects, "My parents had raised me on 'Thou-shalt-nots' and willow switches and John Wayne (even before he became a verb), the Iwo Jima bronze and First and Second Samuel."[6] The placement of John Wayne alongside religious and patriotic icons suggests Hollywood's picture of war was not just important to young boys, but represented a culturally idealized form of masculinity. The nuclear family utilized "John Wayne" and his films as teaching tools, equal to "willow switches" and biblical mandates. Furthermore, the conjunction of John Wayne and the "Iwo Jima bronze" conflates the famous statue glorifying the marines who took the island of Iwo Jima and the film *Sands of Iwo Jima* in which Wayne starred and that vaulted him into the top ten box-office attractions for the next twenty-six years. This conflation reveals the melding of America's military history with popular culture that occurs in and through these films.[7] Kinney suggests in her analysis of John Wayne that "[i]t would be hard to overestimate the influence of this film. More than any other single film, *Sands of Iwo Jima* defined the image not only of John Wayne but of war and the Marine Corps for the generation that fought in Vietnam." The films' influence had material effects on the lives of its viewers, for marine recruiters claimed that, even as late as 1975, they experienced an increase in volunteerism whenever the movie appeared on television.[8]

Later, when American boys actually arrived in Vietnam, the films functioned as an ironic backdrop against which soldiers played their own experiences of war. For these new soldiers found that Hollywood depictions of combat and the masculine codes it upheld did not apply in their war. They were especially disillusioned with Wayne's brand of heroism; they discovered that imitating their boyhood hero only increased their chances of dying. As Heinemann's ironic phrase alludes, "to John Wayne" was to ape the heroes of war films—foolishly and unnecessarily endangering oneself and one's friends and dying stupidly. As cavalryman Harold Bryant recalls in *Bloods: An Oral History of the Vietnam War by Black Veterans*, "I remember this . . . guy . . . [who] was a typical example of a John Wayne complex. It was a week after he had just gotten there that we got into any action . . . We went out and got pinned down by machine guns . . . He saw where the machine-gun net was, and he tried to do the John Wayne thing . . . Charge the machine gun. And never made it. Whoever was firing saw him move and turned the machine gun on him."[9] The bitterly ironic "verbing" of John Wayne points at once to the depth of Hollywood's influence on the Vietnam generation and soldiers' disillusionment with Hollywood's prescriptions for masculinity.

At the same time that young soldiers recognized the unreality of Hollywood's wars—or the inapplicability of the old war films' ideals to the Vietnam War—they were still unable to conceive of war outside of Hollywood's simulacrum. On the one hand, many veterans recount their disappointment at the discontinuity between their arrival in Vietnam and the pictures of World War II soldiers entering Europe. For instance, W. D. Ehrhart writes,

> When I first arrived in Vietnam, I had expected to be greeted by thankful peasants lining the roads, waving and cheering like the newsreels I'd seen as a kid of American GIs liberating French villages from the Nazis. The peace-loving people of South Vietnam were being invaded by cruel communists from the north. I was going to defend them . . . [Instead,] [t]he peasants of Vietnam had greeted me with an opaque silence that looked for all the world like indifference or hostility. And the cruel communists were indistinguishable from the people I thought I had been sent to Vietnam to defend.[10]

In spite of the disillusion experienced by American GIs due to their film-inspired expectations, many of them report an odd feeling of unreality in Vietnam, as if they themselves were starring in a movie. In *The Short-Timers,* Gustav Hasford captures the idea of performativity inherent in American soldiers' concept of war and soldiering when Joker describes how "[a] CBS camera crew appears, [and is] surrounded by star-struck grunts who strike combat-Marine poses, *pretending to be what they are.*"[11] So steeped in the simulacrum of reality presented by a film and televisual culture, soldiers found it difficult to distinguish between reality and celluloid, instead acting their parts, "pretending" to be what they already are. Thus, Vietnam veterans' writing, which constantly points to the mediation of their war experiences via Hollywood combat films, reveals just how deeply Hollywood and television's depictions of war impact their young viewing audiences.

Hollywood and Vietnam: Silence to Embrace

Hollywood's response to the Vietnâm War could not have been more different from its reaction to World War II.[12] Rather than producing reels of interventionist film, Hollywood's "involvement" in the Vietnam conflict fitfully started in the late fifties and early sixties, when such films as *The Quiet American* (1958) and *The Ugly American* (1963) appeared. *The Quiet American,* based on the book by Graham Greene, converts the original message of the book so that American innocence is affirmed, not critiqued as naiveté, and the film implicitly calls for U.S. intervention in Vietnam. *The Ugly American,* however, was much less optimistic, and its unflattering depiction of American diplomats cast doubt on the ability of the United States to successfully intervene in Southeast Asia, at the same time the film presented this intervention as necessary. But this contradiction in the film's message was "perfectly in tune with . . . [the] Kennedy cold-war foreign policy," which "talked about Third World independence and neutrality and the moral struggle against ignorance, hunger, and disease while at the same time doing everything possible to undermine and corrupt such political movements."[13]

As the war got underway, Hollywood's stilted attempts to deal with the conflict gave way to silence; as usual, it found avoidance the best answer to controversial issues. Aside from Wayne's *Green Berets* (1968), which will be discussed below, Hollywood did not directly approach the Vietnam War. Rather, filmmakers chose to address certain issues associated with the war indirectly, through films such as Robert Altman's *M*A*S*H* (1970), which was ostensibly about the Korean War though clearly more about the problems in Vietnam. In addition to embracing countercultural attitudes, films such as Samuel Peckinpah's *Wild Bunch* (1969), Ralph Nelson's *Soldier Blue* (1970), and Arthur Penn's *Little Big Man* (1970) reversed earlier American mythology about the civilizing nature of the West, providing thinly veiled critiques of U.S. actions in Vietnam. In these films, "the state and law now became monstrous entities, inflicting pain and death on rebellious white stand-ins for various oppressed and still largely unseen domestic minorities—and the Vietnamese" (Engelhardt, p. 236). Even the piles of zombies at the end of George Romero's *Night of the Living Dead* (1968) eerily call to mind the pictures of the mass graves and killings in Vietnam.

Despite Hollywood's general reticence to speak aloud the name of the Vietnam War, John Wayne boldly orchestrated a film in the model of the World War II epic, believing—film historians Albert Auster and Leonard Quart suggest—that "only a John Wayne film about the Vietnam War could possibly win the hearts and minds of Americans"

(p. 31). He chose as his subject the Green Berets, a group of cavalry-like men that allowed him to connect "the mythological worlds of his beloved mentor John Ford with a public devotion to the memory of John F. Kennedy's Camelot" (p. 31).[14] Wayne's film casts the Vietnam War as another Western in an exotic setting. While the Green Berets play the cavalrymen of the Westerns, so the Viet Cong are the renegade Indians, who in one scene scale a fort named Dodge City. American soldiers who served in Vietnam frequently found Wayne's movie repulsive. Their old hero, whom many soldiers eventually hated because of his influence on them to go into the military, attempted to force the Vietnam War into a mythology incapable of containing it. Instead of winning their hearts and minds, Wayne's film underscored for them the disingenuousness of American frontier mythology and manifest destiny. In *The Short-Timers*, Joker relates the surreal experience of watching *The Green Berets*—which he dubs "a Hollywood soap opera about the love of guns"—while in country:

> [W]e watch John Wayne leading the Green Beanies. John Wayne is a beautiful soldier, clean-shaven, wearing boots that shine like black glass, sharply attired in tailored tiger-stripe jungle utilities. Inspired by John Wayne, the fighting soldiers from the sky go hand-to-hand with all of the Victor Charlies in Southeast Asia. He snaps out an order to an Oriental actor who played Mr. Sulu on "Star Trek." Mr. Sulu, now playing an Arvin officer, delivers a line with great conviction: "Fire *kill* . . . all stinking Cong . . . then go home." The audience of Marines roars with laughter. This is the funniest movie we have seen in a long time.
>
> Later, at the end of the movie, John Wayne walks off into the sunset with a spunky little orphan. The grunts laugh and whistle and threaten to pee all over themselves. The sun is setting in the South China Sea—in the East—which makes the end of the movie as accurate as the rest of it. (pp. 31–32)

In trying to force the Vietnam War into the earlier film models, Wayne's film lost all claim to verisimilitude. For the soldiers serving in Vietnam, the film is a farce; in Wayne's Vietnam, the soldiers are clean, handsome, and clear on their objectives—as opposed to the dirty, vulgar, and decidedly apolitical troops of *The Short-Timers*; the Vietnamese become space travelers, as Joker conflates George Takei's cinematic and television roles, and the sun sets in the east. At home, though the film was a financial success, it was a critical failure. One review scathingly suggested it was "so unspeakable, so stupid, so rotten and false that it passes through being funny, through being camp."[15] The failure of *The Green Berets* was enough to deter other Vietnam films until the war was safely over. TV networks followed the suit of the Hollywood studios; as TV writer Howard Rodman commented, "Vietnam was like a plague . . . If anyone touched it, your arm would rot away."[16]

Though no other movies or television series dealing directly with the Vietnam War were created during the war years, the Vietnam veteran did become a common character of film, especially exploitational film, during the late sixties and seventies. The veteran made his debut in the *Born Losers* (1967), the first of what would become the Billy Jack series. *The Ravager* (1970); *Dead of Night* (aka *Deathdream*, 1972); *To Kill a Clown*, *Tracks*, and *Rolling Thunder* (all 1976); *When You Comin' Back, Red Ryder?* (1979); and *Don't Answer the Phone* (1980) are typical of early films, which portray "in an exploitative and graphic vein" the emotional trauma of the returning Vietnam veteran who brings his war-driven insanity home.[17] Even in films in which the veteran is a sympathetic character, using his violence to deal in "street enforced justice" as in the *Billy Jack* series (1967–77), he remains incredibly brutal and borders on psychotic (Devine, p. 86).

Auster and Quart convincingly argue that although the "psychotic vet" was certainly present in these late-war and postwar films, the most enduring representation of the Vietnam veteran to finally emerge from this spate of exploitational filmmaking was that of the "superman." The superman veteran was a new symbol who "reflect[ed] the American public's own profoundly ambivalent feelings toward the war and . . . touch[ed] upon its destructive and disturbing aspects without truly dealing with the political defeat of American aspirations." In sum, the superman veteran conveyed the emotional impact of the war without revealing any of the war's true content (p. 57). Interestingly, this superman character is nowhere more apparent than in the art films *The Deerhunter* (Michael Cimino, 1978) and *Apocalypse Now* (Francis Ford Coppola, 1979) in the characters of Michael Vronsky (Robert De Niro) and Colonel Kurtz (Marlon Brando), respectively. An important incarnation of the veteran, the superman allowed moviegoers to see Vietnam as a war fought by a kind of men "morally and physically different from themselves, men whose internal lives remain unfathomable and live on a more-murderous and elevated plane of reality than other men" (p. 71). The focus on the superman veteran allowed the politics behind the war, as well as the moral questions raised by U.S. intervention, to remain unexplored. Even a cursory examination of these early "Vietnam War" movies reveals that they had very little to do with the actual war; instead, they sacrifice details about the war's context, issues, and realities to focus on the superman's quest. Films that dealt with the realities of the war would not appear until the mideighties, and I argue that no films aside from a handful of documentaries seriously explore the larger issues of the war.

The roots of the revisionist 1980s POW and MIA films may be clearly seen in the superman films of the seventies. Although the superman veteran of earlier films, such as *The Deer Hunter*'s Michael, was not without ambiguity, as time moved on, the superman became progressively more uncomplicated, just as the films grew increasingly revisionist. The war films of the eighties, including *Uncommon Valor* (1983), the Rambo trilogy (1982, 1985, 1988), the *Missing in Action* trilogy (1984, 1985, 1988), and *The Hanoi Hilton* (1987), played on the captivity narratives so popular throughout American history.[18] Historian Richard Slotkin's "Myth of the Frontier," in which the redemption of American spirit or fortunes was "something to be achieved by playing through a scenario of separation, temporary regression to a more primitive or 'natural' state, and *regeneration through violence*,"[19] suggests that these films captured the public's imagination because retrofitting the Vietnam War within the frontier myth allowed American males to believe in this mythology and its militarized masculinity once again and to ignore negative images of the United States that emerged during the war itself.

These later films succeeded where Wayne's *Green Berets* had failed because their heroes were also victims, whose violence was a just response to their victimization. The POW films pit Vietnam veterans—tortured by their government's supposed abandonment of their brothers in Vietnam and returning to rescue them—against mercilessly brutal and faceless Asians; these films draw on World War II film depictions of the Japanese, collapsing the differences between them and the Vietnamese. Not only does this distort and erase the historical particularities of the Vietnam War, but it also destroys the political differences between the fascism of the Axis powers and the anticolonial revolutions of the Third World countries.[20] By situating themselves within traditional American myths, the MIA/POW films "allowed the public to perceive for the first time our involvement in Vietnam as both just and victorious." In doing so, these films "actually sought to reverse the results of the war," if only on the screen and in American imaginations (Auster and Quart, p. 99).[21]

Another important change in American attitudes toward veterans and the war, one doubtless catalyzed by the "superman" representation, was the formation of "Vietnam guilt chic." The veterans in the revisionist films are not only fear inspiring (as in the early exploitation films); they are admirable—even enviable—for their courage and fortitude. Not coincidentally, at the time these revisionist films began appearing, many American men who did not serve in Vietnam began to complain of having missed out on a vital experience of manhood. Examples of this newfound envy of veterans are rife. James Fallows, editor of the *Atlantic Monthly* (1979–96) and a draft resistor, claimed, "It's probably true that the [men] who went—who had to cope with permanent irreversible situations in a personal sense—were strengthened and became more mature through the experience."[22] Michael Blumenthal, draft resistor and poet, felt that he had missed out on an integral experience leading to "true" manhood: "To put it bluntly, they (the Vietnam vets) have something we haven't got. It is to be sure, somewhat vague, but nonetheless real and can be embraced under several headings; realism, discipline, masculinity (kind of a dirty word these days), resilience, tenacity, resourcefulness . . . I'm not sure they didn't turn out to be better men in the best sense of the word."[23] Christopher Buckley wrote in a 1983 *Esquire* article, "I didn't suffer with them [veterans] . . . And although I'm relieved, at the same time I feel as though part of my reflex action is not complete . . . I haven't served my country. I've never faced life or death. I'm an incomplete person."[24]

This belief in war as a necessary ingredient of manhood, created by American narratives of masculinity and influenced by World War II propaganda, was encouraged by the writings of some veterans as well as the Hollywood films of the early eighties. In his oft-quoted *Esquire* article, "Why Men Love War" (1984), Vietnam veteran William Broyles Jr. suggests that "[t]he power of war, like the power of love, springs from man's heart. The one yields death, the other life. But life without death has no meaning; nor, at its deepest level, does love without war . . . It is no accident that men love war, as love and war are at the core of man . . . War, like death, is always with us, a constant companion, a secret sharer."[25] He further declares that war is "for men, at some terrible level the closest thing to what childbirth is for women: the initiation into the power of life and death" and that men who do not go to war "now have a sort of nostalgic longing for something they missed, some classic male experience, the way some women who didn't have children worry they missed something basic about being a woman."[26] By figuring war as "the core of man," Broyles denies true masculinity to any man who does not participate in it (just as he and many others deny "true" womanhood to women who do not give birth). With his summation of war as the "classic" rite of manhood, Broyles obscures the fact that only about 8 percent of America's draft-age men served in Vietnam, and only about 3 to 6 percent served in combat.[27] Thus, according to his logic, about 92 percent of Vietnam-generation males are not truly men. And by denying true masculinity to the overwhelming majority of American men, he subtly encouraged male fears of the loss of masculine privilege already present in Reagan America. Hoping somehow to regain the masculinity out of which they had supposedly been cheated, male audiences became even more hungry for film and print narratives of the Vietnam War experience, consuming insatiably not only the countless oral accounts and memoirs, but also the revisionist films.[28] Such accounts appealed to nonveteran men because they attested to this true "core" of masculine identity—the privileging of which the women's movement contested and was accused of having "stolen."

However, at the same time that Vietnam-generation men tried to recover an experience they had missed (or in the case of younger audiences, imbibed as eagerly as their fathers had World War II films), the film and print accounts confronted them with the message that no civilian (or even more pointedly, no one who had not experienced combat in Vietnam) could truly understand the war.[29] According to Broyles, the "specialness" of the veteran's experience cocoons him so that no civilian is allowed to question his actions; he writes about the war story, "Its purpose is not to enlighten but to exclude. Its message is not its content but to put the listener in his place. I suffered, I was there. You were not. Only those facts matter. Everything else is beyond words to tell."[30] This assertion of the civilian's unavoidable ignorance precludes him or her from questioning the politics and morality of war itself, for to do so would be to make judgments about an experience of which civilians can have no true knowledge.

Thus, the early revisionist films of the eighties not only rewrote the war so that America could "win it" through the rescue of POWs, but they also encouraged the process of valorizing the veteran as a noble man who was a double victim of his government, sent to fight a war he could not win, then abandoned when the war became inconvenient. He became a man hauntingly traumatized by his war experience, yet because of it, he occupied a higher moral plane than nonparticipants, especially the feminized men who had actively resisted the war—figured as the core of manhood. It was during this period that the veteran began to be seen as the only "authentic" spokesperson for the war, and it was the figure of the veteran as both hero and *victim* that enabled a revision of the war itself into a "noble" cause[31] and, as Jeffords argues, a concurrent "remasculinization of America."

The Late Eighties: Revision Goes Big Budget

The influx of veteran films of the early eighties, together with influence of the hawkish Reagan administration, opened the door for a more thorough filmic approach to the Vietnam War.[32] For aside from *The Deer Hunter* and *Apocalypse Now*, no widely seen films were actually set during the war; the early eighties films—the *Rambo* trilogy, *Uncommon Valor*, and the like—while retuning to Vietnam, all took place in the postwar years. These films were also notably "low-brow"—heavy on physical action, muscle-bound male bodies, and jingoistic rhetoric while light on plot, character development, and realism. However, the fiscal success of these films proved the American public's willingness to revisit the topic of the Vietnam War, and big-name filmmakers began to make serious Vietnam War films with high production value.[33] Such films include *Platoon, Hamburger Hill, Full Metal Jacket, Casualties of War, Born on the Fourth of July,* and *Heaven and Earth.* Several of these films are adaptations of the literary works discussed earlier, and the remainder of this chapter will compare those films with their literary counterparts. I will show the specific moments of erasure and rewriting that successfully allow audiences to forget sexual abuse against women, abuse to which literature had explicitly witnessed and explored.

Platoon

Oliver Stone's *Platoon* (1986) hit the American market with a huge splash. Garnering critical accolades, four Academy Awards (including best film and best director), and the praise of often-finicky veterans, the film ushered in a new era of Vietnam War filmmaking. Capitalizing on the now popular belief that only a veteran could "authentically" speak on the war, *Platoon's* advertising campaign stressed that its writer-director was "a decorated infantryman who spent fifteen months in Vietnam."[34] MGM went so far as to claim that Stone's was, in fact, "the first *real* film about Vietnam."[35] Although Stone's Vietnam film (it eventually became the first of his Vietnam War trilogy) was not adapted from literary sources as were his two later films but from his own experiences, it is necessary to analyze this early effort, for the importance of *Platoon* to all subsequent Vietnam War films cannot be overstated. As Andrew Martin argues, Stone demonstrated that filmmakers no longer needed to worry over the political implications of Vietnam, for he provided them a "usable past . . . in the codes set forth" in *Platoon* (p. 131). Dubbed a "noble grunt" film by critics, *Platoon* began the trend of microcosmically focusing on the individual soldiers of the war much like the realistic novels discussed in chapter 4. With their myopic concentration, these films ignored the political machinations behind the war, the reasons it was lost, and the long-term devastation wreaked on the countries in which it was fought; rather, they focused on combat and "war as hell" (for the soldier). Featuring ensemble casts without well-known stars (like the De Niros and Brandos of the seventies films), the soldiers of *Platoon* and its imitators were ordinary, unlike the superman-soldiers of earlier Vietnam films. Yet the "noble grunt films," as they came to be called, arrived at the same conclusion as their predecessors: the American soldier was a victim. The formula worked so well in *Platoon* that, as Martin says, "[t]he masculinity of war—shot through with the melodramatic tropes of male rivalry and . . . oedipalized rites of passage, and concluding with a nod in the direction of the tragic waste of it all—would now, in the late 1980s, become the conventional way of constructing the Vietnam War in American culture" (p. 131).

In addition to *Platoon*'s redevelopment of the Vietnam War soldier as a typical American kid, another important feature is its extraordinary use of the trope of friendly fire. For not only the metanarrative but also the storyline of *Platoon* is centered on friendly fire—the accidental or purposeful killing of Americans by Americans. Two sergeants, whom the film's protagonist, Chris Taylor (Charlie Sheen), refers to as "two fathers," struggle for Taylor's soul. The kind-hearted, "good" sergeant is killed by the brutal, "evil" sergeant, and Taylor must ultimately kill the "evil" sergeant. Beyond this personalized occurrence of friendly fire, the trope further plays itself out in the final, apocalyptic battle in which Taylor's captain calls for an air strike on his company's own position in order to destroy the NVA who have invaded his encampment's perimeter. Figured as one long incident of friendly fire, Taylor's voiceover summation of the war at the film's conclusion makes perfect sense, "I think now looking back that we did not fight the enemy, we fought ourselves and the enemy was within us."

While today this friendly fire rhetoric seems benignly naturalized, its consequences are nonetheless pernicious. To suggest that the true battle was between Americans reduces the war and the Vietnamese to mere metaphors. It becomes a myth—dehistoricized—and its mythical status allows Americans to forget the historical and political realities of the war. Forgotten are the horrible consequences of the war for the working class and people of color, who were drafted, fought on the front lines, and died in much larger proportion than they should have. Even more thoroughly erased are the costs of the war to the

Vietnamese: incredible numbers of people killed, missing, displaced, and exiled; agricultural lands and industry devastated; cities destroyed; and the proliferation of sociological problems ranging from prostitution to unwanted interracial children.[36] Moreover, by erasing the United States's real enemy—the NVA and NLF—such works deny, as the revisionist films did differently, that the United States actually lost the war, since America only fought itself. Denying the true enemy and that enemy's victory allowed America to retain the mantle of righteousness that its military superiority supposedly confirmed.

In *Friendly Fire: American Images of the Vietnam War* (2000), Kinney unravels the significance this trope has had for American culture and narratives of the Vietnam War. She makes the undeniable claim that the repetitious image of Americans killing Americans is "virtually the only story that has been told by Americans about the Vietnam War" (p. 4). Similar to my argument that the erasure of Vietnamese women's rape has been necessary in the preservation of American ideals of militarized masculinity, Kinney contends that the ubiquity of friendly fire in Vietnam War representation reflects the war's deep connection to the contemporary domestic challenges to American authority, such as women's liberation, black power, and Chicano movements. As American world hegemony was apparently breaking down in the jungles of Vietnam, the categories—race and gender—that defined and upheld that power were concurrently being attacked domestically. Thus, the fraggings and other incidents of friendly fire so frequent in Vietnam War literature and film represent not the Vietnam War so much as the domestic battles being waged. Though friendly fire tropes might therefore be seen as subversive of traditional American categories of meaning, Kinney suggests that ultimately such a metaphor merely reinstates Slotkin's pattern of "regeneration through violence." In *Platoon*, for example, it is through the violent murder of his "father" that the protagonist achieves a more refined knowledge. For as Taylor continues in the voiceover at the end of the film (literally on a higher plane as he rises in a helicopter), "those of us who did make it have an obligation to build again, to teach to others what we know, and to try with what's left of our lives to find a goodness and meaning to this life." Born again through violence, Taylor is ready to return home and share his message with others.

Building on Kinney's claims, the argument of this project is that the trope of friendly fire in film is often particularly used to obscure and lessen the significance of sexual violence against women. Even when films include violence against women, these incidents primarily reveal the conflicts between soldiers rather than demonstrating the military's widespread acquiescence to the abuse of women or investigating soldiers' motivation to commit such acts. *Platoon* provides an excellent example of how rape is erased by the foregrounding of friendly fire; with strategic scene placement, fast-paced editing, and sublimated content, Stone emotionally and visually denies viewers the ability to process war rape, even as he films it. Just prior to *Platoon*'s rape scene, Stone confronts viewers with one of the most gut-wrenching scenes in all of Vietnam War film. Taylor, angry and afraid when his platoon finds guns and ammunition in a village, discovers a mentally handicapped Vietnamese man hiding with his mother in their home bunker. Rage overtaking him, Taylor rapidly fires his machine gun at the man's only foot (he is an amputee), forcing him into a macabre dance. As the mother pleads in Vietnamese for the soldiers to leave her son alone, Taylor screams obscenities and continues firing. This sickeningly misplaced display of American power horrifies viewers as it is meant to. Even after Taylor regains control of himself, realizing with revulsion his own capacity for atrocity, he and viewers watch agape as a fellow soldier completes the trajectory of brutality initiated by Taylor. The soldier viciously bashes in the Vietnamese man's head with his rifle—callously exclaiming about the novelty of seeing human brains—and then shoots the now prostrate old mother. The horrifying impact of this scene cannot be exaggerated.

After the draining experience of watching Taylor's descent into animalism, Stone's fast-paced editing leaves viewers no opportunity to regroup their emotions or analytic capacities before encountering the subsequent scenes of soldiers' burning the village, murdering occupants, and finally raping a woman. In fact, after the horror show of Taylor's ghoulish demand that the amputee "Dance, fucker, dance!" everything after feels like denouement. Emotionally depleted and dazed, it is possible for viewers to miss the rape entirely, especially as the film's *mise-en-scene* and camerawork obscure it. Following Taylor as he polices up the villagers while the platoon destroys their homes, the camera suddenly focuses on a group of soldiers (identified at this point in the film as the "bad seeds"), who are standing in a tight knot. Viewers hear the cries of a Vietnamese girl, though with the wails continuously raised in the background, viewers do not realize at first that anything special is afoot. When Taylor rushes to the men and screams, "Get the fuck off, you fucker . . . Don't do it, don't do it," shoving the men, it becomes apparent that *something* is happening, though it is still not clear what. Attentive viewers might notice the flash of a soldier's bare legs when Taylor pushes him onto his backside, indicating the soldier's dropped pants. As Taylor continues berating his fellow soldiers, the camera catches the merest glimpse of a Vietnamese woman's naked body, blocked instantly from the screen by Taylor's movement. Though focusing on the young girl who was screaming earlier (presumably the victim's younger sister), never does the camera reveal the face of the violated woman. Even at the scene's end, as Taylor grasps both of the girls protectively by their necks, their heads remain bent, and when the camera zooms in for a close-up of Taylor's face, only their tousled black hair is visible in the bottom of the frame, visually accenting their peripheralism even as they are ostensibly the subject.

Besides the visual absence of both the sexual violence and the rape victim, mention of "rape" is conspicuously missing from the dialogue. Instead, the already exhausted audience must piece the rape together from elliptical dialogue. Taylor screams at the men not to "do it," leaving the "it" unexplained, and to "get off," rather than "Get off *her*"; these omissions and obfuscations verbally erase the rape even as it occurs. Because the men complain that "she's only a fucking dink," viewers may realize that the subject of the fracas is a woman. Taylor accuses the men of being "fucking animals," but he does not explain why. As these quotations demonstrate, instead of directly addressing the sexual nature of the crime, Stone sublimates sexual violence into the language of the dialogue instead. In this brief scene—approximately fifty-four seconds long—the word "fuck" in various forms is used fourteen times. Even in Vietnam War films and literature, in which this sexualized word is a favored expletive, such prolific usage is unusual and therefore meaningful.

While I certainly do not advocate a voyeuristic exploitation of rape for the titillation of audiences, I argue that Stone's portrayal of the rape is so muted and understated as to be nearly invisible. Numbed viewers may even miss the fact that a rape even occurred, instead interpreting it as yet another scene of Americans' abusing Vietnamese villagers and squabbling with each other. Building on Kinney's argument, I suggest that Stone's obfuscation of this crime's sexual nature is proof neither of his directorial incompetence nor his sensitivity to rape victims; rather the camera work and dialogue in the scene as well as the force of the entire film suggest that this rape was muted intentionally so as not to distract from the scene's real import. For the rape ultimately functions as a stage on which Stone shows audiences that Taylor has not lost his humanity after all, despite the horrible act he committed just moments before. Moreover, the scene is yet another example of Americans' fighting Americans—Taylor's conflict with the rapist-soldiers is meant to be a literal fight, but also symbolic of America's and humanity's struggle with its "dark side" during the moral chaos of war. Stone is not interested in unraveling rape's causes or portraying the astonishingly wide extent of this crime, either in the film or in his personal life. In one interview about his own war experience, Stone offhandedly tacked onto the end of a somewhat lengthy list of heroic exploits he committed on behalf of his fellow soldiers, "And I saved villagers from being killed when I could, or raped."[37] His mention of these atrocities does not register the surprise or horror of most veterans' recollections, either at civilian killing or rape; Stone apparently broaches the topic only in order to display evidence of his miraculously intact moral compass, as the rape scene's placement in *Platoon* similarly does for Taylor.

Indeed, Stone's use of the rape as a site of conflict between Americans—if audiences are careful enough to realize the scene involves a rape—is itself misleading. In Stone's version, the normalized American soldier attempts to stop the rape, but in the majority of American accounts of war rape, soldiers rarely recall trying to prevent or halt rapes. Instead, these veterans either openly admit to "taking their turn," or they speak of passively or helplessly watching. Rather than sites of American conflict, rapes actually functioned as gruesome moments of American bonding, building on the way recruits were encouraged to relate to each other via verbal abuse of women in basic training. Take for instance, one of the most terrible incidents related in Mark Baker's *Nam*. In this excerpt, a veteran describes how his unit stopped a Vietnamese man and his daughter. On searching the civilians, the soldiers found a can of pears, which the man explained had been given to him by a GI. Being field soldiers, they did not get many "luxuries" such as canned fruit, and the fact that a Vietnamese peasant possessed what they were being denied enraged them. So, they said,

> "The GIs gave you pears? Oh, yeah? For that, we're going to screw your daughter" . . . She was crying. I think she was a virgin. We pulled her pants down and put a gun to her head.
>
> Guys are taking turns screwing her. It was like an animal pack. "Hey, he's taking too long to screw her." Nobody was turning their back or nothing. We just stood on line and we screwed her . . .
>
> We turned back to the father and we said, "So you got pears. GIs are nice enough to give them to you" . . . So we ripped up [his] ID card. "Hey, we got a VC here, fellas. A VC stealing government stuff, huh? So you must be an infiltrator." We shot him . . .
>
> Baby-san [the daughter], she was crying . . . Then we start pumping her with rounds. After we got finished shooting her, we started kicking them and stomping on them. That's what the hatred, the frustration was. After we raped her,

> took her cherry from her, after we shot her in the head, you understand what I'm saying, we literally start stomping her body . . . Then we start cutting the ears off. We cut her nose off. The captain says, "Who's going to get the ears who's going to get the nose? So-and-so's turn to get the ears."[38]

Even when soldiers did not actively participate in the war rapes—did not become part of the "animal pack"—they rarely tried stop them. One speaker in Baker's collection offers a reason for this. After describing a rape his friends had almost committed, the speaker says, "I don't know what I would have done if I had been faced with that sort of thing. I don't think I would have taken part in it, but I also don't think I would have tried to stop it. That would have been encouraging your own sudden death. These are the guys who get in fire fights with you. It would have been too easy to get blown away" (p. 190).

Thus, according to veterans' oral accounts, raping Vietnamese women, rather than functioning a divisive event for American soldiers as Stone suggests, in reality provided the soldiers a monstrous bonding opportunity. They literally became a pack with one mind—the teller of the pear story likens his unit to a pride of lions as they kicked and mutilated the body of the murdered girl. And according to the second speaker, disapproving soldiers were unlikely to voice their misgivings about such rapes precisely for *fear* of "friendly fire." Keeping its complete reversal of this situation in mind, the rhapsodized realism of Stone's film seems suspect. While preserving the façade of reality by apparently being open and honest about the terrible atrocities, such as rape, that occurred in the war, Stone nonetheless denies the typical outcome and motivation of such violences by having Taylor, his normalized American soldier-hero defend the girl, rather than joining the rape or watching helplessly.

From Rape Victim to Prostitute: Full Metal Jacket

The year 1987 saw an enormous number of Vietnam War films claiming realism more or less in the mold of *Platoon,* among them *Hamburger Hill; The Hanoi Hilton; Good Morning, Vietnam;* and *Full Metal Jacket.* The films took their cue from Stone's serious treatment of the war, rather than the comic-book heroics of the *Rambo* and *MIA* films. Stanley Kubrick's *Full Metal Jacket* (1987) has ultimately garnered the most attention of the more "realistic strain of Vietnam films";[39] it is based on Hasford's *The Short-Timers* and, despite some interpersonal conflict, adapted for the screen by Kubrick, Hasford, and Michael Herr (Vietnam War correspondent and author of *Dispatches* [1977]). Two important points prevent

Jacket's being classed unproblematically with these other "realistic films." First, Kubrick's Brechtian techniques of distancing to "make strange" are the polar opposite of the film techniques of *Platoon* and its ilk, which encourage—even demand—deep identification with their protagonists. Kubrick's distancing results in flat, nonrealistic characters much like the "mannequin figures" of the novel from which they were adapted. Second, as the use of Brechtian techniques indicates, this film puts forth a different view of the war, one that is more openly negative rather than ambiguously "descriptive." While viewers have claimed that *Platoon* is an antiwar film, it along with the other "buddy" war films from every era—with their focus on the exploits of individual soldiers—ultimately glorify war, even as they attest to the human waste and carnage inherent in it. *Jacket*, however, is meant to be an antiwar film, with an explicitly critical—though unnuanced and facile—look at American intervention. In fact, many critics sniped about the film's "overt" antiwar message, though this says more about the conservatively hawkish cultural attitudes of the eighties than the film's ideological content. The British *Observer*'s review of the film claimed that audiences would "receive [their] regular, liberal anti-war inoculation," and the *New Yorker* asserted that *Jacket* supplied "a neat parcel of guilt," in contrast to *Hamburger Hill*, which the reviewer extolled for its portrayal of boys who "fight because their country tells them to fight . . . and the movie['s] respec[t] [for] their loyalty to each other."[40]

However, many have made the argument that even explicitly antiwar films finally serve to promote war through their presentation of it as an attractive and enjoyable spectacle (attractive and enjoyable, or audiences would not watch), and this argument certainly applies to *Jacket*. Anthony Swofford, a combatant in the first Gulf War, specifically points to Kubrick's Vietnam film as part of the "warnography" so important to promoting militarized masculinity among American boys. He claims that although "[t]here is talk that many Vietnam films are antiwar, that the message is war is inhumane and look what happens when you train young American men to fight and kill . . . actually, Vietnam war films are all pro-war, no matter . . . what Kubrick or Coppola or Stone intended." For soldiers and soldiers-to-be "watch [those] films and are excited by them, because the magic brutality of the films celebrates the terrible and despicable beauty of their fighting skills. Fight, rape, war, pillage, burn. Filmic images of death and carnage are pornography for the military man; with film you are stroking his cock, tickling his balls with the pink feather of history, getting him ready for his First Fuck. It doesn't matter how many Mr. and Mrs. Johsnsons are antiwar—the actual killers who know how to use their weapons are not."[41] Beyond the inherent inability to speak effectively against war-as-spectacle to which Swofford points, Kubrick's adaptation of *The Short-Timers* eviscerates much of the meat of Hasford's scorching analysis even as it attempts to capture the novel's critique. In particular, changes made to women's roles and the soldiers' interactions with them are especially important in the "toning down" of Hasford's narrative, making it palatable to the American public. Thus, even in what is probably the most thoughtful of Hollywood's Vietnam War films, the sexual abuse of women—and its roots in basic training—are erased from the story.

As discussed in the preceding chapter, Hasford's novel makes explicit basic training's dependence on the absolute degradation and destruction of women, revealing in the later sections of the novel the real, physical consequences this has for the women who fall prey to the soldiers in country. Kubrick's film depicts the drill instructor's degradation of recruits as women and queers as in the novel; it also underscores basic training's mixing of sex and violence via the rifle-gun chant with a very memorable scene in which the recruits march through their barracks to the cadence "this is my rifle, this is my gun, one is for fighting, and one is for fun," dressed in their white skivvies and grasping their crotches in one hand and their weapons in the other. However, the detrimental effects of such a linkage remain unexplicated by the film. Perhaps having difficulty translating Hasford's magical realism to the screen, Kubrick leaves out the novel's fantastic elements, such as the speaking rifles. Certainly Joker's sanity and thus his trustworthiness as a narrator are never doubted, as they are in the novel. Also as a consequence of Kubrick's excision of nonrealistic elements, the film's Leonard does not develop the same relationship with Charlene, his rifle. His love for "her" is left out entirely; the murder-suicide he commits is depicted simply as an unstable, feeble-minded man's reaction to the cruelly brutal treatment of Gerheim and the other recruits, rather than a lover's jealous rage.

Thus, while Kubrick demonstrates the cruelty of basic training tactics, he represses the gendered specificities of these strategies, which demand a destruction of the feminine and cancerously links sex and violence. As I argued in chapter 4, the lethal nature of rifle-love is essential to Hasford's critique of basic training, as he traces its ultimate consequences for women in Vietnam. Kubrick's failure to incorporate fully the sex/violence link reduces his critique of military training tactics to a mere complaint of over-zealous brutality, rather than a demonstration of a dangerous and defective ideology of gender division. Furthermore, the film's emphasis on Leonard's mental deficiency subtly suggests that his personal inadequacy caused the training to fail, again brushing aside Hasford's claim that basic training is fundamentally flawed. In the end,

Kubrick incorporates those aspects of the novel's basic training section that emphasize its brutality and create the most memorable, visceral scenes. However, when such scenes appear in isolation from the other events of Hasford's novel, they form only a half-critique, which may even bolster dangerous myths about the military. Gone are the ominous suggestions that basic training is a kind of "suburban death camp." Instead the film replaces Hasford's intimation of neofascist production with the suggestion that only the mentally and physically tough (the "real" men) can and deserve to make it through basic training, denying the military's destructively misogynist ideology.

Jacket's unwillingness to develop the full and deadly consequences of basic training is apparent in the alterations to the in-country portion of the film. While the film portrays Animal Mother as viciously murderous toward his fellow soldiers and the Vietnamese enemy, it edits out his predilection for raping and/or butchering young Vietnamese girls. The film similarly jettisons Mother's equation of killing women and raping them. This whitewashing of Mother functions not only as a simple act of erasure of American sexual crimes in Vietnam, however. As Jeffords notes, Kubrick's omission regarding Animal Mother's behavior toward women is consequential for our understanding of Joker's subsequent killing of the film's female sniper, who is a conflation of both of the novel's snipers (the female sniper and the unseen sniper of the book's final episode). Recall that, in the novel, because the killing of the female sniper follows the discussion of Mother's "blowing [a girl's] motherfucking face off" as an equally erotic substitute for raping her, Joker's shooting of the female sniper has sexual overtones. He, too, has shot a woman in the face, effectually raping her in Animal Mother's equation of sex and violence. In the film, however, because there has been no discussion of Animal Mother's sexual exploits, there is likewise no suggestion that Joker's killing of the sniper is in any way sexual. This omission thus further undermines Hasford's insightful critique of masculinist basic training techniques that are based on the linkage of sex and violence and demand the destruction of the feminine. The trajectory of violence Hasford so carefully drew from the sexual indoctrination in basic training to the sexual violence committed upon innocents is equally carefully erased from the film.

Additionally, the encounter between Joker and the sniper, which forms the climax of the film, rewrites through the prostrated female body the entire outcome of the war. In the novel, Joker's final encounter with the unseen sniper involves his refusal to carry out a heroic (and suicidal), John Wayne-worthy rescue of his downed comrade. Instead, he reverses the conventional Hollywood soldierly action by shooting dead his best friend, Cowboy. With this conclusion, Hasford bluntly disavows the masculine codes of honor that have long been used to glorify war. Kubrick's film, however, ignores the novel's final scene, instead concluding with the scene of Joker and his comrades' triumph over the female sniper. By amputating Hasford's ultimate scene, Kubrick avoids blaspheming against the long-treasured ideal of the noble soldier, an ideal he preserves even in this "anti-war" film. Moreover, this ending rewrites the outcome of the war, showing the Americans as dominant, hovering over the body of the dead Vietnamese girl-soldier. As Lorrie Goldensohn persuasively argues, "For Kubrick and for Hollywood, heroic masculinity demands the presence of a subjugated female to displace the center of quarreling warrior brothers and, if not the confirmation of heroic rescue, than [sic] at least its elision. And once again the most unpleasant realization is dodged: that the Vietnamese enemy, undertechnologized and frequently feminine, won over superior American force."[42]

Similar to the way in which the film shows the military's use of sex in basic training, but refuses to reveal the negative consequences of its use, so it incorporates the novel's running joke between Cowboy and Joker about Cowboy's sister—who functions as an acceptable object of mediation for the two men's homosocial, and possibly erotic, desire. Importantly, however, the film omits Cowboy's final confession that his sister never existed. This omission obscures Joker and Cowboy's use of the sister as a *metaphorical* buffer. The negotiation of male relationships via women is never subjected to scrutiny, and the potential for disruptive male-male desire is never broached. Instead of Hasford's careful revelation of the true nature of Cowboy and Joker's relationship, which critiques American standards of masculinity that require such mediation of male relationships to make them acceptable, the film's audience receives merely a restatement of the very masculine ideals Hasford questions. The mediation of male relationship via the sister's sexuality is presented as innocuously acceptable and even desirable. Kubrick uncritically presents Cowboy's trading of his "sister's" body as humorous and evidence of the soldiers' safe "buddy" relationship.

Full Metal Jacket does not only omit important incidents concerning women, however. It also invents another, different kind of woman. Hasford's novel is unusual for Vietnam War literature in that it includes no prostitutes; *Jacket* remedies this "problem" by inventing two. The film's in-country half opens with the first of these prostitutes. The woman's garish Western clothing and her vulgar pandering represent her as a corrupter and an extremely unsympathetic character. Her infamous dialogue, including the lines, "Me so horny. Me fuckee, fuckee. Me love you long time," builds on and reinforces stereotypes about Asian woman as prostitutes, and her infantile use of English suggests her mental inferiority to the Americans she propositions. Even more, the childlike quality of her diction juxtaposed with her speech's very adult content seems almost pedophilic and certainly revolting. The second prostitute is not as obnoxious as the first one; however, rather than having much consequence in itself, her appearance is designed to afford the film opportunity to reveal racism between male soldiers within the military. Similar to the rape scene in *Platoon*, the disgusting and insulting struggle between *Jacket*'s white and black soldiers over who gets first rights to the prostitute provides a stage on which to show another kind of "friendly fire" rather than to reveal anything about the terrible suffering of women under the widespread prostitution for which the American military was almost solely responsible.

Both of these prostitutes precede the female sniper from the last part of the film and contextualize her appearance. As Jeffords insightfully notes, after the film's female sniper is killed, one of the squad members looks down at her and says, "No more boom-boom[43] for this baby-san," a phrase not in the book and the language of which links this woman warrior to the prostitutes seen earlier (p. 177). No longer a "grunt" equal to the American soldiers she has killed and who kill her, as is the novel's sniper, this woman is reduced in status to a prostitute. In this way then, Kubrick and his scriptwriters retool Hasford's sexualization of the sniper-killing (recall that in the novel, Joker's killing of the sniper is sexualized because of the sex-killing linkage made explicit by Animal Mother). *Jacket* safely transforms the female sniper from a victim of American sexual violence to a prostitute. Because of prostitution's transgressive nature, the woman is deserving of her death. Additionally, the conflation of the deadly sniper with the prostitutes echoes and justifies American soldiers' fear of women (in Vietnam, rumors proliferated of women, especially prostitutes, who bore weapons in their vaginas to destroy an unsuspecting soldier's penis). Thus, *Jacket*, in its adaptation, does what so many Hollywood films do—shows sexual contact between American soldiers and Vietnamese women as consensual and mercenary; ultimately, it suggests that all Vietnamese women were, in the end, prostitutes.

One might simply chalk these changes up to the difficulties inherent to filmic adaptation. Despite the fact that all film adaptations must abridge their stories and use the formal devices available to their medium, which are quite different than those of written narrative, I submit that such adaptation nonetheless affords the perfect opportunity to study how Vietnamese women's stories are transformed. For, by looking at who and what get omitted and incorporated (not to mention who/what is added), one can see the moments of erasure and transformation in remembering the war. This does not only apply to the film's portrayal of women, however. For example, many other incidents are left out of *Jacket,* the inclusion of which would have resulted in a much more radical critique of the war and the military; however, these also would have been very difficult images to sell to a public who had been urged for the last decade to believe that Vietnam was not an unjust war. Surely audiences would not have responded well to images of American soldiers' cannibalizing their dead and souveniring body parts or to constant comparisons of Americans to Nazis in terms of propaganda, ideals, and activities.

This consciousness of audience desire, as well as the need for the filmmakers and studio to make a profit, which results from an audience's responding well to a film, is a driving force in what is shown in film. Kubrick was undoubtedly conscious of the commercial aspect of his art. Timothy Corrigan even suggests that Kubrick's career is exemplary of the way in which film's interaction with literature became, from the late seventies onward, "more blatantly enmeshed in the commercial shapes that determined their artistic possibilities. The value and meanings of . . . film . . . [were] increasingly determined by [its] status as [a] saleable commodity[y]." In 1980, Kubrick's adaptation of Stephen King's *The Shining* marked a change in the filmmaker's previous "auterist experiments to collaborate with and creatively remake the literary as filmic." Though initially excited by Kubrick's desire to film his novel, King became increasingly angry at Kubrick's rewriting and particularly with the casting of Jack Nicholson to play the lead; Kubrick explained that this choice was economic as Nicholson was "bankable," but this marketability was no consolation to King who saw the film "as a beautiful image emptied of its inner meaning."[44]

However, the success of Kubrick's earlier films, including the bitterly antiwar *Paths of Glory* (1957) and *Dr. Strangelove* (1964), an edgy condemnation of superpower behavior during the Cold War, indicates that something more than concern for commercial success was at stake in his conventionalization of his Vietnam War film. Specifically, it is important for this project to note that one of the main themes Kubrick jettisons is that of woman abuse and basic training's teaching of it. Not only does Kubrick's film eliminate these themes, but he takes the further step of replacing abused women—victims—with prostitutes, who are then presented as corruptors of American innocence. Such a move denies the military's reliance on the repression of the feminine in the making of the soldier and the deadly consequences such a construction of militarized masculinity has on women. Perhaps even more important than mere denial of women's abuse, the film's revision of the feminine in Hasford's novel allows Kubrick to present an account of the war in which Americans dominate, thus adding *Full Metal Jacket* to the ever-growing tradition of Hollywood films refighting—and winning—the Vietnam War. For after the climax involving the killing of the female sniper, the soldiers march off, dirty and soiled by the war, but holding their weapons high and walking in formation. They have survived the terrible battle for Hue, and the film's final shot suggests they will survive and dominate the war. Based on the area in which he chose to undercut Hasford's critique—the condemnation of an oppressively masculinist ideology—I argue that Kubrick's conventionalization was part of the national move to restore masculine ideals and American dominance, even as he suggests Vietnam was the wrong environment in which to enact these ideals. In doing so, the film mirrored and supported trends in national culture to shore up masculinity against the advancements made by the women's movement in the previous decade.

Containing the Threat: War Rape as Social Deviance in Casualties of War

In 1989, Brian De Palma added to the ever-growing list of Vietnam War films with his drama *Casualties of War*, based on Andrew Lang's 1969 report, which was discussed in chapter 3. Lang details the terrible events that occurred in Vietnam during a 1967 reconnaissance patrol by an army squadron. This squad kidnapped, gang raped, and murdered a Vietnamese girl named Phan Ti Mao. Lang reports not just on the rape and murder, but also on the only partially effective attempts of Sven Eriksson—the one squad member who refused to participate in the gruesome crimes—to see the responsible men punished. Lang's book was strictly journalistic, very different in narrative form and devices as well as in scope from Hasford's *The Short-Timers*. This almost certainly made Lang's work simpler to adapt for the screen, and one notices far fewer overt changes from the original story to the film. One might wonder then, how a movie whose sole purpose is to depict the horrific kidnapping, rape, and murder of a Vietnamese woman—and that closely represents the originally reported facts—can be accused of erasing or mitigating the importance of Vietnamese women's sexual abuse in the war. I would suggest that several important details added to or omitted from the film, as well as the adjustments to fit Eriksson's story into a conventional Hollywood framework, function to do just that.

To begin, whereas Lang's report picks up the story of Eriksson's squad at the moment that it is sent out on the fateful patrol, De Palma invents a Vietnam sequence as a background to the squad's actions. These early scenes ultimately justify the men's actions. First, the background sequence shows Tony Meserve (Sean Penn) heroically rescuing several men during a firefight. These scenes' lionization of Meserve is important, for it mitigates the audience's harsh feelings for him as they later see him hatching and directing the scheme to kidnap, rape, and murder the girl. Second, De Palma adds another scene in which the men see one of their favorite friends killed by enemy fire as their platoon patrols through a village. Presenting this killing as a traitorous act by supposedly friendly Vietnamese who did not warn the soldiers of a Viet Cong presence in a village, the scene justifies their hatred of the Vietnamese. Third, after the soldiers have suffered this bitter loss, they attempt to leave their camp and travel to "Dogpatch," an encampment where the men can access Vietnamese prostitutes. To their great ire, however, the soldiers are turned away by the MPs. The placement of this scene—it directly precedes the squad's crimes—suggests that if the men had been allowed to take out their anger, aggression, and sexual need upon prostitutes, the soldiers would not have plotted to abuse and murder a Vietnamese girl. By forwarding the atrocity with these invented sequences, De Palma plants a seed of justification for the events involving the Vietnamese girl. Thus, although he admirably treats the actual subject of the soldiers' brutal crimes against the girl, his preface to these crimes disables what could have been a radically critical picture by falling back into the damaging logic employed by military leaders and noted by Susan Brownmiller, that in war there shall "[*u*]*nquestionably* . . . be some raping," an attitude that assumes soldiers simply cannot control their sexual urges.

Another aspect that undermines the film's critique is De Palma's binary portrayal of Eriksson (Michael J. Fox) as the "good" squad member in contrast to the "bad" squad members. In the report, most of the soldiers who participated in the rape-murder are complex subjects whose natures do not seem to predispose them to their brutal actions.[45] Lang's readers are shocked, for instance, to read that two of the men were married, and one had a baby daughter, relationships that, in the report, normalize the men, suggesting they were not previously homicidal rapists, but family men who could and did love women. The film's audience never receives this humanizing information (which would also add greater complexity to the men's crime); rather, only Eriksson's personal life is mentioned in the film: the other men are understood only in terms of their actions within the war.

A more subtle means of strengthening the binary opposition between the "good" and "bad" squad members is the association of Eriksson with the middle class. While in Lang's book, all the squad members are revealed to be equal on the socioeconomic scale—they are working-class men from small towns, who have very limited educations; two of them are men of color—in the film version, Eriksson is solidly middle class. He speaks perfectly grammatical, unaccented English. Fox, the actor playing Eriksson, had starred in the sitcom *Family Ties* for seven years at the time of the film's release, and his televisual background conferred an air of bourgeois morality and values to the character that simply does not exist in Lang's Eriksson. Meserve, played by Hollywood bad boy Penn, on the other hand, is marked by many working-class indicators, such as his ungrammatical English spoken with a heavy, northeastern accent and his penchant for chewing tobacco. The other filmic squad members are equally nonnormative: one is Meserve's sadistic and knife-obsessed henchman; one is a mentally deficient, malleable Neanderthal; and the other is a Latino overly concerned with issues of machismo. Thus, all squad members but Eriksson are aberrations from what the film presents as the "good" American soldier, typified by Eriksson as white, middle-class, and protestant (the film mentions Eriksson's Lutheranism more than once). In this way, the film, even as it attests to the occurrence of rape, works diligently to ensure that the soldiers who committed these crimes are perceived as deviant rather than normative.

Furthermore, one of the larger purposes of Lang's narrative was to demonstrate the army's tacit approval of such atrocities as evidenced by its unwillingness to hold its soldiers accountable. De Palma, however, is more interested in Eriksson's psychological trauma and his unimpeachable character; Phan Ti Mao's rape and murder are important only insofar as they provide the stage upon which Eriksson's heroism is played. For instance, Lang's book emphasizes Eriksson's powerlessness to help the girl; Eriksson himself makes it very clear that he did not attempt to help her escape. In the film, however, Eriksson attempts to help Mao escape, even though his effort must ultimately be aborted. This addition to the film increases the audience's perception of Eriksson as a hero. Thus, De Palma's film insists on Eriksson's heroism, righteousness, and definitive action, while Lang's report suggests Eriksson's failings, as well as the ineffectualness of the individual against the behemoth military bureaucracy. Similarly, in Lang's book, Eriksson reports his fear that he had been the purposeful target of friendly fire after reporting the crime. However, this suspicion was not confirmable, for in the incident in question, Eriksson's entire platoon was fired upon, and it could not be proved that his old squadmate was the one who began the volley. The film, however, makes this questionable murder attempt concrete—and much more spectacular. In the film, Clark, the most bloodthirsty of the criminal squad members, stalks Eriksson and tosses a grenade in the latrine with him while he is alone. Eriksson escapes seconds before the latrine is blown apart. With these subtle alterations, the film transforms the largely passive Eriksson of the report to an active, heroic character: not only did he refuse to participate in the rape and murder, but he dashingly assists the victim in (a failed) escape and then withstands violent persecution in order to bring her murderers to justice. As a chronicle of a heroic individual, the emphasis of the film is on Eriksson and his trials and tribulations, rather than on bringing the atrocity itself to light and condemning the military's willingness to overlook and forgive the act.

The film's heroicizing of Eriksson and his actions necessitates the most crucial, glaring alteration of the film: ignoring the commutations of the soldiers' sentences. After watching the harrowing experience of Mao and then Eriksson as he struggles to attain justice, the film's audience finds great relief and satisfaction when the four squad members are rightfully convicted of rape and murder. While the sentences, which are flashed on the screen underneath the squad members' pictures, seem paltry prices for the soldiers' crimes, the audience cheers Eriksson's commitment to seek justice for the victim. It appears that lawfulness and American ideals have prevailed, largely due to the moral integrity and steadfast heroics of the middle-class Everyman. Never does the film's audience discover that these sentences, already ridiculously short, were commuted to less than half or overturned within two years. By omitting this vital piece of information, De Palma creates a film that willfully denies the military and the public's acceptance of the sexual abuse of women and itself participates in the erasure of such abuse. Although *Casualties of War* gives every appearance of informing the public of abuse against women, it clearly works to portray the rape of Mao as a singular event, an event that, in the film, was corrected (and correctable) because of the persistence of a normalized American soldier.

By forcing the story of Mao's rape to fit conventional narrative patterns of the heroic individual against a larger, stronger enemy, De Palma's film denies, rather than reveals, the military's acceptance of woman abuse. The film lionizes Eriksson and the middle-class morality he represents as well as lauding the power of the individual to bring about change. Further, in portraying the "bad" squadmates as nonnormalized Americans and thus inherently different from Eriksson, the film also suggests that the rape of Mao was an act of deviants. The attribution of such behavior to deviance denies the sexist and racist modes of thinking prevalent in American culture that allowed these men to believe their scheme acceptable, that allowed them to deny Mao's humanity and her right to live unviolated. Further, imputing sexual abuse of women only to deviant Americans covers over the systemic abuse of women by the American military and insinuates that no further attention to rape by the military is necessary. Knowing the true, final outcome of the story—in which rapist-murderers are given minimum punishments or acquitted entirely—gives the lie to such sentiments: the military institution does not sufficiently punish its sexual criminals, nor can individuals cause significant changes in such institutions.

Heaven and Earth: *Hayslip's Story through the Camera of Oliver Stone*

The final film I will analyze is Oliver Stone's third Vietnam-oriented production, *Heaven and Earth* (1993). Offering a different perspective from his earlier Vietnam War films, which focused on active duty soldiers and a veteran, in this film Stone adapts Vietnamese American Le Ly Hayslip's two autobiographies, in order to add the perspective of the "other side" to his filmic oeuvre. Unlike his previous Vietnam films, which enjoyed great financial and critical success, *Heaven and Earth* was a failure, both with the critics and with popular audiences. Variously described as sprawling yet plotless, beautifully shot but full of visual clichés, overly long and dragging yet also frenziedly paced, the film is certainly the weakest of Stone's Vietnam films in terms of narrative structure. Despite its shortcomings, however, the film is frequently recommended to viewers as the only non-American perspective on the war offered by American cinema.[46] This reputation is precisely the reason the film is important to my project: Stone's filmic rewriting is the version of Hayslip's story most influential on American culture. And this reshaping has ideological implications, for it casts Hayslip—one of the strongest spoken, most tenacious voices in women's autobiography—as a powerless victim, diminishes her indictment of both Vietnamese and American culture for their abuse of women, and erases her plea for reconciliation between her nations.

Even as Stone attempts to be sensitive to Hayslip's story and to make the public aware of it by placing it on the big screen, he destroys her beautiful, skillfully written memoir in which the private details of her personal history provide a metaphor for the politics of her two countries. Hayslip's narrative, though organized around her sexual victimization by many types of men, reveals her not as a broken woman but an active and cunning survivor. Stone, however, transforms Hayslip into a passive victim (a move that also ruins the film's pacing). Janet Maslin, who reviewed the film for the *New York Times*, called Hayslip's "an essentially passive experience," and Marjorie Baumgarten wrote in the *Austin Chronicle* that in Stone's film, "Le Ly becomes a long-suffering heroine, first brutalized by Americans in her homeland, then further brutalized by Americans once she arrives on their shores."[47] Maslin suggests part of the reason for the film's inability to realize an active center is that by treating his "Vietnamese heroine as both sexual martyr and national metaphor, [Stone] so overburdens her story that Le Ly disappears as a real person." Thus, although Stone attempts to capture Hayslip's careful construction of her personal story as a national metaphor—this is certainly how she conceives of her first autobiography—he clumsily represents her only as a disempowered victim, much like the soldier-victims of his earlier two works.

Though Hayslip's first memoir chronicles the sexual abuse—the sexual torture, rapes, molestations, attempted rapes, and spousal abuse—she experienced during and after the war, she never represents herself as a passive victim or as lacking in agency. Rather, readers come away from her incredible story inspired by the fact that a woman can not only survive such hardships and abuse but also accomplish great things. In Stone's film, however, Hayslip becomes merely a victim for several reasons. First, Stone obscures Hayslip's early, active role as an NLF sympathizer/participant. While he does show the entire village's apparent acceptance of the NLF (which he arrogantly presents as a simple peasant people accepting the crude propaganda of the communist leaders),[48] he does not reveal that Hayslip, along with the other village children, received an education in guerilla warfare from them. They were not only propagandized but also taught to steal weapons and munitions from the ARVN soldiers who occupied their village. Hayslip herself was considered a heroine by the NLF for a clever warning she gave of incoming enemy troops; they credited her with saving many guerilla lives. This is also one of the incidents for which she was imprisoned by the Republican army, which was correctly suspicious that she had given the warning. Hayslip's work for the NLF is not portrayed in the film, however. Instead of the events described above, audiences see only Hayslip's imprisonment, which seems inexplicable and cruel. While certainly the army's imprisonment of a child, and especially its torture of her, was indeed horrific and brutal, in reality her imprisonment was not unmotivated, nor was Hayslip an innocent victim. Moreover, because the film erases Hayslip's Viet Cong activities, her refusal to give her torturers information does not result from the resolve of a politically committed subject as in her narrative, but because she is only an ignorant child with no information to give.

As Hayslip's original narration of these events is more dramatic and revealing of her strong character, one must assume that Stone felt it necessary to tone down these events for his audience. Perhaps he believed a woman who had actively worked for the NLF would still be repulsive to American audiences. Indeed, Hayslip herself had faced such criticism as she struggled to write her first autobiography. In *Child of War, Woman of Peace*, Hayslip recalls an argument she had with her husband when she told him that she wanted to write her story: "People think they know who the Viet Cong were, but they really don't." Her husband replied, "I'll tell you this: you start talking about the VC and the Commies over there and they'll take away your kids."[49] Though the state did not seize her children, Hayslip did experience many negative reactions when her first book was published in 1989, both from Americans and from the Vietnamese exile community. Hayslip, as well as the *LA Times*, which ran an excerpt from the book, received death threats and hate mail in regard to her story.[50] Thus, Stone's fear of an American audience's possible rejection of Hayslip's past alliance with the Viet Cong was probably justified; however, changing his portrayal of Hayslip's activities in deference to such concerns hides important evidence of Hayslip's activism and agency, as well as seriously impairing her books' message of reconciliation and understanding, as will be discussed later.

Similar to its presentation of the child Hayslip as a passive victim, the film's quick succession of scenes portraying Hayslip's black market career, her brief dip into prostitution, and her bargirl career do not adequately reveal the intelligence and resourcefulness she used to lift herself into these lucrative positions and then extricate herself from them when they became overly dangerous. Stone's film depicts her activities as demeaning and desperate measures taken by an outcast Hayslip. Hayslip presents this difficult time very differently in her book; readers see her as a hardworking, constantly evolving entrepreneur, who gradually gains confidence and the skills to deal with all types of people. In her memoirs, readers follow the movements of a young woman with a growing sense of self, and especially an increasing understanding of her rights to protect herself from men who believe they are entitled to her body. Stone's film erases Hayslip's development from clever child to strong woman. The very events that Hayslip presents as a series of obstacles or struggles, the overcoming of which better enables her to navigate her dangerous world, Stone positions as outside forces in which a passive and childish Hayslip becomes unwittingly caught and which sweep her along, moving her from one terrible situation to another. There is no sense that, through these struggles, Hayslip has grown, changed, or evolved over the course of the film.

Particularly germane to my argument here is Stone's treatment of Hayslip's prostitution. While in the book, Hayslip makes it clear that because of the large amount of money she was offered for prostituting herself to two men—enough to completely support herself, her mother, and her son for an entire year—she saw this as the way out of her dangerous, hand-to-mouth existence as a black marketeer. She also described the transaction as a way to strike back at the men who had taken so much from her. As I quoted earlier, "[T]o make [the money], I wouldn't even have to . . . risk going to jail or getting blown up by a mine or blown away in ambush. Just lie down and let these two American boys be men. What could they do to me that hadn't been done already? Maybe it was time some men paid me back for what other men had taken" (*Heaven*, p. 258). And though Hayslip struggles against negative feelings about the encounter, she never regrets it, for it puts her on the road to escape.

Stone's film, however, depicts a downtrodden Hayslip who submits without much struggle to what is merely a further degradation (not financial salvation for her family). Furthermore, the camera's lingering focus on Hayslip's naked toddler son, whom she leaves unattended in the dust beside the dangerously busy road when she goes with the men, impugns Hayslip's mothering. The son's presence in this scene is an insertion by Stone, for readers of her memoir know that Hayslip's mother kept her grandson at home while her daughter worked. The only purpose the gratuitous inclusion of the son serves is to paint Hayslip further as a helpless victim as well as allowing normalized Americans to feel smugly superior. For while viewers are encouraged to feel disgust at the bad mothering of which the film's Hayslip is guilty, the film's previous scenes and the viewers' sympathy for Hayslip require that they also see this as another—perhaps the primary—example of Hayslip's wartime victimization. Thus, the message of this incident in the film directly contradicts that of Hayslip's story. In her book, she makes it clear that her act of prostitution, as much as she disliked it, allowed her to secure a much safer and more profitable position in an American-run hospital, and the connections established there eventually led her to America. Thus, what Stone presents as just one more victimization of—and passive acceptance by—Hayslip, the woman herself positions as an act of vengeance that propelled her to financial safety and began her global journey.

Stone's portrayal of Hayslip's life in America continues to deny her agency. Though Hayslip records continuing abuse after her arrival in the United States—she was the victim of terrible spousal abuse, had her children kidnapped, was scammed out of several thousand dollars, and taken financial and emotional advantage of by numerous men—she also achieved great accomplishments. These achievements are left out of the film entirely or mentioned only briefly in the film's final voiceover. Though Stone alludes to Hayslip's attempts to open a deli (one of her most insignificant entrepreneurial endeavors, which failed because of the interference of her husband), this story is interrupted by scenes of her victimization at the hands of her husband, which culminates with his suicide. After Hayslip's recovery from the suicide, the film ends with her traveling to Vietnam, cutting an important, several-year span from her life. During the period withheld from the film's audience, Hayslip became an establishing partner in a successful Chinese restaurant and a wealthy real estate investor; she wrote and published her life story, traveled numerous times to Vietnam, and, after selling her interest in the restaurant, devoted her time and energy to the creation of a charity, the East Meets West Foundation, which fosters a relationship of healing between the United States and Vietnam. Never does the film suggest the extent of Hayslip's remarkable achievements. Instead, it presents her as a person of interest for her victimization and mere survival.

Besides crippling Hayslip's presentation of herself as a woman—who overcomes her continuously difficult situations and eventually comes to have a material impact on the lives of thousands of people through her work to promote understanding and healing between her countries and the individuals involved in the war—Stone enfeebles her feminist critique of the sexist cultures of which she is a part. Though Stone depicts Hayslip's rape by the NLF cadre as well as an attempted rape/extorted sexual encounter by an American man in Vietnam, this is the range of the sexual trauma she faces in the film. He does not reveal the tremendous extent of the abuse and harassment to which she was subjected at the hands of numerous men. *When Heaven and Earth Changed Places*, on the other hand, is relentless in its assertion of systemic sexual abuse, both in Vietnam and in the United States, as discussed in chapter 2. In its limited depiction of the abuse Hayslip experienced, the film denies this message.

Moreover, one of the characters who abuses Hayslip in the film is her husband, Steve (Tommy Lee Jones), a composite character Stone creates from several American men with whom Hayslip was either involved or married. In the film, Steve romantically pursues a lonely Hayslip and dramatically plucks her from the collapsing South. He seems kind and very much in love with her, but when they begin their lives in America, Steve changes. He is often unsupportive of Hayslip in the face of his racist family, and his lack of support gradually changes to abuse. The abuse culminates when he holds a rifle to Hayslip's head and then turns it on himself, threatening suicide. Viewers often cite this as the film's most powerful scene, for it ends with Steve's tearful confession of his terrible role in psy-ops warfare, which has left him unable to deal with his past. Unable to make their marriage work, Steve kidnaps the children he and Hayslip share and then kills himself. He is a perfect example of the veteran suffering from PTSD, and the "America" portion of the film is dominated by his story. Thus, even in this film about "the Vietnamese perspective," Stone cannot retrain his focus from the veteran and his ravaged psyche. Most ironic about this portion of the film, however, is the fact that according to Hayslip's memoir the real person to whom the "psy-ops" confession belonged was a conman named Cliff, a man she met only briefly and who used this story to win her trust and bilk her out of a great deal of money. Her memoirs suggest then that this story (a little too stereotypical for the initiated reader) was completely false. Stone's use of the psy-ops fabrication as the pièce de résistance for Steve's character, then, is shocking. While Hayslip's book invites a certain skepticism toward the pitiable, victimized veteran, Stone latches on to the false story to make his veteran seem exactly the pathetic victim Hayslip's book denies.[51]

Similarly, Hayslip's first autobiography is full of discussions about, and sympathy for, the women who were forced (by their situation, relatives, or enslavers) to prostitute themselves. Her narrative represents institutionalized prostitution as a horrible circumstance necessitated by Vietnam's wartime economy and its destroyed agricultural lands, which could no longer support the villagers who lived there, sending them fleeing to overcrowded cities. The only prostitutelike person, aside from Hayslip, in Stone's film is her sister Lan, renamed Kim in the film. Kim is a bargirl, and for viewers uneducated in the various jobs Vietnamese women filled during the war, she probably appears to be a prostitute, made up and dressed in skimpy Western clothing; she clearly has an American "boyfriend" who supports her in exchange for sex. Though she is Hayslip's sister, Kim is an extremely unsympathetic character, bratty to the point of cruelty, especially when she turns a very pregnant Hayslip out onto the street. She also insults her venerable father in order to keep her boyfriend. Thus, in this uncompelling representation of the "typical" prostitute, the audience does not receive Hayslip's sympathetic message about prostitutes nor her critical analysis of the roots and causes of institutionalized prostitution in wartime. Instead, the film uses this unappealing character to offset Hayslip's own meritorious qualities and to reveal Hayslip as a victim once again, persecuted even by her sister. Hayslip's own description of her sister fills a different purpose in her memoir. While Lan is equally mean, Hayslip suggests that the war changed her sister; its pressures forced Lan to support herself by unpleasant means rather than remaining at home among her family.

Hayslip contrasts the older Lan to her memories of her caring sister as a youngster. Within Hayslip's narrative, Lan's bad behavior exemplifies the wartime destruction of traditional Vietnamese culture in which family and respect for elders was the preeminent value. In Stone's film, such concerns are jettisoned, and viewers are exposed to yet another negative representation of the selfish, avaricious Vietnamese prostitute typical of Vietnam War film.

Finally, Stone's film alters the political message of Hayslip's memoirs, in which she carefully sets up a call for reconciliation between her old country and her new one. Such a call was quite radical in 1989, when her first memoir appeared. This was before movements toward normalizing relations between the United States and Vietnam had begun, and in fact, demands for the return of MIAs were still being made. Hayslip's call for reconciliation and to rebuild was perhaps even more shocking to the Vietnamese-in-exile community, many of whom still believed that the South would someday rise again, and who were training anti-Communist guerilla fighters to send to Vietnam to continue the war.[52] Even many of the exiled Vietnamese who were not so fanatically right-wing thought Hayslip was terrible to suggest laws and financial help which would aid the Communist government in Vietnam.

Hayslip's radical stance on the need for normalized relations between the countries is erased from Stone's film, however. In fact, after she comes to America, Vietnam seems far from Hayslip's concerns. As stated earlier, Steve's trauma dominates this portion of the film, and when Hayslip does regain the spotlight, the film focuses on the psychological drama of immigration. Her return visit to Vietnam, shown at the very end of the film, appears as strictly a familial visit. Hayslip's first memoir, however, is carefully drawn as an interwoven narrative, one thread focusing on her dramatic personal story of victimization, survival, and escape from war-torn Vietnam, and the other, retrospective thread more thoughtfully following a middle-aged Hayslip as she makes her first frightening journey back to Vietnam to see how her country and her family have fared. The story of her girlhood and young adulthood are punctuated with her philosophizing about the war and its effects on both her countries as she travels through Vietnam. Her epilogue, entitled "A Song of Enlightenment," explicitly calls for reconciliation and for readers to recognize the continued suffering of the Vietnamese as a direct result of the war, and through their need, she offers opportunities for American healing. Hayslip solicits any readers who have been moved by her story to contact her charity (p. 367). The book ends with contact information for aid organizations. While one would not expect Stone's film to end with a plea for charitable support, his complete dropping of Hayslip's political, social interests in rebuilding Vietnam is surprising. His interest in the "Vietnamese perspective," like that of many Americans, extends only to their wartime experience, not to a recognition of America's continuing and unfulfilled responsibilities.

Although Stone deserves some credit for his attempt to screen a Vietnamese perspective on the war, his film does a grave disservice to Hayslip's story. By clumsily forcing Hayslip's story into a combined immigrant story and victimized veteran story form, *Heaven and Earth* represents Hayslip as a passive victim, one who must be rescued by a strong American and then must learn to survive without him (which she can do because she has come to America, the land of plenty). In pressing Hayslip's story into this form, Stone's film drops her feminist critique of sexist Vietnamese and American male cultures, which leave her and other women constantly in danger of being raped and sexually abused at every turn and then condemn the women for their abuse. What is more, the film's extensive focus on the amalgamated Steve character, with his war trauma, draws audiences' attention once again to American male suffering. With this focus on Steve, Hayslip's value in the film derives from the healing she can bring to Steve, rather than what she can bring to her countries, as in her own works. Thus, the film ends by turning about itself in the hermetic circle of American rhetoric spoken of by Renny Christopher: though the film sets out to portray a Vietnamese perspective on the war, it ultimately merely sounds the same "tired notes" Americans have often heard.

In looking specifically at films adapted from literary sources—sources that are very interested in the systemic abuse of women by the military—viewers may see the particular moments this abuse is excised from or justified by film, simultaneously eradicating it as a problem from American cultural memory. By analyzing these moments of erasure, one may also recognize how such elimination serves to ameliorate the character of the Vietnam War soldier and veteran. For in all of the films discussed above, American soldiers are, on the whole, considered as victims, traumatized by a vicious war they did not ask to fight. While admitting there are some "bad apples" among the lot—such as Animal Mother in *Jacket* and Clark in *Casualties*—most soldiers are presented as hapless boys who become caught up in a situation over which they had no control. They have not irreversibly transgressed against American norms, and indeed, many soldiers redeem themselves in the films. For example, Joker's mercy killing of the Vietnamese woman seems a kindness, and

Taylor's halting the rape and his love for the "good father" equalize his momentary bad act of terrorizing the mentally handicapped amputee. At the time they were produced, these filmic redemptions encouraged a reinstatement of American benevolence toward real-life veterans. The unproblematic acceptance of veterans encouraged by the films would not be possible, however, if viewers saw the systemic abuses of women American soldiers perpetrated in these films' literary sources. This sanitization of the Vietnam veteran and the war, making them reclaimable, is an important difference between the antiwar literary sources discussed previously and the "antiwar" films adapted from them: the written narratives make no attempt to redeem American soldiers—they do not explain or justify soldiers' actions; rather they condemn them and the systems that enabled soldiers' capacity for such atrocities. Instead of trying to enhance the veterans' reputation in American culture, the literature on which these films are based asks readers to recognize America's complicity in its soldiers' actions.

Clearly, films asking viewers to recognize their own potential culpability in such actions—so heinous they do not even want to believe their soldiers capable of them—would not sit well with audiences, a fact of which filmmakers are constantly aware. As Oliver Stone told one interviewer, who had just classified Stone as "both radical and conservative," as someone whose movies "shake people up, but . . . also . . . restore the community to itself and its true story": "Movies have to make money, you've got to make them so they're exciting, they're gripping, people want to go see them . . . So how do you make it exciting to tell the story? Well first of all you have to make the character strong so that people can follow that. And then hopefully that character can integrate with the background of the social situation that people can recognize."[53] Stone thus points to the reason Vietnam War film transforms its soldiers into traumatized heroes rather than depicting them as brutal victimizers: audiences must be able to identify with the film's leading character and to recognize him as part of their own social situation in order for the film to make money, which he lists as the obvious leading concern of any Hollywood production.

The erasure, containment, and denial of American brutalization of Vietnamese women in these films—all considered respectable by popular and critical audiences and utilized by teachers of the Vietnam War—did not end with them. Predictably, the tendency toward erasure of sexual abuse and a demonization of Vietnamese women filtered to television, and television's first Vietnam War series—CBS's *Tour of Duty*, which ran from 1987 through 1990—relied on the formula set forth in the second wave of Vietnam films. The series was produced in the wake of *Platoon*'s successful revision of the war and, like the film, was premised on the concept of American soldiers in Vietnam as a lovable, though often traumatized, all-American kids. Also as in *Platoon*, friendly fire plays a primary role in *Tour of Duty*, with most episodes centering on soldiers' conflicts with other Americans, either within the platoon or between soldiers and American culture (represented by parents or antiwar protestors, for example). Never are the politics of the war seriously questioned. Ironically, the series specifically used soldiers' kindly actions toward peasant women to buttress its argument that the war and American forces were well intentioned toward the Vietnamese. The series suggests that the only harm Americans caused civilians was not gratuitous but was committed, usually accidentally, because of the terrible necessities of guerilla warfare.

Thus, Hollywood's erasure of abuse toward women has been consequential for all future representations of the war. Its portrait is reflected in television, which in turn mirrors and voices the desires of American culture. And American cultural narratives and beliefs are then reflected and voiced yet again by Hollywood. So a pernicious circle of misunderstanding and disremembering continues. Not only has the erasure of woman abuse from representations of the war enabled a sympathetic but ultimately crippling portrait of the veteran as victim, but it has also been a key part of the rewriting of the war, a rewriting that necessitated denial of the systemic abuse of women and the genocidal characteristics of the war. Though these aspects were spoken of frequently during the war and have been written of since—with a vocal segment of veterans pleading with the public to recognize the immorality of the war as well as of the social class and gender systems that prepared American boys to commit atrocities—the Hollywood productions discussed here deny the dialogue these veterans tried to begin. Operating within the confines of neoconservative, "remasculinized" culture, these films deny the damaging excesses of a militarized masculinity that is based on the destruction of whatever is considered "feminine," by erasing, justifying, or containing incidences of sexual abuse. In doing so, these films make even more difficult the creation of a healing public that can conceive of the veteran as something other than a helpless victim, making true acceptance of the veteran ever less a possibility.

Afterword

Legacies

While the Vietnam War has left varying legacies—physical, geographical destruction in Vietnam; Vietnamese American children; veterans suffering from PTSD; a (short-lived) loss of national bravado—one of the unacknowledged but enduring legacies is the sexual abuse of women by men in the military. While the abuses I have analyzed in the preceding chapters were committed mainly against "other" women, namely, Vietnamese, the same sorts of abuse continue today; now, however, as the geopolitical field has shifted, and our recent wars have occurred in Muslim-dominated areas, soldiers have been restrained for the most part from committing such abuses on the women of the countries they occupy. Instead, American soldiers now unleash their frustrations and the violent sexuality they have learned upon their fellow female soldiers. As national guardswoman Mickiela Montoya, who was deployed to Iraq, claims, "This guy out there [in Iraq], he told me he thinks the military sends women over to give the guys eye candy to keep them sane. He said in Vietnam they had prostitutes to keep them from going crazy, but they don't have those in Iraq. So they have women soldiers instead."[1]

The belief that men must be able to satisfy their sexual frustration on a woman coupled with the sexualized violence and contempt for women that soldiers are indoctrinated with during basic training creates an admixture of desire and resentment that encourages sexual assault. However, such a climate is preventable if the military as a whole would implement leadership and a new attitude that clearly shows such behavior as antithetical to its purpose. For instance, national guardsman Demond Mullins, who served in Iraq from 2004 to 2005, told *Salon.com* reporter Helen Benedict that while rapes occurred in other units in his camp, such as when a woman was raped in the shower by one soldier while a group of fellow soldiers held the door shut, no rapes occurred in his unit because his commander simply did not tolerate such behavior. Other interviewees also reported to Benedict that if commanders did not put up with the mistreatment of women, it did not occur.[2] Unfortunately, the harassment and assault of female soldiers are all too often practiced by commanders themselves, so often, in fact, that women call it "command rape." And even when commanders do not engage in such practices themselves, they often ignore or downplay the threat or violence against their female soldiers.

Such commanders both participate in and reflect the ethos of the military as a whole, which does not aggressively punish or attempt to prevent sexual assault. As noted in the introduction, from 1992 through 2002, about half of all sexual assault offenders were given administrative punishment; an average of 22 percent faced courts-martial. A substantial percentage of sexual assault case outcomes, approximately 27 percent, were simply not recorded. The shoddy record keeping in such cases again points to the military's determined ignorance on the subject and to the flawed, hierarchical justice system in which the commanders who report and order investigations of cases stand to benefit from hiding the presence of sexual assault problems.

After the *Denver Post's* series "Betrayal in the Ranks" was published in late 2003, congressional hearings on the problems of military sexual assault were held in 2004, and in response to panel findings, the Department of Defense created the Office of Sexual Assault Prevention and Response (SAPRO) in October 2005 to function as "the single point of accountability for Department of Defense (DoD) sexual assault policy."[3] The SAPR website proclaims that "the Department of Defense does not tolerate sexual assault and has implemented a comprehensive policy that reinforces a culture of prevention, response and accountability that ensures the safety, dignity and well-being of all members of the Armed Forces. Our men and women serving throughout the world deserve nothing less, and their leaders-military and civilian-are committed to maintaining a workplace environment that rejects sexual assault and attitudes that promote such behaviors."[4] Thus, it would seem that the DoD is finally at least acknowledging that there is a problem with sexual assault in the military and is perhaps willing to respond to the problem.

However, a breakdown of the DoD's most recent report on sexual assault in the military—from fiscal year 2007—reveals interesting trends that controvert its claims of "reinforc[ing] a culture of . . . response and accountability." Of the 1247 completed dispositions of male-on-female sexual assault, only eighty-seven offenders received courts-martial [within the year], only about 6.97 percent of cases. Thirty-five percent of the cases were actually closed with no action taken at all (439), and 390 cases were labeled as "pending."[5] Thus, under the newly instituted

SAPRO, the number of cases prosecuted to the fullest extent has actually *dropped* rather than climbed as one would have expected with more diligent oversight. However, the DoD's report shows that courts-martial were pursued significantly more often in cases of male-on-male sexual assault—about 15.5 percent of the time. For the very few cases of female perpetrated violence (there were nine female-on-male sexual assaults and four female-on-female sexual assaults reported), the percentage of courts-martial was also higher, 11.11 percent and 25 percent respectively. Thus, these findings suggest that the military still radically underprosecutes male-on-female violence, while being slightly more willing to prosecute male-on-male or female-perpetrated violence. The military's willingness to prosecute the much more rare female-perpetrated violence is reminiscent of Hollywood films' reversal of the Vietnamese woman's role in the Vietnam War narratives, moving her from sexual victim to sexual aggressor and despoiler of American youth. This repetition of narrative reversals reveals the importance of pinpointing such important narrative patterns in our history to increase awareness of their reoccurrence in the present.

The narratives of W. D. Ehrhart and Larry Heinemann in which they portray the negative effect military indoctrination had upon soldiers' interaction with women "on the homefront" is also an important predictor of another alarming problem facing today's military: domestic abuse. While studies of military domestic-abuse trends compared to civilian trends have been not been decisive, an early 1990s study suggested that domestic abuse might be twice as high as in the civilian world, and a 1999 study showed that army domestic-abuse cases had a tendency to be more severe than civilian cases.[6]

However it may compare with the civilian rate of abuse, domestic abuse is pervasive in the military. The *Denver Post* reporters found that "[b]etween 1997 and 2001, more than 10,000 cases of spouse abuse a year have been substantiated in the armed forces. Of those cases, 114 were homicides of adults, according to military records" (p. 20). Judy Neal-Post, an ex-military wife, points to the simple reason for this violence against women: "In the military, you are rewarded for violent behavior. This indoctrinates people to a certain state of mind, that they can do this even at home" (p. 51). She told her story to writers for the *Denver Post* after the military dropped the investigation of her ex-husband, Ross Gobel, a lieutenant colonel who attacked and choked Neal-Post during a visit to his children.

Not only is this abuse severe and frighteningly prevalent, but the military once again shows a lack of concern for the victims. When investigating domestic abuse, the *Post* reporters found "a secretive justice system tightly controlled by commanders that routinely fails to prosecute domestic-violence offenders and creates obstacles for victims, sometimes leaving them unprotected" (p. 20). Over the decade-spanning reports the *Post* reporters reviewed, even in the most severe cases—murder—military offenders were administratively punished, with demotion or letters filed in the offender's permanent record, as often as they faced courts-martial. In the 2002 case of sailor David DeArmond, who threatened his wife's life, the military did not respond to the threat he posed his wife, who had taken out a civilian restraining order on him. They did not restrict DeArmond to military barracks or provide his wife with a victim's advocate who could provide her with a safety plan. DeArmond eventually bludgeoned his wife with an iron skillet and stabbed his mother-in-law, killing both. When DeArmond was court-martialed for the murders, the charge was reduced to manslaughter and a panel of sailors sentenced him to twenty-two years, with parole eligibility in eight (p. 30).

In response to a series of domestic-abuse homicides at Fort Cambell in the late 1990s, Congress created the Defense Task Force on Domestic Violence, designed to look into the military's handling of domestic-abuse cases and make suggestions on improving the military's response to such cases (Herdy and Moffeit, p. 21). One of the committee's recommendations was that fatality reviews be conducted after domestic-abuse murders to locate the failings of the military's safety system. A year after the task force made its recommendations, Fort Bragg had a spate of five domestic-abuse homicides. Task force members contacted the secretary of defense asking that a review be set in motion; however, the secretary had already set a team in motion—not to conduct a fatality review, but to investigate the relation of the murders to the soldiers' postcombat stress (p. 25). Thus, in the same way I have argued that Vietnam veterans' medical plight of PTSD has been used to overwrite memories of civilian women's trauma in the Vietnam War, the military in this case focused attention on current veterans' PTSD to the exclusion of veteran domestic abuse. In each case, the military's attitudes and policies toward women that underwrite the criminal behavior of male soldiers are ignored in favor of a medicalized explanation of their behavior.

The American people and its military's continuing tendency to look away from the victims created by the military's training system and ethos as demonstrated by new statistics on military sexual assault and domestic abuse demonstrate the necessity of public acknowledgement of a problem with and demand for a change in the military's attitude toward and its protection of women. As a nation, we must insist that our military take responsibility for its gross negligence in relying on a basic training system that is rhetorically abusive toward women, inculcating hatred of woman as the ultimate enemy of the American military core. The ability to see and hear the current victims begins with acknowledgment that the abuse of women is a decades-old, systemic problem within the U.S. military, one that can be traced back at least to the basic training of GIs prepared for the Vietnam War.

It has been the purpose of this project to bring to light one very particular type of atrocity systemically committed by American soldiers during that war—rape and sexual abuse of Vietnamese women. I have shown how, though an important and vocal segment of veterans have themselves made attempts to publicize the routine nature of sexual abuse through testimony, literature, and oral remembrance, their American audiences—from congressional members, to the press, to literary scholars and historians—have repeatedly ignored this testimony. By tracing the erasure/containment of this atrocity in recent American reimaginings of the war via Hollywood film, it becomes clear how even this most unjustifiable of crimes becomes appropriated. Vietnamese women are, for the most part, transformed into the victimizers and corrupters of innocent American youth in Vietnam War cinema, and their aggressors become innocent victims. I would argue that this representation damages not only Vietnamese women, but also many Americans veterans; by refusing to listen and accept the trauma of guilt to which they have repeatedly borne witness, the nation continues to refuse true healing and acceptance to these veterans.

I hope that my work reveals the importance of remembering the events and policies of the war itself, as well as the war's most basic victims. A more complete picture of the male veteran is necessary than the one now embraced by the American public; however uncomfortable it is, the nation must move beyond its simplistic vision of the veteran as a victim to recognize him also as a possible aggressor, created by the multiple, often-oppressive social systems in which he was caught. I am not suggesting that America should condemn its Vietnam veterans; certainly it must not silence or ignore veteran testimony, as has been consistently patterned. Rather, new publics must be formed that can openly hear and accept the confessions of all veterans. A true acceptance of the Vietnam veteran will entail the nation's recognition of its culpability for the atrocities that occurred in the war—a far different process than the saccharine acceptance of the Vietnam veteran as the ultimate victim that occurred in the early eighties. I hope that this project may serve as an early step in bringing the histories of the true victims of the war—Vietnamese civilians—to light, as well as revealing many veterans' unsung heroism in "endur[ing] . . . mockery, . . . disgrace, [and] patriotic ridicule" to witness to the war's terrible events and their own complicity in them. By forwarding Vietnamese women's and veteran testimony and antiwar literature, I hope to reverse the trend to justify, mitigate, and erase stories of American brutality that is evident in Hollywood's filming of the war.

Onscreen depictions of the Vietnam War, while certainly not alone in erasing militarized masculinity's violent excesses or representing the veteran as a victim, have played a crucial role in the distribution of such narratives. Hollywood, as a market-driven industry, reflects what its consumers are willing to watch and hear. It seems, then, as long as Americans seem content to "remember" the Vietnam veteran only as a victim of the war (and the peace movement as a kind of brutalizer), there is little hope that the film industry will contribute any effort to correcting this faulty memory. And, as Anthony Swofford suggests in *Jarhead*, perhaps dramatic antiwar-war film is truly impossible. However, through the affordability of in-home media, mail-order services such as Netflix, and online forums such as YouTube.com, the distribution opportunities for independently produced films and documentaries have recently exploded. In this format, non-Hollywood endorsed and therefore nonmarket-driven viewpoints and narratives have found their way to the small screen, including a different kind of Vietnam War film. One such film is Barbara Sonneborn's 1998 documentary, *Regret to Inform.*

Regret to Inform records the journey of Sonneborn, widowed by the Vietnam War in 1968, to locate the area in Vietnam where her husband was killed. Although the subject of the film is Sonneborn's survival of loss and grief, her story is interwoven with those of several other American and Vietnamese war widows. In this unique "war film," there is no bloody carnage, no combat footage. Rather, it mostly consists of widows sitting quietly, often in their homes, telling of the pain the war has caused them. For the Americans, this is the pain of loss and the niggling thought that their husbands died for a purposeless—perhaps even an immoral—cause. Overshadowing the American women's stories, however, are those of the Vietnamese, upon whom Sonneborn allows her camera to linger. In these women's stories, it is clear that, while the war caused terrible pain, suffering, and loss for American women, it has been far worse for the Vietnamese women. The pain in their stories does not only stem from the uncertainty of not knowing where or how their husbands died; rather, they document the life-and-death struggles of survival in a war zone. They tell of losing, not just their husbands, but all of their children and extended families to bombing and village raids. One older woman tells Sonneborn matter-of-factly that she was lucky to be older, for the younger women lived in constant fear of being raped: "[I]f you weren't dead, you weren't safe." As one woman says, "The cruelty we experienced was longer than a river, higher than a mountain, deeper than an ocean."

The film's most moving testimony is that of Nguyen Ngoc Xuan, Sonneborn's friend and translator. Nguyen is a Vietnamese woman whose husband was killed while serving in the ARVN and who later married an American GI and became an American citizen. Like Holocaust survivors had done earlier, she recalls the hellish burden of choosing her own survival over helping others, a burden that continues to haunt her. She explains, "I decide[d] who lived and who died . . . [For several days,] my girlfriend was hiding with me [in a bunker], and she was wounded, and we don't have lots of food left. I took her portion because I'm going to live. She badly wounded, she's going to die. So I took her food for me. I'm 14 years old. Why [was] I . . . forced to make that decision like that? I don't even trust my 24-year-old son with the lawn mower sometimes. But I have to decide who's going to live and who's going to die." Like American veterans, Nguyen demonstrates that war's lasting trauma is not due to combat exposure but is a complex psychological reaction; her decision to pursue her own survival haunts her, despite her intellectual rationalization. When recalling her interactions with GIs as a prostitute, Nguyen movingly speaks of the deeply damaging inability to communicate with these men who were both her tormentors and her saviors. With a perplexity like that of the Vietnamese peasants in Hess's collection, Nguyen mournfully recalls, "Sometimes the soldier hit me, and I don't know enough English to say, 'Why do you hit me?'" She suggests, as do many veterans, that if only the Americans and the Vietnamese could have spoken, could have understood each other, so much violence would have been avoided. Sonneborn's film moves toward crossing that gulf of communication; hers is an attempt to truly allow both sides to hear and understand the voice of the other side.

In focusing its lens on the war's legacy for women, Sonneborn's film suggests that veterans are not the only subjects who have authority to speak on the war. Vietnamese and American women, the ignored and the forgotten, regain their voices, and unlike Hollywood films and realistic novels, they do not speak of war's gloriousness, but only of the pain and suffering it causes, suffering that continues for generations. Perhaps most important, Sonneborn's film does not allow the other side to be forgotten, as Swofford suggests usually happens in national interpretations of war. He claims that "the problem with believing your country's battle monuments and deaths are more important . . . is that the enemy disappears . . . and [the war] becomes a trophy."[4] While Sonneborn shows the war's effect on women of both sides, she does not suggest that any woman's suffering is more important than another's.

Rather, in the film, it is the recognition and acknowledgment of the commonality of her pain with that of the other women that allow Sonneborn to heal. Even Nguyen is an example of this when she talks of her long battle against suicide and depression. Despite her pain and guilt, she understands that she is only one of many who have suffered in the war. "My husband has a scar on his face. I don't have a scar. It's so deep . . . In Vietnam, my neighbor's husband died. My neighbor's son died too. Sometimes you're ashamed to cry, because, What makes my pain greater than my neighbor's?" Here Nguyen compares the pain of her husband—which is written in the scar on his face—with her internal pain, a pain she supposes should pale in comparison to that of her neighbor who suffered more than she. Her assertion that there are always people who have suffered more suggests that measuring one's (or a nation's) victimization is not the answer, but rather, empathizing with others' pain is the way to prevent future suffering, as she earlier wished for mutual empathy with the GIs who sometimes abused her. It is only the recognition that the pain in others is similar to the pain we ourselves feel that can make war impossible. In promoting this kind of thinking, Sonneborn's film points the way to a new understanding of the Vietnam War, one in which there are victims beyond American veterans; moreover, it suggests, as the Winter Soldier veterans did in earlier years, that from reconciliation and mutual understanding springs new hope for true regeneration.

Notes

Preface

1. "Friendly fire" is the euphemism for a military's accidental destruction of its own troops in combat.

2. Larry Heinemann, *Paco's Story* (New York: Farrar, Straus, Giroux, 1986), p. 174. Subsequent references will be to this edition and will appear parenthetically within the text.

3. Of all the numerous works on various aspects of the literary and film culture that has grown from the Vietnam War, only a handful of critics have discussed the rape scene in *Paco's Story*, namely Susan Jeffords in *The Remasculinization of America* and Katherine Kinney in *Friendly Fire: American Images of the Vietnam War*, though both only afford the incident a few pages. However, Jeffords' later essay "Tattoos, Scars, Diaries, and Writing Masculinity," included in *The Vietnam War and American Culture,* elaborates upon her reading of the rape scene(s) in *Paco's Story* (eds. John Carlos Rowe and Rick Berg [New York: Columbia University Press, 1991], pp. 208–25). Thomas Meyers mentions the novel briefly in his afterward, though he, as the reader Orrin Judd cited below, seems to have missed Heinemann's point, with his language suggesting Paco's problems emanate from the "single soul-destroying night" in which his company is wiped out (*Walking Point: American Narratives of Vietnam* [New York and Oxford: Oxford University Press, 1988], pp. 223–24).

4. Orrin C. Judd, "distant and derivative," *Amazon Online Review*, 30 Nov. 2000, <http://www.amazon.com/gp/product/customer-reviews/1400076838/ref=cm_cr_dp_2_1/104-7704756-1032755?%5Fencoding=UTF8&customer-reviews.sort%5Fby=-SubmissionDate&n=283155> (accessed 7 July 2005).

5. Qtd. in Noam Chomsky, preface to *Against the Crime of Silence: Proceedings of the International War Crimes Tribunal* (New York: Clarion Books, 1968), p. xiii.

6. Although the terms *rape*, *sexual* or *gendered violence*, and *sexual assault* clearly are not interchangeable, in this context they are equally meaningful as violence of a sexual nature, perpetrated against women solely because of the fact that they are women. I do not include in my discussion of rape and sexual abuse the institutionalized prostitution in Vietnam that developed during the U.S. occupation (though one might certainly argue for its inclusion), but I do include violence and sexual assaults against sex workers.

7. Vietnam Veterans against the War, *The Winter Soldier Investigation: An Inquiry into American War Crimes* (Boston: Beacon, 1972), p. 14. Subsequent references will be to this edition and will appear parenthetically within the text.

8. Sara Corbett, "The Women's War," *The New York Times Magazine*, 18 March 2007, 1–16. Subsequent references will appear parenthetically within the text.

9. Amy Herdy and Miles Moffeit, "Betrayal in the Ranks," *The Denver Post*, 18–16 November 2003. Quotations taken from Digital Newsbook "Betrayal in the Ranks," <http://extras.denverpost.com/justice/tdp_betrayal.pdf>.

10. Carol Burke, *Camp All-American, Hanoi Jane, and the High-and-Tight: Gender, Folklore, and Changing Military Culture* (Boston: Beacon, 2004), p. 131.

11. Amy Street and Jane Stafford, "Military Sexual Trauma: Issues in Caring for Veterans," *Iraq War Clinician Guide* (Department of Veteran Affairs: 2004), p. 66.

12. The Joint Economic Committee, "Helping Military Moms Balance Family and Longer Deployments," 11 May 2007, <http://jec.senate.gov/Documents/Reports/MilitaryMoms05.11.07Final.pdf>.

13. Helen Benedict, "The Private War of Women," *Salon.com*, 7 March 2007. <http://www.salon.com/news/feature/2007/03/07/women_in_military/>, p. 1.

14. Mickiela Montoya, qtd. in Benedict, p. 2.

15. Undoubtedly one of the reasons military rapes go unpunished is because many take the form of "command rape," a term used to denote a female soldier being asked or commanded to have sex with a superior, making the victim feel threatened or coerced into sexual intercourse. As army specialist Suzanne Swift reported to Corbett, "You can tell another E-4 [specialist] to go to hell . . . But you can't say that to an E-5 [a sergeant] . . . If your sergeant tells you to walk over a minefield, you're supposed to do it" (Corbett, p. 2).

16. Cynthia Enloe, "Women after Wars: Puzzles and Warnings," in *Vietnam's Women in Transition*, ed. Kathleen Barry (New York: St. Martin's, 1996), p. 313.

Chapter 1

1. Anne Llewellyn Barstow, *War's Dirty Secret: Rape, Prostitution, and Other Crimes against Women* (Cleveland: Pilgrim, 2000), p. 3. Subsequent references will appear parenthetically within the text.

2. "Toilet" was the Japanese soldiers' name for comfort women (Barstow, p. 8).

3. *Bananas, Beaches, and Bases: Making Feminist Sense of International Politics* (1990), *The Morning After: Sexual Politics at the End of the Cold War* (1993), and *Maneuvers: The International Politics of Militarizing Women's Lives* (2000).

4. Qtd. in Susan Brownmiller, *Against Our Will: Men, Women, and Rape* (New York: Simon and Schuster, 1975), p. 31. Subsequent references will appear parenthetically within the text.

5. Brownmiller tends to overlook how other factors—such as race, class, and sexual orientation—have also played into the ways women have variously been subjected to rape throughout history. For a contemporaneous response voicing this critique, see Alison Edwards's *Rape, Racism, and the White Women's Movement: An Answer to Susan Brownmiller* (Chicago: Sojourner Truth Organization, n.d.).

6. Madeline Morris, "By Force of Arms: Rape, War, and Military Culture," *Duke Law Journal,* 45, no. 4 (February 1996): p. 653.

7. Catherine N. Niarchos, "Women, War, and Rape: Challenges Facing the International Tribunal for the Former Yugoslavia," *Human Rights Quarterly* 17, no. 4 (November 1995): p. 665.

8. Jocelyn Campanaro, "Women, War, and International Law: The Historical Treatment of Gender-Based War Crimes," *Georgetown Law Journal* 899 (August 2001): p. 2584.

9. Cynthia Enloe, *The Morning After: Sexual Politics at the End of the Cold War* (Berkeley: University of California Press, 1993), p. 239

10. Ibid.

11. Karen Engle, "Feminisim and Its (Dis)contents: Criminalizing Wartime Rape in Bosnia and Herzegovina," *The American Journal of International Law,* 99, no. 4 (October 2005): p. 794.

12. Atina Grossmann, "A Question of Silence: The Rape of German Women by Occupation Soldiers," *October* 72 (Spring 1995): p. 45.

13. Ibid.

14. It is possible the same erasure is already occurring in America's present war. Even after the Abu Ghraib prison abuse story broke, the fact of Iraqi women's presence in the prison was widely underreported. A 12 May 2004 *Guardian* story reported that a woman suspected of having been sexually assaulted while detained is now believed to have been killed by her own family (Luke Harding, "Focus Shifts to Jail Abuse of Women"). In the Taguba Report, widely available online, the investigator found one of the improprieties committed at Abu Ghraib to be a "male MP guard having sex with a female detainee." Of course, the graphic pictures of male sexual humiliation and torture at the hands of female guards received much greater attention than any treatment of female prisoners. Might the American public's horror at the pictures have as much to do with American males' fear of degradation at the hands of women than of genuine regard for the prisoners' well-being and their religious sensibilities? (Article 15–6 Investigation of the 800th Military Police Brigade, p. 17).

15. Keith Beattie, *The Scar That Binds: American Culture and the Vietnam War* (New York and London: New York University Press, 1998), p. 61. Subsequent references will be to this edition and will appear parenthetically within the text.

16. Interestingly, the possibly mythical "spitter" is figured not only as a war protester but also usually a woman. See Jerry Lembcke's fascinating investigation

of what he deems the spitting "myth" in *The Spitting Image: Myth, Memory, and the Legacy of Vietnam* (New York: New York University Press, 1998), especially the chapter entitled "Women, Wetness, and Warrior Dreams."

17. Arthur Egendorf, *Healing from the War: Trauma and Transformation after Vietnam* (Boston: Houghton Mifflin, 1985), pp. 26, 27, 29.

18. Of course, the United States is certainly not the only nation that has experienced attempts—both popular and governmental—to rehabilitate the national image. A wealth of literature exists on Japan's struggle to reconceptualize itself after World War II, with trends toward self-castigation creating a backlash of conservative rehabilitation, especially recently. See Roger B. Jeans, "Victims or Victimizers? Museums, Textbooks, and the War Debate in Contemporary Japan," *The Journal of Military History*, 69, no.1 (January 2005): 149–95.

19. See Robert Buzzanco's discussion of Vietnam studies scholar Keith Taylor's assertion that "The United States lost the Vietnam War because 'the American people came to hate the war' and, hence, 'they hated themselves'" ("Fear and [Self] Loathing in Lubbock, Texas, or How I Learned to Quit Worrying and Love Vietnam and Iraq," *CounterPunch*, 17–16 April 2005, <http://www.counterpunch.org/buzzanco04162005.html>).

20. Lembcke, p. 141. He further notes that "[e]ncoded in the image of the spat-upon veteran are the country's collective 'memories' of Vietnam returnees being assaulted by aggressive anti-war females and effeminate males. The loss of war is represented in the image as emasculation, the loss of manhood" (p. 140). Lembcke suggests that "the stories functioned to rehabilitate the warrior identity of the Vietnam generation of American males: were it not for the soft, female side of American culture (manifested in the women's movement, longhaired males, the gay rights movement, etc.) we would have won" (p. 139).

21. See, for instance, Ruth Leys, *Trauma: A Genealogy* (Chicago: University of Chicago Press, 2000), pp. 3–5; Cathy Caruth, *Trauma: Explorations in Memory* (Baltimore: Johns Hopkins University Press, 1995), pp. 3–11; and Ann Cvetkovich, *An Archive of Feelings: Trauma, Sexuality, and Lesbian Public Cultures* (Durham: Duke University Press, 2003), pp. 15–20.

22. James William Gibson, *The Perfect War: Technowar in Vietnam* (Boston: Atlantic Monthly, 1986), pp. 3–4, 6.

23. The popular understanding of the PTSD-suffering veteran as male is yet another site in which male suffering overwrites female trauma. A large proportion of female Vietnam veterans also have suffered from severe forms of PTSD. The landmark Vietnam Veterans Readjustment Study found that 26.9 percent of "women serving in the Vietnam theater had the full-blown disorder at some time during their lives," a number surprisingly close to the 30.6 percent of male veterans who have suffered from PTSD at some point (Richard A. Kulka, et. al., *Trauma and the Vietnam War Generation: Report of the Findings from the Vietnam Veterans Readjustment Study,* Brunner/Mazel Psychosocial Stress Series, no. 18 [New York: Brunner/Mazel, 1990], p. xxvii). Such data must draw attention to the fact that—though generally not threatened with death through combat in the way male veterans were—women veterans, especially nurses, were often terribly traumatized by their daily and overwhelming contact with the dead, dying, and dismembered soldiers they cared for. Such

women veterans were often denied the medical treatment for PTSD that did eventually become available to male veterans. See Lynda Van Devanter's *Home before Morning* (1983; 2001) for the chronicle of one nurse's struggle with PTSD after her military career.

24. Bush made the reworking of Vietnam vis-à-vis the Gulf War explicit on several occasions, including a 1992 speech in which he told listeners, "[A]fter Desert Storm, when our troops came home to a hero's welcome, the outpouring of love and honor was a grateful Nation's way of saying thanks. But it was something more. It was a reaching out, a warm embrace, a welcome home to all who wear the uniform, including the unsung heroes of another war, those who till that moment had not been recognized, a long-overdue recognition of gratitude to the veterans of the Vietnam war. And the country rallied behind them and at long last gave them their proper honor" ("Remarks to the American Legion National Convention in Chicago, Illinois." 25 August 1992. <http://www.presidency.ucsb.edu/index.php>). For examples of "kicking the Vietnam syndrome" rhetoric, see Bush's speeches of 1 March 1991, 2 March 1991, and 4 March 1991.

25. Cvetkovich, p. 16.

26. Kalí Tal, *Worlds of Hurt: Reading the Literatures of Trauma* (Cambridge: Cambridge University Press, 1996), p. 14. Subsequent references will appear parenthetically within the text.

27. One important exception is Rachel M. MacNair's *Perpetration-Induced Traumatic Stress: The Psychological Consequences of Killing* (Westport: Praeger, 2002), esp. chapter 2. In her investigation, MacNair suggests that what she terms "Perpetration-Induced Traumatic Stress" (PITS) must be considered by mental health workers as they study the effects of war. She makes the case that perpetrators of violence can and do develop psychological and physiological symptoms that are just as real as those of PTSD sufferers. Her contribution is important, for to my knowledge, she is the only researcher who has broken out "perpetrators" suffering from PITS from "combat veterans" suffering from PTSD. Her more nuanced recognition that it is not just exposure to violence but some veterans' perpetration of violence that creates traumatic stress allows researchers to begin to uncover the true causes of veteran suffering, including violence against civilians, while at the same time not denying the very real psychological stress from which such veterans suffer.

28. The language of "co-ownership" may be found in Dori Laub and Shoshana Felman, *Testimony: Crises of Witnessing in Literature, Psychoanalysis, and History* (New York: Rutledge, 1992), p. 57.

29. Leys, *Trauma*, p. 7.

30. Caruth, *Unclaimed Experience*, p. 11.

Chapter 2

1. Renny Christopher, *The Viet Nam War/The American War: Images and Representations in Euro-American and Vietnamese Exile Narratives* (Amherst: University of Massachusetts Press, 1995), p. 2.

2. See Robert B. Ray's discussion of this mythologization and how it has affected—and is in turn influenced by—Hollywood productions in *A Certain Tendency of the Hollywood Cinema, 1930–1980* (Princeton: Princeton University Press, 1985). He notes that Hollywood's use of these imaginative structures dictates "the conversion of all political, sociological, and economic dilemmas into personal melodramas" (p. 57).

3. Christopher, p. 2.

4. Ann Cvetkovich, *An Archive of Feelings: Trauma, Sexuality, and Lesbian Public Cultures* (Durham: Duke University Press, 2003), p. 7.

5. Kalí Tal, *Worlds of Hurt: Reading the Literatures of Trauma* (Cambridge: Cambridge University Press, 1996), p. 20.

6. Ibid.

7. Kathleen Barry, Introduction to *Vietnam's Women in Transition*, ed. Barry (New York: St. Martin's, 1996), p. 11.

8. Lê Tuan Hùng, "Hue and Tài Tu Music of Viet Nam: The Concept of Music and Social Organisation of Musicians," *ePapyrus*, Australia Asia Foundation, 31 January 2006, <http://home.vicnet.net.au/~aaf/ch2.html>.

9. Ibid. For further development of the restrictive effect of Confucian Buddhism in contemporary Vietnamese women's lives, see Trinh T. Minh-ha's film *Surname Viet, Given Name Nam* (1989).

10. Lynne Goodstein, "Sexual Assault in the United States and Vietnam: Some Thoughts and Questions," in *Vietnam's Women in Transition*, p. 277. Subsequent references will appear parenthetically in the text.

11. Khuat Thu Hong," Sexual Harassment in Vietnam: A New Term for an Old Phenomenon," in *Gender Practices in Contemporary Vietnam*, ed. Lisa Drummond and Helle Rydstrøm (Singapore: NIAS, 2004), p. 121. Subsequent references will appear parenthetically in the text.

12. Barry, p. 12.

13. See, for instance, Le Ly Hayslip, who notes that when her American boyfriend pulled a gun on her, "It didn't occur to me to call the police because, in Vietnam, domestic problems were nobody else's business and violent husbands were part of almost every marriage" (*Child of War, Woman of Peace* [New York: Doubleday, 1993], p. 118). In her account of her childhood, Hayslip remarks upon the one time she remembers her father making a show of his male power, what the Vietnamese refer to as *do danh vo*. Hayslip notes that *do danh vo* "was usual behavior for Vietnamese husbands but unusual for my father" whom "violence in any form offended" (with Jay Wurts, *When Heaven and Earth Changed Places: A Vietnamese Woman's Journey from War to Peace* [New York: Plume, 1989], p. 28). Subsequent references will appear parenthetically within the text.

14. Le Thi Quy, "Domestic Violence in Vietnam and Efforts to Curb It," in *Vietnam's Women in Transition*, p. 264.

15. Ibid., p. 267.

16. In her first memoir, Hayslip recounts being raped twice by NLF cadre (*Heaven*, pp. 93–97) and nearly raped twice more, once by her boss, and once by a street gang (pp. 106–07, 171).

17. Similar to the Soviet Union's *perestroika*, *Đổi mới* refers to the economic reforms by the Socialist Republic of Vietnam in the mideighties, which permitted and encouraged many free market enterprises at the same time that Communist authorities abandoned the push to collective industrial and agricultural operations.

18. In her second memoir, *Child of War, Woman of Peace*, Hayslip narrates the events of a bus ride she took in the last days before the South fell. When the bus was boarded by ARVN soldiers, Hayslip notes, "Thanh [her domestic help] and several other girls on the bus . . . were in the bloom of youth: stewbones dangling before hungry dogs." She gave Thanh medicine to make her sick and unappealing. Though Thanh was saved from the soldiers, they removed another girl from the bus and raped her beside the road (pp. 79–80). Hayslip's certainty of the soldiers' intentions, as indicated by her prepping of Thanh, reveals the danger of which every Vietnamese woman was aware.

19. Karen Gottschang Turner, *Even the Women Must Fight: Memories of War from North Vietnam* (New York: Wiley and Sons, 1998), p. 43. Subsequent references will appear parenthetically within the text.

20. It is important to remember that America's war with Vietnam was only one in a series. After the colonizing French fled Vietnam during WWII, Vietnam was subsequently invaded by the Japanese, whom the Vietnamese eventually drove out; Vietnam was then recolonized by France, whom the Viet Minh successfully overthrew in 1954, only to have their country invaded by the United States and its allied forces (officially in 1963, but beginning unofficially at the signing of the Geneva Accords). Eventually North Vietnamese forces and their southern supporters toppled the American-backed Republic of South Vietnam in 1975. They then went to war in Cambodia to overthrow the Pol Pot regime and conducted a brief war with China in 1978–79.

21. The standard requiring women to work outside the home and still complete the majority of care for children and home remains firmly in place even after completion of the socialist revolution. See Le Thi Quy for statistics on this issue, p. 265.

22. Cynthia Enloe, *The Morning After: Sexual Politics and the End of the Cold War* (Berkeley: University of California Press, 1993), p. 239.

23. Ibid.

24. Written in the late eighteenth century by Nguyễn Du, *The Tale of Kieu* is considered the national poem of Vietnam and is memorized and quoted widely.

25. Qtd. in Anne Llewellyn Barstow, *War's Dirty Secret: Rape, Prostitution, and Other Crimes against Women* (Cleveland: Pilgrim's, 2000), p. 58.

26. The exception to this is the aid Vietnam continues to request in treating the lingering effects of Agent Orange. The United States maintains its denial that Agent Orange is responsible for the birth defects and other health and reproductive problems in Vietnam (Talk by Peter Peterson, former ambassador to Vietnam, at Thirty Years after Conference, November 2005).

27. For an example of contemporary North-South tensions, see Andrew Lam's article "Vietnamese Media Bare Their Teeth—Carefully," *Pacific News*

Service, 17 January 2003, <http://news.pacificnews.org/news/view_article.html?article_id=63f3e3150d9d4a3b6fae42a725d12d5b>.

28. For instance, see James M. Freeman's *Hearts of Sorrow: Vietnamese-American Lives* (Stanford: Stanford University Press, 1989). His interviewees, if South Vietnamese, are urban, and most interviewees are from the North. Nguyễn Ngoc Ngan's *The Will of Heaven: A Story of One Vietnamese and the End of His World* is the autobiography of a Saigon schoolteacher (New York: Dutton, 1982). Nguen Quí Đuc's *Where the Ashes Are: The Odyssey of a Vietnamese Family* (Reading: Addison-Wesley, 1994) similarly chronicles the struggles of a wealthy Saigonese family.

29. Duong Thu Huong, *Novel without a Name*, trans. Nina McPherson and Phan Huy Duong (New York: Penguin Books, 1995), pp. 2–3.

30. This sex-death linkage interestingly forms both a difference and a parallel to American soldiers' war narratives. As we will see in subsequent chapters, for Americans soldiers, violence and sex became inextricably linked so that one may substitute for the other. While within the Vietnamese idea of death as the ultimate act of intimacy with the nationalist cause, sex was the *metaphor* for what the sacrificial death act achieved, in American narratives, sex functions as a stand-in for the deadly aggression soldiers could not act out on an enemy.

31. Bao Ninh, *The Sorrow of War: A Novel of North Vietnam*, trans. Phan Thanh Hao, ed. Frank Palmos (New York: Riverhead Books, 1993), p. 207.

32. Ibid., pp. 191–92.

33. Martha Hess, introduction to *Then the Americans Came: Voices from Vietnam* (New York: Four Walls Eight Windows, 1993), p. 12. Subsequent references will appear parenthetically within the text.

34. John Duffett, ed., *Against the Crime of Silence: Proceedings of the International War Crimes Tribunal* (1968; New York: Clarion Book, 1970), pp. 568, 570, 571.

35. Mark Baker, *Nam: The Vietnam War in the Words of the Men and Women Who Fought There* (1981; New York: Cooper Square, 2001), p. 191. Subsequent references will appear parenthetically within the text.

36. For a fascinating critique of this aspect of the memoir, see Leslie Bow's "Third-World Testimony in the Era of Globalization: Vietnamese Sexual Trauma and Le Ly Hayslip's Art of Neutrality," in *Haunting Violations: Feminist Criticism and the Crisis of the Real*," ed. Wendy S. Hasford and Wendy Kozol (Urbana: University of Illinois Press, 2001), pp. 169–74. Bow suggests that "[u]surping tactics of masculinist nationalism by linking femininity to a nationalist imaginary, *When Heaven and Earth Changed Places* attempts to invoke a maternal space that transcends national divisions" (p. 171).

37. Hayslip does not seem to have expected or desired this outcome. Instead, apparently, she thought by informing the MPs, Jim would receive some type of counseling. She was upset and bewildered upon his deportation.

Chapter 3

1. In his opening statement at the Winter Soldier Investigation, Lt. William Crandell said, "We went to defend the Vietnamese people and our

testimony will show that we are committing genocide against them. We went to fight for freedom and our testimony will show that we have turned Vietnam into a series of concentration camps." Naming the war a "genocide" continued throughout the three days of testimony by other veterans (Vietnam Veterans against the War, *The Winter Soldier Investigation: An Inquiry into American War Crimes* [Boston: Beacon, 1972], p. 1).

2. In Ralph Schoenman's forward to the Stockholm Tribunal transcript, he summarizes the charges of contemporary critics: "[T]he Tribunal was a 'kangaroo court' in which the evidence offered was such as could only service a pre-determined judgment . . . [I]t would be little more than a mock trial in which Johnson, Rusk and McNamara would be tried and found guilty *in absentia*. Also . . . the Tribunal was not interested in the crimes of the Vietcong; the Tribunal fulfilled none of the accepted canons of judicial procedure; it was self-appointed; it lacked legal standing and, most damning of all, every aspect of its work from its composition to its *modus operandi* betrayed an absence of that impartiality and objectivity on which Western jurisprudence has been founded" (*Against the Crime of Silence: Proceedings of the International War Crimes Tribunal*, ed. John Duffet [New York: Clarion, 1970], p. 6).

Schoenman's answer to this critique is that the "Tribunal never pretended to be a trial. How could we have had a trial? We lack state power . . . That is why we called the body a Tribunal rather than a court. The Tribunal functioned as a Commission of Inquiry" (p. 7).

3. See, for example, Aryeh Neier's letter to the editor in *The New York Review of Books* 40, no. 18 (4 November 1993), in which István Deák calls the Stockholm Tribunal a "sorry example" of an international tribunal, namely, because "[n]o testimony contradicting the predetermined conclusions was allowed, and after eight days, the tribunal solemnly declared the US guilty of war crimes in Vietnam." Available at <http://www.nybooks.com/articles/2416>.

4. James Landers, *The Weekly War: Newsmagazines and Vietnam* (Columbia: University of Missouri Press, 2004), pp. 4–5. Landers also notes that an important turning point in news media reportage occurred in late 1969 when the uncovering of the My Lai massacre gave way to more negative portrayals of the American troops, including "more frequent reports of misconduct, drug abuse, and poor morale" (p. 4).

5. Bertrand Russell, "Introduction by Bertrand Russell," in *Against the Crime of Silence*, pp. 3–4.

6. Duffet, ed., *Against the Crime of Silence,* p. 440. Subsequent references will appear parenthetically within the text.

7. See Karen Engle, "Feminism and Its (Dis)contents: Criminalizing Wartime Rape in Bosnia and Herzegovina," *The American Journal of International Law*, 99, no. 4 (October 2005): 778–816.

8. Sara Evans, *Personal Politics: The Roots of Women's Liberation in the Civil Rights Movement and the New Left* (New York: Vintage Books, 1980), p. 182.

9. Ibid., p. 188.

10. "An SDS Statement on the Liberation of Women," *New Left Notes*, 10 July 1967, p. 4. Rpt. in Miriam Schneir, ed., *Feminism in Our Time: The*

Essential Writings, World War II to the Present (New York: Vintage Books, 1994), pp. 104–07.

11. Richard Stacewicz, *Winter Soldiers: An Oral History of the Vietnam Veterans against the War* (New York: Simon and Schuster, 1997), p. 14. Subsequent references will appear parenthetically within the text.

12. Nelson Adkins, ed., *Thomas Paine: Common Sense and Other Political Writings*, American Heritage Series (New York: Macmillan, 1953), p. 55.

13. Although the transcript has been published in book form, the bound version has been greatly abridged. The only full-text version widely accessible is the online text. Thus, unless otherwise indicated, all quotations from the Winter Soldier Investigation transcript will refer to the online version, housed at the Sixties Project, which is sponsored by Viet Nam Generation and the University of Virginia at Charlottesville at <http://lists.village.virginia.edu/sixties/HTML_docs/Resources/Primary/Winter_Soldier/WS_entry.html>. Each quotation will be footnoted, providing panel information.

14. Although there were several women panelists, none testified about GI treatment of Vietnamese women. Because these women were aid workers or nurses, they most likely never accompanied troops during village searches or firefights, which is when most rapes and sex abuse seem to have occurred.

15. I have chosen not to cover, in this chapter on early veteran testimony, Mark Lane's *Conversations with Americans* (New York: Simon and Schuster, 1970). This collection of oral interviews, like the transcript of the Winter Soldier Investigation, includes many horrifying accounts of brutally sexualized mistreatment of women. However, Lane's book was widely discredited from the time it was published and reviewed. As Joe Urgo, one of the investigation coordinators told Stacewicz, Lane "never checked with the VVAW people to put his vets through our process of checking out their story. Essentially what he did was, he printed a book that was full of flaws." The discrediting of Lane's book proved an important lesson for the VVAW, who meticulously checked out the stories of its investigation witnesses, asking them to locate corroborating witnesses who would also testify and to bring evidentiary documents with them to the investigation when possible. As Urgo noted, the lesson they learned from Lane's experience was that "we'd better do our work right. We'd better talk to these vets and weed out the bullshitters so that we can't get set up, because we're going to come under attack" (p. 236). Urgo was correct; most recently, during the 2004 presidential election, John O'Neil, leader of the anti-Kerry group Swift Boat Veterans for Truth, took up his 1971 accusations that testimony given at the WSI was patently false. However, the current claim by conservatives that the WSI has been discredited can be traced to Guenther Lewy, a revisionist historian, whose 1978 history of the war argued that the U.S. actually won the Vietnam War. For more information on Lewy's, O'Neil's, and others' accusations against the Investigation and its participants, see John Prados, "Winter Whether," *The Veteran*, 34, 2 (Fall 2004), p. 19. Also available at <http://www.vvaw.org/veteran/article/?id=481>.

16. Please note that my ellipses have been enclosed in brackets. Other ellipses are from the original text, indicating perhaps a gesture or a word the

transcriber was unable to understand. Miscellaneous Panel, Part III.

17. POW Panel, Part IV.

18. First Marine Division, Part II.

19. First Marine Division, Part IV.

20. First Air Cav., Part III.

21. Miscellaneous Panel, Part I.

22. Third Marine Division, Part III.

23. Of course, such murder directly violates the Geneva Convention, whose rules guarantee the humane treatment of prisoners (though the conventions do not protect women from rape).

24. Miscellaneous Panel, Part I.

25. First Marine Division.

26. First Marine Division, Part II.

27. First Marine Division, Part III.

28. See the accounts of Luu Thi Nao, Nguyen Thi Duc, and Le Van Ky in Martha Hess, *Then the Americans Came: Voices from Vietnam* (New York: Four Walls, Eight Windows, 1993), pp. 145–47.

29. First Marine Division, Part IV.

30. Americal Division Panel, Part II.

31. First Marine Division Panel, Part IV.

32. Third Marine Division Panel, Part II.

33. First Marine Division Panel, Part IV.

34. First Marine Division, Part IV.

35. This assumption has long been used to excuse the sexual abuse of women in war; see Susan Brownmiller's discussion of General Patton's comments from WWII in chapter 1, for example.

36. Racism Panel, Part II.

37. Racism Panel, Part I.

38. "Rudely" here (obviously a vast understatement of the nature of women's treatment by soldiers) is again indicative of people's extreme tentativeness in even approaching the subject of women's sexual treatment in war.

39. First Fourth, and Ninth Infantry Divisions Panel, Part II.

40. Emphasis added. First Marine Division Panel, Part IV.

41. Richard R. Moser, *The New Winter Soldiers: GI and Veteran Dissent during the Vietnam Era* (New Brunswick: Rutgers University Press, 1996), p. 26. Subsequent references will appear parenthetically within the text.

42. Twenty-fifth Infantry Division and Public Information Office Panel, Part III.

43. What Are We Doing to Ourselves? Panel, Part III.

44. Ibid.

45. "Rap groups" were created when Jan Barry, then president of the VVAW, contacted Lifton about two projects the VVAW had in mind, one of which evolved into the Winter Soldier Investigation, and the other was to do something to deal with "the severe psychological problems of many Vietnam veterans because of their experiences" (qtd. in Robert J. Lifton, *Home from the War: Vietnam Veterans, Neither Victims nor Executioners* [New York: Simon

and Schuster, 1973], p. 75). Members of the VVAW had already been meeting informally at their headquarters to "rap" about war-related issues; thus, Lifton joined the group, and they began meeting formally once a week for periods of at least two hours. See Lifton, pp. 76–77.

46. Lifton, *Home from the War*, p. 18.

47. What Are We Doing to Ourselves? Panel, Part V.

48. Ibid.

49. Emphasis added. Americal Division Panel, Part I.

50. Emphasis added. Closing Statements, I.

51. This is, of course, yet another dehumanization of the Vietnamese, although this time due to a "noble savage"-like stereotype.

52. At the WSI, though veterans witnessed to a packed audience, the VVAW did not receive the media attention it desired. Although reporters were present, outside the Midwest, the media "ignored this story or deliberately buried it" (Stacewicz, p. 240). It is indicative of the difficulty inherent in presenting such disturbing and damning evidence of U.S. crimes, for other of the VVAW events, such as Dewey Canyon III, received enormous press coverage.

53. Congressional Record, 17 May 1971, Folder 01, Box 09, Douglas Pike Collection: Unit 03–Antiwar Activities, the Vietnam Archive, Texas Tech University, p. E4465. Subsequent references to this source will appear parenthetically in the text by page number.

54. American soldiers' perception of the Vietnamese women as sexually inadequate is interesting in itself. Enloe has pointed out that "the entire R&R policy and its dependent industry only work if thousands of Asian women are willing and able to learn what American military men rely on to bolster their sense of masculinity; [it all] depend[s] on Asian women to be alert to the differences among masculinities" ("It Takes Two," in *Let the Good Times Roll: Prostitution and the U.S. Military in Asia*, Saundra Pollock Sturdevant and Brenda Stoltzfus [New York: New, 1992], p. 25). While prostitutes by necessity learned to navigate the desires of American masculinity (and many of them commented on how different American male expectations were from those of Vietnamese), what reason would a typical South Vietnamese village woman have to learn what American men expected from their sex partners? This again demonstrates American soldiers' tendency to perceive all Vietnamese women as prostitutes and as "owing" them something.

55. Feminists did begin to make such connections soon thereafter, as evidenced by the publication of Cynthia Enloe's groundbreaking *Does Khaki Become You? The Militarization of Women's Lives* (Boston: South End, 1983), though never specifically in terms of the military in Vietnam.

56. Despite his original life sentence, Nixon paroled Calley after he had served only three years of house arrest (Wilson, "I Had Prayed," pp. 162–63).

57. Qtd. in James S. Olson and Randy Roberts, *My Lai: A Brief History with Documents*, Bedford Series in History and Culture (Boston: Bedford Books, 1998), p. 17. Subsequent references will appear parenthetically within the text.

58. Joseph Lelyveld, "The Story of a Soldier Who Refused to Fire at Songmy," *New York Times*, 14 December 1969, SM32.

59. Uniform Code of Military Justice. Title 10. Subtitle A, Part II, Ch. 47. Subch. X. 920 Art. 120 Rape and Carnal Knowledge.

60. Wilson, William. "I Had Prayed to God That This Thing Was Fiction," in *My Lai*, ed. Olson and Roberts, p. 162.

61. Schneir, p. 125.

62. Wilson, "I Had Prayed," p. 163.

63. Daniel Lang, *Casualties of War* (New York: Pocket Books, 1989), pp. 22, 26.

64. Kathy J. Phillips, *Manipulating Masculinity: War and Gender in Modern British and American Literature* (New York: Palgrave MacMillan, 2006), p. 3.

65. Phillips, p. 7.

66. Whether the individual testifying actually committed the crimes he described matters little. He certainly was guilty by association in the minds of most Americans, as well as in his own mind.

67. None of these veterans was tried for war crimes (for admitting them as war criminals would be admitting to the illegality of the war in Vietnam); however, the Nixon administration persecuted antiwar veterans mercilessly with wiretapping, surveillance, and confrontations designed to intimidate both veteran activists and their families. For instance, FBI agents repeatedly contacted Barry Romo's mother hoping to elicit information regarding her son's activities (Stacewicz, p. 318).

Chapter 4

1. Larry Heinemann, *Black Virgin Mountain: A Return to Vietnam* (New York: Doubleday, 2005), p. 37. Subsequent references will appear parenthetically within the text.

2. John F. Kennedy, "Inaugural Address." 20 Jan. 1961, The American Presidency Project. <http://www.presidency.ucsb.edu/ws/index.php?pid=8032&st=ask+not+what+your+country&st1=>.

3. American belief in the essentialness of war to masculinity ran so deep that even those actively opposed to the war were tempted into enlistment. In *Stiffed: The Betrayal of the American Man* (New York: Harper Perennial, 1999), Susan Faludi relates that antiwar protestor Gordon Dalbey, after a stint in the Peace Corps, "impulsively applied to the army and lined up a commission to missile-launch training school," despite his continued opposition to the war. When asked the cause of his "enlistment fervor," Dalbey replied, "You don't get to be a *man* unless you go to war. I opposed the Vietnam War, I oppose *war* itself . . . And yet . . . all my life I had longed for a war that I could be part of" (pp. 314, 315).

4. Faludi, p. 319.

5. As one veteran argued, "It could have been over within six months . . . We could have took the 57,000 troops that got killed and put them

all in a line behind tanks and APCs instead and just started them at one end and walked across the country" (Peter Goldman and Tony Fuller, eds., *Charlie Company: What Vietnam Did to Us* [New York: Ballantine, 1983], p. 102).

6. James Webb, *Fields of Fire* (New York: Bantam, 1979), p. 25.

7. Qtd. on jameswebb.com, <http://www.jameswebb.com/reviews/fields.htm>.

8. Thomas Meyers, *Walking Point: American Narratives of Vietnam* (New York: Oxford University Press, 1988), p. 39. Subsequent references will appear parenthetically within the text.

9. Don Rignalda, *Fighting and Writing the Vietnam War* (Jackson: University Press of Mississippi, 1994), p. 25. Subsequent references will appear parenthetically within the text.

10. This overfilling results in quite lengthy novels. As points of comparison, Webb's novel is 452 pages, and Del Vecchio's hefty tome contains a whopping 606 pages; the more "antiwar" works that will be discussed later average around 200 pages.

11. Susan Jeffords, *The Remasculinization of America: Gender and the Vietnam War* (Bloomington: Indiana University Press, 1989), p. 168. Subsequent references will appear parenthetically within the text.

12. Lucas Carpenter, "'It Don't Mean Nothin'': Vietnam War Literature and Postmodernism," *College Literature* 30, no. 2 (2003): p. 36.

13. Fredric Jameson, *Postmodernism: or, the Cultural Logic of Late Capitalism* (Durham: Duke University Press, 1991), pp. 44–45. Jameson's suggestion that the Vietnam War was an entirely new and different kind of war is part of the pernicious tendency in academic and popular American culture alike to classify the Vietnam War and its effects as completely outside past American experience, a classification that denies the fact that Vietnam was one in but a series of wars America fought against various nations and people across time, and the existence of the traditional, realistic Vietnam War novel belies his claim of the breakdown "of all previous narrative paradigms." However, Jameson's comments on Michael Herr's *Dispatches* and his recognition of the postmodern "breakdown of . . . shared language" are instructive in considering the formal devices of this literature.

14. Tim O'Brien, *The Things They Carried* (New York: Penguin Books, 1991), p. 89.

15. Walter Clemons, "Killing Ground," *Newsweek,* 1 January 1979.

16. "One Step Forward in the Fledgling Art of the Vietnam War Novel," *Kirkus Reviews,* 1 November 1978.

17. J. B., "Death Becomes a Bore," *The New Republic*, 27 January 1979.

18. Peter Greenberg, "Death Overkilled in Vietnam War," *Los Angeles Times,* 22 April 1979. In a letter to the editor, Hasford—who did not take criticism well—accused Greenberg (probably not unfairly) of plagiarism and unoriginality in his negative review (Hasford, unpublished letter to the editor of *LA Times,* 28 May 1979, <http://www.gustavhasford.com/letter05–28–79.htm>).

19. These names were a major sticking point with the *New Republic* reviewer, who apparently misunderstood both Hasford's strategies and purpose.

20. Gustav Hasford, *The Short-Timers* (New York: Harper and Row, 1979), pp. 1, 50. Subsequent references will appear parenthetically within the text.

21. O'Brien, *If I Die in a Combat Zone, Box Me up and Ship Me Home* (New York: Delacorte, 1973), p. 59.

22. Christian G. Appy, *Working Class War: American Combat Soldiers and Vietnam* (Chapel Hill: University of North Carolina Press, 1993), pp. ix, 101. Subsequent references will appear parenthetically within the text.

23. And the idea that the feminine—the unmasculine, the cowardly—was contagious is rampant within Vietnam War rhetoric. In Bo Hathaway's novel, *A World of Hurt*, the DI says in reference to a recruit who attempts suicide in order to leave basic training, "I don't know if this fairy *infected* any of the rest of you . . ." ([New York: Taplinger, 1981], p. 20). In the film *Full Metal Jacket*, the DI threatens to "cut [a recruit's] balls off to keep [him] from infecting the rest of the world" with his "softness."

24. Lucinda Franks, *Waiting Out a War: The Exile of Private John Picciano* (New York: Coward, McCann, and Geoghegan, 1974), p. 57.

25. Eve Kosofsky Sedgwick, *Between Men: English Literature and Male Homosocial Desire* (New York: Columbia University Press, 1985), p. 40. Subsequent references will appear parenthetically within the text.

26. Cowboy kills the wounded soldiers in order to prevent the rest of the squad from being sucked into the sniper's range.

27. Katherine Kinney, "Women, War, and the Pacific," in *Post-Nationalist American Studies*, ed. John Carlos Rowe (Berkeley: University of California Press, 2000), pp. 90–91.

28. Appy reports that "Marine Corps basic training in the Vietnam years, conducted in only two places . . . was a highly standardized and predictable cycle . . . [from which can be drawn] a . . . clear-cut model of essential elements" (p. 90). See Appy, pp. 101–03. Veteran accounts of Marine BT suggest that this particular training tactic was widely practiced during the Vietnam War.

29. Larry Heinemann, *Close Quarters* (New York: Penguin Books, 1986), p. 4. Subsequent references will appear parenthetically within the text.

30. Kurt Jacobsen, "Larry Heinemann in Conversation with Kurt Jacobsen," *Logos* 2, no. 1 (Winter 2003). http://logosonline.home.igc.org/heinemann.htm.

31. Ibid.

32. Sarah Evans, *Personal Politics: The Roots of Women's Liberation in the Civil Rights Movement and the New Left* (New York: Vintage Books, 1979), p. 178.

33. Heinemann, *Paco's Story* (New York: Vintage Contemporaries, 2005), p. xii. Subsequent references will refer to the first edition of the novel (New York: Farrar Straus Giroux, 1986) and will appear parenthetically within the text.

34. And Appy calls the Vietnam War specifically a working-class war because "[r]oughly 80 percent [of American troops in the Vietnam War] came from working-class and poor backgrounds" (Appy, p. 6).

35. Recall here the testimony from the Winter Soldier Investigation about the American military's careful suppression of news stories about successful female enemy combatants.

36. Ernest Hemingway, *A Farewell to Arms* (New York: Scribner, 1995), p. 243.

37. W. D. Ehrhart, *Vietnam-Perkasie: A Combat Marine Memoir* (Jefferson and London: McFarland, 1983), p. 10. Subsequent references will appear parenthetically within the text.

38. Kalí Tal, *Worlds of Hurt: Reading the Literatures of Trauma* (New York: Cambridge University Press, 1996), p. 103.

Chapter 5

1. Clayton R. Koppes and Gregory D. Black, *Hollywood Goes to War: How Politics, Profits, and Propaganda Shaped World War II Movies* (Berkeley: University of California Press, 1987), p. 64. Subsequent references will appear parenthetically within the text.

2. Tom Engelhardt, *The End of Victory Culture: Cold War America and the Disillusioning of a Generation* (New York: Basic Books, 1995), p. 45. Subsequent references will appear parenthetically within the text.

3. Christian G. Appy, *Working-Class War: American Combat Soldiers and Vietnam* (Chapel Hill: University of North Carolina Press, 1993), p. 60.

4. Ron Kovic, *Born on the Fourth of July* (New York: McGraw-Hill, 1976), p. 55.

5. Toshio Whelchel, *From Pearl Harbor to Saigon: Japanese American Soldiers and the Vietnam War* (London: Verso, 1999), p. 117. Asian American military recruits were routinely forced to model "the gook" enemy while in basic training. They were often referred to as "gooks" even when in Vietnam; Asian Americans thus experienced a dissonance between received notions of the American military's essential "good[ness]" and the racism they encountered there. See Whelchel, pp. 18–19, 104, 107, 131.

6. Larry Heinemann, *Close Quarters* (1977; New York: Penguin Books, 1986), p. 53.

7. The raising of the flag on Mt. Suribachi, depicted in the final scenes of the film and immortalized in the bronze statue and *Life* photographs, itself conflated reality and representation. The flag-raising spectacle captured in the famous photograph had to be reenacted especially for the camera (the "real" flag-raising had occurred earlier with a less impressively sized flag and was itself "an undramatic and, in many respects, rather staged and phony affair."). Philip D. Beidler, *The Good War's Greatest Hits: World War II and American Remembering* (Athens and London: University of Georgia Press, 1998), p. 58. See pp. 58–65 for further discussion.

8. Katherine Kinney, *Friendly Fire: American Images of the Vietnam War* (Oxford: Oxford University Press, 2000), pp. 18 and 20. Subsequent references will appear parenthetically in the text.

9. Wallace Terry, *Bloods: An Oral History of the Vietnam War by Black Veterans* (New York: Random House, 1984), p. 25.

10. W. D. Ehrhart, *Busted: A Vietnam Veteran in Nixon's America* (Amherst: University of Massachusetts Press, 1995), p. 13.

11. Emphasis added. Gustav Hasford, *The Short-Timers* (New York: Harper and Row, 1979), p. 70. Subsequent references will appear parenthetically within the text.

12. For an excellent selected filmography of the Vietnam War, see appendix B in *From Hanoi to Hollywood: The Vietnam War in American Film*, Dittmar and Michaud, eds. (New Brunswick: Rutgers University Press, 1997), pp. 350–73. Another extremely useful source on films of and about the war is Jeremy M. Devine's *Vietnam at Twenty-four Frames a Second: A Critical and Thematic Analysis of Over Four Hundred Films about the Vietnam War* (Jefferson: McFarland, 1995). Subsequent references will appear parenthetically within the text.

13. Albert Auster and Leonard Quart, *How the War Was Remembered: Hollywood and Vietnam* (New York: Praeger, 1988), p. 21. Subsequent references will appear parenthetically within the text.

14. JFK single-handedly popularized the Green Beret as his "new 'counterinsurgency' warrior," a figure who "could be mythologized and publicized." He also proclaimed the Green Berets his "favorite unit" and personally oversaw their reoutfitting in updated and flashy uniforms and equipment (Engelhardt, p. 162).

15. Renata Adler, *A Year in the Dark* (New York: Berkeley Books, 1969), pp. 199–200.

16. Qtd. in Todd Gitlin, *Inside Prime Time* (New York: Pantheon Books, 1985), p. 227.

17. One might add to this list Martin Scorsese's *Taxi Driver* (1976), though it seems much less exploitational than the violence-driven B-movies above (Devine, p. 123).

18. H. Bruce Franklin's fascinating study *M.I.A., or Mythmaking in America: How and Why Belief in Live POWs Has Possessed a Nation*, in which he examines Americans' still-extant belief in Vietnam POWs and MIAs (and the U.S. government's encouragement of this belief) despite undeniable evidence that no living soldiers were abandoned in Vietnam, reveals America's need to believe in the captivity mythology (Brooklyn: Hill Books, 1992).

19. Richard Slotkin, *Gunfighter Nation: The Myth of the Frontier in Twentieth-Century America* (New York: HarperPerrenial, 1992), p. 13.

20. Linda Dittmar and Gene Michaud, "America's Vietnam War Films," in *From Hanoi to Hollywood: The Vietnam War in American Film*, Dittmar and Michaud, eds. (New Brunswick: Rutgers University Press, 1997), p. 4.

21. For further argument about filmic revision of the Vietnam War as noble (and won by the Americans), see Michael Klein, "Historical Memory and Film," in *From Hanoi to Hollywood*, p. 23.

22. Qtd. in Myra MacPherson, *Long Time Passing: Vietnam and the Haunted Generation* (New York: Signet, 1985), pp. 180–81.

23. Qtd. in MacPherson, p. 183. Of course, this quotation makes clear the trend toward "remasculinization" as it implicitly critiques the women's movement for dirtying the word *masculinity,* a quality obviously prized by Blumenthal. Clearly he asks readers to re-evaluate the feminist critique of the word.

24. Qtd. in John Wheeler, *Touched by Fire: The Future of the Vietnam Generation* (New York: Avon, 1984), p. 124.

25. William Broyles Jr., "Why Men Love War," *Esquire,* November 1984, p. 62.

26. Ibid., p. 61.

27. Susan Faludi, *Stiffed: The Betrayal of the American Man* (New York: Perennial, 2000), p. 292. Faludi credits Appy for helping her interpret the often difficult-to-decipher and conflicting numbers for military participation in this period.

28. As Susan Jeffords notes, *Rambo: First Blood, Part Two* had the third highest opening gross up to that time (1985); it collected $100 million in its first month. Its novelization made it to the *New York Times* best-seller list (*The Remasculinization of America: Gender and the Vietnam War* [Bloomington: Indiana University Press, 1989], p. 187n3). Subsequent references will appear parenthetically within the text.

29. In the discussion of who has authority to speak on the Vietnam War, a distinction is made between Vietnam War veterans and Vietnam era veterans.

30. William Broyles Jr., *Brothers in Arms: A Journey from War to Peace* (New York: Knopf, 1986), p. ix.

31. In his 28 May 1984 Memorial Day speech, Ronald Reagan said that "the veterans of Vietnam . . . were never . . . defeated in battle and were heroes as surely as any who have ever fought in a noble cause." The "unknown" soldier of this war "saw the horrors of war, but bravely faced them, certain his own cause and his country's cause was a noble one; that he was fighting for human dignity, for free men everywhere." "Remarks at Memorial Day Ceremonies Honoring an Unknown Serviceman of the Vietnam Conflict." The American Presidency Project at UC Santa Barbara. <http://www.presidency.ucsb.edu/ws/index.php?pid=39975&st=noble+cause&st1=vietnam>.

32. Films and political culture certainly played off each other during Reagan's administration. President Reagan, in a speech preparing the nation for the possibility of intervention in the Middle East, declared, "Boy, I saw *Rambo* last night; now I know what to do next time" (qtd. in the *New York Times,* 1 July 1985).

33. Although Oliver Stone began his attempts to bring the Vietnam War to the big screen via an adaptation of Ron Kovic's *Born on the Fourth of July* around 1978, that film was canceled, shelved until Stone's successful release of *Platoon* (Andrew Martin, *Receptions of War: Vietnam in American Culture* [Norman: University of Oklahoma Press, 1993], p. 111). Subsequent references to this source will appear parenthetically within the text.

34. Qtd. in Klein, p. 24.

35. Qtd. in Harry W. Haines, "They Were Called and They Went": The Political Rehabilitation of the Vietnam Veteran," in *From Hanoi to Hollywood,* p. 81.

36. The editor of *Unwinding the Vietnam War: From War into Peace* claims that between 1965 and 1973, approximately one in thirty Indochinese was killed; one in twelve wounded; and one in five made a refugee. There were an estimated 200,000 prostitutes and 300,000 orphans in South Vietnam alone. The United States used 15,500,000 tons of bombs and munitions in Vietnam

(compared to the 6,000,000 used during all of World War II) and sprayed over 18,000,000 gallons of herbicides over South Vietnam's forests and croplands (Ed. Reese Williams for Washington Project for the Arts [Seattle: Real Comet, 1987], pp. 7–8).

37. Appy, *Patriots: The Vietnam War Remembered from All Sides* (New York: Viking, 2003), p. 256.

38. Mark Baker, *Nam: The Vietnam War in the Words of the Men and Women Who Fought There* (1981; rprt., New York: Cooper Square, 2001), pp. 210–11. Subsequent references to this source will appear parenthetically.

39. Gaylyn Studlar and David Desser, "Never Having to Say You're Sorry: *Rambo*'s Rewriting the Vietnam War," in *From Hanoi to Hollywood*, p., 104.

40. Qtd. in Klein, p. 29.

41. Anthony Swofford, *Jarhead: A Marine's Chronicle of the Gulf War and Other Battles* (New York: Scribner, 2003), pp. 6–7.

42. Lorrie Goldensohn, *Dismantling Glory: Twentieth-Century Soldier Poetry* (New York: Columbia University Press, 2003), p. 300.

43. "Boom-boom" was the slang word used by American soldiers and prostitutes for sex.

44. Timothy Corrigan, *Film and Literature: An Introduction and Reader* (Upper Saddle River, NJ: Prentice Hall, 2000), pp. 68, 67.

45. The exception to this is the soldier Clark, who appears in both versions as a sociopath.

46. Such recommenders are apparently unaware of the excellent documentaries that include Vietnamese perspectives on the war, including Peter Davis's *Hearts and Minds* (1974) and Barbara Sonneborn's *Regret to Inform* (1998).

47. Janet Maslin, "A Woman's View of Vietnam Horrors," *The New York Times* (24 December 1993); Majorie Baumgarten, "Review of *Heaven and Earth*," *Austin Chronicle* (24 December 1993).

48. Hayslip makes it very clear that Americans continue to misunderstand the meaning of the war for the South Vietnamese peasants, for whom the concepts 'democracy' and 'communism' meant little, but who desperately desired a united Vietnam. For them, the war with the Americans was merely a continuation of the colonial wars Vietnam had been fighting throughout its long history (see Le Ly Hayslip, with Jay Wurts, *When Heaven and Earth Changed Paces: A Vietnamese Woman's Journey from War to Peace* [New York: Plume, 1990], pp. x–xiv). Subsequent references to this source will appear parenthetically within the text.

49. Hayslip, with James Hayslip, *Child of War, Woman of Peace* (New York: Anchor Books, 1993), p. 163.

50. Ibid., pp. 227–29.

51. Indeed, just as she does not wish herself to be understood as merely a victim, she encourages American veterans to avoid such circumscription. She says, "I learned that you were only a victim—truly a victim—when you felt like one: when you got knocked down and didn't even try to get up. The . . . GIs who began to hate themselves for simply answering their country's call were also victims" (*Heaven*, p. 227).

52. See Rajiv Chandrasekaran's discussion of the problems recently caused in Vietnam by militant exile community groups. "Waging War from California," *Washington Post,* 29 July 2001.

53. Harry Kreisler, "History and the Movies: Conversation with Oliver Stone" (17 April and 27 June 1997), University of California at Berkeley, <http://globetrotter.berkeley.edu/Stone/stone-con5.html>.

Afterword

1. Helen Benedict, "The Private War of Women," *Salon.com*, 7 March 2007. <http://www.salon.com/news/feature/2007/03/07/women_in_military/>, p. 2.

2. Benedict, p. 5.

3. "Home," SAPR Home Page, United States Department of Defense, 21 March 2008, <http://www.sapr.mil/>.

4. "General Information," SAPR Home Page, United States Department of Defense, 21 March 2008, < http://www.sapr.mil/HomePage.aspx?Topic=About%20SAPRO>.

5. Department of Defense, "FY07 Report on Sexual Assault in the Military," 13 March 2008, <http://www.sapr.mil/contents/references/2007%20Annual%20Report.pdf>, p. 29.

6. Amy Herdy and Miles Moffeit, "Betrayal in the Ranks," *The Denver Post*, 18-16 November 2003. Quotations taken from Digital Newsbook "Betrayal in the Ranks," <http://extras.denverpost.com/justice/tdp_betrayal.pdf>, p. 21. Subsequent references will appear parenthetically in the text.

Bibliography

Adkins, Nelson, ed. *Thomas Paine: Common Sense and Other Political Writings.* American Heritage Series. New York: Macmillan, 1953.

Adler, Renata. *A Year in the Dark.* New York: Berkeley Books, 1969.

Appy, Christian G. *Patriots: The Vietnam War Remembered from All Sides.* New York: Viking, 2003.

———. *Working-Class War: American Combat Soldiers and Vietnam.* Chapel Hill and London: University of North Carolina Press, 1993.

Auster, Albert, and Leonard Quart. *How the War Was Remembered: Hollywood and Vietnam.* New York: Praeger, 1988.

Baker, Mark. *Nam: The Vietnam War in the Words of the Men and Women Who Fought There.* 1981; New York: Cooper Square, 2001.

Barry, Kathleen, ed. *Vietnam's Women in Transition.* New York: St. Martins, 1996.

Barstow, Anne Llewellyn. *War's Dirty Secret: Rape, Prostitution, and Other Crimes against Women.* Cleveland: Pilgrim, 2000.

Beattie, Keith. *The Scar That Binds: American Culture and the Vietnam War.* New York and London: New York University Press, 1998.

Beidler, Philip D. *The Good War's Greatest Hits: World War II and American Remembering.* Athens and London: University of Georgia Press, 1998.

Benedict, Helen. "The Private War of Women," *Salon.com*, 7 March 2007.

Black, Gregory D., and Clayton R. Koppes. *Hollywood Goes to War: How Politics, Profits, and Propaganda Shaped World War II Movies.* Berkeley: University of California Press, 1987.

Bow, Leslie. "Third-World Testimony in the Era of Globalization: Vietnam, Sexual Trauma, and Le Ly Hayslip's Art of Neutrality." *Haunting Violations: Feminist Criticism and the Crisis of the "Real,"* Ed. Wendy S. Hesford and Wendy Kozol. Urbana and Chicago: University of Illinois Press, 2001, 169–194.

Brownmiller, Susan. *Against Our Will: Men, Women, and Rape.* New York: Simon and Schuster, 1975.

Broyles, William Jr. *Brothers in Arms: A Journey from War to Peace.* New York: Knopf, 1986.

Burke, Carol. *Camp All-American, Hanoi Jane, and the High-and-Tight: Gender, Folklore, and Changing Military Culture.* Boston: Beacon, 2004.

Buzzanco, Robert. "Fear and (Self) Loathing in Lubbock, Texas, or How I Learned to Quit Worrying and Love Vietnam and Iraq," *Counterpunch*, 17–16 April 2005.

Campanaro, Joceyln. "Women, War, and International Law: The Historical Treatment of Gender-Based War Crimes," *Georgetown Law Journal* 899 (August 2001): 2557–92.

Caputo, Philip. *A Rumor of War.* New York: Ballantine Books, 1977.

Carpenter, Lucas. "'It Don't Mean Nothin': Vietnam War Literature and Postmodernism," *College Literature* 30.2 (2003): 30–50.

Caruth, Cathy, ed. *Trauma: Explorations in Memory.* Baltimore and London: Johns Hopkins University Press, 1995.

Christopher, Renny. *The Viet Nam War/The American War: Images and Representations in Euro-American and Vietnamese Exile Narratives.* Amherst: University of Massachusetts Press, 1995.

Corrigan, Timothy. *Film and Literature: An Introduction and Reader.* Upper Saddle River, NJ: Prentice Hall, 2000.

Cvetkovich, Ann. *An Archive of Feelings: Trauma, Sexuality, and Lesbian Public Cultures.* Ser. Q. Durham and London: Duke University Press, 2003.

Del Vecchio, John M. *The Thirteenth Valley.* New York: St. Martin's, 1982.

Devine, Jeremy M. *Vietnam at Twenty-four Frames a Second: A Critical and Thematic Analysis of over Four Hundred Films about the Vietnam War.* Jefferson NC: McFarland, 1995.

Dittmar, Linda, and Gene Michaud, eds. *From Hanoi to Hollywood: The Vietnam War in American Film.* New Brunswick and London: Rutgers University Press, 1997.

Duffett, John, ed. *Against the Crime of Silence: Proceedings of the International War Crimes Tribunal.* 1968; New York: Clarion Book, 1970.

Edwards, Alison. Rape, *Racism, and the White Women's Movement: An Answer to Susan Brownmiller.* Chicago: Sojourner Truth Organization, n.d.

Egendorf, Arthur. *Healing from the War: Trauma and Transformation after Vietnam.* Boston: Houghton Mifflin, 1985.

Ehrhart, W. D. *Busted: A Vietnam Veteran in Nixon's America.* Amherst: University of Massachusetts Press, 1995.

———. *Vietnam-Perkasie: A Combat Marine Memoir.* Jefferson and London: McFarland, 1983.

Engle, Karen. "Feminism and Its (Dis)contents: Criminalizing Wartime Rape in Bosnia and Herzegovina," *The American Journal of International Law* 99, no. 4 (October 2005): 778–816.

Engelhardt, Tom. *The End of Victory Culture: Cold War America and the Disillusioning of a Generation.* New York: Basic Books, 1995.

Enloe, Cynthia. *Bananas, Beaches, and Bases: Making Feminist Sense of International Politics.* Berkeley and Los Angeles: University of California Press, 1990.

———. *Does Khaki Become You? The Militarisation of Women's Lives.* Boston: South End, 1983.

———. *The Morning After: Sexual Politics at the End of the Cold War.* Berkely and Los Angeles: University of California Press, 1993.

———. "Women after Wars: Puzzles and Warnings." In *Vietnam's Women in Transition.* 299–313.

Evans, Sara. *Personal Politics: The Roots of Women's Liberation in the Civil Rights Movement and the New Left.* New York: Vintage Books, 1980.

Faludi, Susan. *Stiffed: The Betrayal of the American Man.* New York: Harper Perennial, 1999.

Franklin, H. Bruce. *M.I.A., or Mythmaking in America.* New York: Lawrence Hill Books, 1992.

Franks, Lucinda. *Waiting Out a War: The Exile of Private John Picciano.* New York: Coward, McCann and Geoghegan, 1974.

Freeman, James A. *Hearts of Sorrow: Vietnamese-American Lives.* Stanford: Stanford University Press, 1989.

Fuller, Tony, and Peter Goldman, eds. *Charlie Company: What Vietnam Did to Us.* New York: Ballantine, 1983.

Gibson, James William. *The Perfect War: Technowar in Vietnam.* Boston: Atlantic Monthly, 1986.

Gitlin, Todd. *Inside Prime Time.* New York: Pantheon Books, 1985.

Goldensohn, Lorrie. *Dismantling Glory: Twentieth-Century Soldier Poetry.* New York: Columbia University Press, 2003.

Goodstein, Lynne. "Sexual Assault in the United States and Vietnam: Some Thoughts and Questions." In *Vietnam's Women in Transition.* 275–296.

Grossman, Anita. "A Question of Silence: The Rape of German Women by Occupation Soldiers," *October* 72 (Spring 1995): 43–63.

Haines, Harry W. "They Were Called and They Went": The Political Rehabilitation of the Vietnam Veteran." In *From Hanoi to Hollywood.* 81–97.

Hasford, Gustav. *The Short-Timers.* New York: Harper and Row, 1979.

Hathaway, Bo. *A World of Hurt.* New York: Taplinger, 1981.

Hayslip, Le Ly. *Child of War, Woman of Peace.* New York: Doubleday, 1993.

———, with Jay Wurts. *When Heaven and Earth Changed Places: A Vietnamese Woman's Journey from War to Peace.* New York: Plume, 1989.

Heinemann, Larry. *Black Virgin Mountain: A Return to Vietnam.* New York: Doubleday, 2005.

———. *Close Quarters.* New York: Penguin Books, 1986.

———. *Paco's Story.* New York: Farrar Straus Giroux, 1986.

Hemingway, Ernest. *A Farewell to Arms.* New York: Scribner, 1995.

Herdy, Amy, and Miles Moffeit, "Betrayal in the Ranks," *The Denver Post,* 18–16 November 2003.

Herr, Michael. *Dispatches.* New York: Vintage International, 1991.

Hess, Martha, ed. *Then the Americans Came: Voices from Vietnam.* New York: Four Walls Eight Windows, 1993.

Hong, Khuat Thu. "Sexual Harassment in Vietnam: A New Term for an Old Phenomenon." In *Gender Practices in Contemporary Vietnam.* Ed.

Lisa Drummond and Helle Rydstrøm. Singapore: NIAS Press, 2004. 117–36.

Hùng, Lê Tuan. "Hue and Tài Tu Music of Viet Nam: The Concept of Music and Social Organisation of Musicians," *ePapyrus*. Australia Asia Foundation. 31 January 2006. <http://home.vicnet.net.au/~aaf/ch2.html>.

Huong, Duong Thu. *Novel without a Name*. New York: Penguin, 1996.

Jacobsen, Kurt. "Larry Heinemann in Conversation with Kurt Jacobsen," *Logos* 2, 1 (Winter 2003). <http://logosonline.home.igc.org/heinemann.htm>.

Jameson, Frederic. *Postmodernism, or, the Cultural Logic of Late Capitalism*. Post-Contemporary Interventions. Durham: Duke University Press, 1991.

Jason, Philip K., ed. *Fourteen Landing Zones: Approaches to Vietnam War Literature*. Iowa City: University of Iowa Press, 1991.

Jeans, Roger B. "Victims or Victimizers? Museums, Textbooks, and the War Debate in Contemporary Japan," *The Journal of Military History*, 69.1 (Jan. 2005): 149–95.

Jeffords, Susan. "Masculinity as Excess in Vietnam Films: The Father/Son Dynamic of American Culture." *Genre* 21 (Winter 1988): 487–515.

———. *The Remasculinzation of America: Gender and the Vietnam War*. Theories of Contemporary Culture 10. Bloomington and Indianapolis: Indiana University Press, 1989.

———. "Tattoos, Scars, Diaries, and Writing Masculinity." In *The Vietnam War and American Culture*. Ed. John Carlos Rowe and Rick Berg. New York: Columbia University Press, 1991. 208–225.

Kinney, Katherine. *Friendly Fire: American Images of the Vietnam War*. Oxford: Oxford University Press, 2000.

———. "Women, War, and the Pacific." In *Post-Nationalist American Studies*, ed. John Carlos Rowe. Berkeley: University of California Press, 2000.

Kovic, Ron. *Born on the Fourth of July*. New York: McGraw-Hill, 1976.

Kulka, Richard A., et al. *Trauma and the Vietnam War Generation: Report of Findings from the National Vietnam Veterans Readjustment Study*. Brunner/Mazel Psychosocial Stress Ser. 18. New York: Brunner/Mazel, 1990.

Landers, James. *The Weekly War: Newsmagazines and Vietnam*. Columbia and London: University of Missouri Press, 2004.

Lane, Mark. *Conversations with Americans*. New York: Simon and Schuster, 1970.

Lang, Daniel. *Casualties of War*. New York: Pocket Books, 1989.

Laub, Dori, and Shoshana Felman. *Testimony: Crises of Witnessing in Literature, Psychoanalysis, and History*. New York: Rutledge, 1992.

Lembcke, Jerry. *The Spitting Image: Myth, Memory, and the Legacy of Vietnam*. New York: New York University Press, 1998.

Leys, Ruth. *Trauma: A Genealogy*. Chicago and London: Chicago University Press, 2000.

Lifton, Robert J. *Home from the War: Vietnam Veterans: Neither Victims nor Executioners*. New York: Simon and Schuster, 1973.

MacNair, Rachel M. *Perpetration-Induced Traumatic Stress: The Psychological Consequences of Killing*. Westport: Praeger, 2002.

MacPherson, Myra. *Long Time Passing: Vietnam and the Haunted Generation.* New York: Signet, 1985.

Mariscal, George, ed. *Aztlan and Viet Nam: Chicano and Chicana Experiences of the War.* American Crossroads. Berkley and Los Angeles: University of California Press, 1999.

Martin, Andrew. *Receptions of War: Vietnam in American Culture.* Norman: University of Oklahoma Press, 1993.

Meyers, Thomas. *Walking Point: American Narratives of Vietnam.* New York and Oxford: Oxford University Press, 1988.

Moser, Richard R. *The New Winter Soldiers: GI and Veteran Dissent during the Vietnam Era.* New Brunswick: Rutgers University Press, 1996.

Ngan, Nguyễn Ngoc with E. E. Richey. *The Will of Heaven: A Story of One Vietnamese and the End of His World.* New York: EP Dutton, 1982.

Nguen, Quí Đuc. *Where the Ashes Are: The Odyssey of a Vietnamese Family.* Reading: Addison-Wesley, 1994.

Niacharos, Catherine N. "Women, War, and Rape: Challenges Facing the International Tribunal for the Former Yugoslavia," *Human Rights Quarterly* 17, no. 4 (Nov. 1995): 649–690.

Ninh, Bao. *The Sorrow of War: A Novel of North Vietnam.* Trans. Phan Thanh Hao. Ed. Frank Palmos. New York: Riverhead Books, 1993.

O'Brien, Tim. *If I Die in a Combat Zone, Box Me up and Ship Me Home.* New York: Delacorte, 1973.

———. *The Things They Carried: A Work of Fiction.* New York: Penguin Books, 1990.

Olson, James S., and Randy Roberts, eds. *My Lai: A Brief History with Documents.* Bedford Ser. in History and Culture. Boston and New York: Bedford/St. Martin's, 1998.

Phillips, Kathy J. Manipulating *Masculinity: War and Gender in Modern British and American Literature.* New York: Palgrave MacMillan, 2006.

Powell, Mary Reynolds. *A World of Hurt: Between Ignorance and Arrogance in Vietnam.* Cleveland: Greenleaf Enterprises, 2000.

Ray, Robert. B. *A Certain Tendency of the Hollywood Cinema, 1930–1980.* Princeton: Princeton University Press, 1985.

Rignalda, Don. *Fighting and Writing the Vietnam War.* Jackson: University Press of Mississippi, 1994.

Rowe, John Carlos, ed. *Post-Nationalist American Studies.* Berkley and Los Angeles: University of California Press, 2000.

Russell, Bertrand. *War Crimes in Vietnam.* New York: Allen and Unwin, 1967.

Sajor, Indai Lourdes, ed. *Common Grounds: Violence against Women in War and Armed Conflict Situations.* Quezon City, Philippines: Asian Center for Women's Human Rights, 1998.

Santoli, Al, ed. *Everything We Had: An Oral History of the Vietnam War by Thirty-Three American Soldiers Who Fought It.* New York: Balantine Books, 1981.

Schneir, Miriam, ed. *Feminism in Our Time: The Essential Writings, World War II to the Present.* New York: Vintage Books, 1994.

Sedgwick, Eve Kosofsky. *Between Men: English Literature and Male Homosocial Desire*, Gender and Culture. New York: Columbia University Press, 1985.

Slotkin, Richard. *Gunfighter Nation: The Myth of the Frontier in Twentieth-Century America*. New York: Atheneum, 1992.

Stacewicz, Richard. *Winter Soldiers: An Oral History of the Vietnam Veterans against the War*. New York: Simon and Schuster, 1997.

Stiglmayer, Alexandra, ed. *Mass Rape: The War against Women in Bosnia-Herzegovina*. Trans. Marion Faber. Lincoln and London: University of Nebraska Press, 1994.

Stoltzfus, Brenda, and Saundra Pollock Sturdevant. *Let the Good Times Roll: Prostitution and the U.S. Military in Asia*. New York: New, 1992.

Street, Amy, and Jane Stafford, "Military Sexual Trauma: Issues in Caring for Veterans," *Iraq War Clinician Guide*. Department of Veteran Affairs, 2004.

Studlar, Gaylyn and David Desser. "Never Having to Say You're Sorry: *Rambo*'s Rewriting the Vietnam War." In *From Hanoi to Hollywood*. 101–12.

Stuhldreher, Karen. "State Rape: Representations of Rape in Viet Nam." *Viet Nam Generation* 5, nos. 1–4 (March 1994). <http://lists.village.virginia.edu/sixties/HTML_docs/Texts/Scholarly/Stuldreher_Rape.html>. Accessed 2 March 2005.

Swofford, Anthony. *Jarhead: A Marine's Chronicle of the Gulf War and Other Battles*. New York: Scribner, 2003.

Tal, Kalí. *Worlds of Hurt: Reading the Literatures of Trauma*. Cambridge Studies in American Literature and Culture. Cambridge: Cambridge University Press, 1996.

Terry, Wallace. *Bloods: An Oral History of the Vietnam War by Black Veterans*. New York: Random House, 1984.

Turner, Karen Gottschang, and Phan Thanh Hao, eds. *Even the Women Must Fight: Memories of War from North Vietnam*. New York and Chichester: Wiley and Sons, 1998.

Van Devanter, Lynda. *Home before Morning: The Story of an Army Nurse in Vietnam*. New York: Warner Books, 1983.

Vietnam Veterans against the War. *The Winter Soldier Investigation: An Inquiry into American War Crimes*. Boston: Beacon, 1972.

Webb, James. *Fields of Fire*. New York and Toronto: Bantam Books, 1978.

Wheeler, John. *Touched by Fire: The Future of the Vietnam Generation*. New York: Avon, 1984.

Whelchel, Toshio. *From Pearl Harbor to Saigon: Japanese American Soldiers and the Vietnam War*. London: Verso, 1999.

Williams, Reese, ed. *Unwinding the Vietnam War: From War into Peace*. Seattle: Real Comet Press, 1987.

Wright, Stephen. *Meditations in Green*. New York: Scribner, 1988.

Index